STUDIES IN EUROPEAN HISTORY

X

# SWORD AND MITRE

## GOVERNMENT AND EPISCOPATE
## IN FRANCE AND ENGLAND
## IN THE AGE OF ARISTOCRACY

*by*

### NORMAN RAVITCH

*University of California, Riverside*

1966
**MOUTON & CO.**
THE HAGUE · PARIS

*Printed in The Netherlands*

PREFACE

This study in the comparative institutional history of 18th-Century France and England is the product of my interest in the Gallican Church of the Old Régime and in the current emphasis among historians of the period on the problem of the aristocratic resurgence. The original stimulus for this work was the graduate history seminars of Professor Robert R. Palmer at Princeton University, and it is preeminently to Professor Palmer, now Dean of the Faculty of Arts and Sciences at Washington University in Saint Louis, Missouri, that my thanks and acknowledgment must go — for his interest, his time, his encouragement, and his careful criticism and advice.

For the opportunity to spend a year in France I must thank the Institute of International Education for a Fulbright Grant during the academic year 1960-61. Of great help and encouragement to me in Paris was the advice of Professors René Rémond of the Ecole des Sciences Politiques and André Latreille of the Université de Lyon. I also acknowledge with thanks the help of Mgr. le Chanoine J. Leflon of the Institut Catholique, and the assistance and great patience of the archivists and staff of the Bibliothèque Nationale, the Bibliothèque de la Sorbonne, the Archives Nationales, the Archives du Ministère des Affaires Etrangères, and the Archives Départementales du Rhône.

Back in this country, I am indebted to the staffs of the Firestone Memorial Library of Princeton University, the Bancroft Library of the University of California at Berkeley, and the library of the University of California at Riverside. Through an Intercampus Opportunity Fund the University of California made possible a summer of work at Berkeley for which I am thankful. I am also indebted for reading certain parts of this study to Professor David D. Bien of Princeton University, and to Professors Ernst Ekman and Jeffrey B. Russell of the University of California at Riverside. Finally, I thank the editorial boards of *Church History, The Catholic Historical Review* and *The Historical Journal* for publishing material from this study in article form in their periodicals.

Riverside, California
June, 1965

N. R.

# TABLE OF CONTENTS

# LIST OF TABLES

# INTRODUCTION

There are at least two fundamental justifications for offering a comparative study of the English and French episcopates in the 18th Century. First of all, there is a constant interest in comparing the history and institutions of the two greatest European democracies, in seeking to understand why the British nation has been able to develop a liberal, democratic society endowed with a political system renown for its relative lack of violent upheaval and its realization of progress with order, while the French nation has won its precious and inspiring liberties more conspicuously at the cost of violence and bloodshed and has never yet been able to reconcile progress with order and political stability. The quest for an understanding of these divergencies needs no further justification. In avoiding explanations involving such uncertain concepts as *the Latin temperament* and Anglo-Saxon *sangfroid*, if even it can be established to what extent racially the French are indeed Latins and the British Anglo-Saxons, the historian will necessarily seek comprehension in the more scientific domain of historical events and institutions.

Secondly, in understanding the causes and implications of the 18th-Century Revolutions which gave birth to liberal society as we know it, contemporary historical research has put the emphasis on the nature of 18th-Century society and specifically on the role of the aristocracies within it: the democratic Revolutions are seen to have been the alternative to seizures of power by aggressive aristocratic corporations and classes as the successors of the despots who had in varying degrees been absolute and enlightened. The 18th-Century established Churches of France and England and particularly their leadership were members of the ruling class of the nation, a part of the national aristocracy. No comprehension of the French and English aristocracies and their relationship to the rest of society would be complete without ample consideration of this ecclesiastical aristocracy. It is, then, as a contribution to the comparative study of France and Britain in general and to the study of their aristocratic constitutions under the Old Régime in particular that this study is offered.

In any comparative analysis of French and British institutions the moderate observer usually expresses some notion of the superiority and greater liberalism of the latter this has been all the more true when the observer in question has been an English. Recently, in expanding upon what he considered to have been the "myth" of the French Revolution, Alfred Cobban offered these thoughts on the France and Britain of the 18th Century:

A comparison with England in the eighteenth century is not unilluminating. . . .; if one considers the differing prospects that offered themselves to men of ability, lacking what is in all societies so much more valuable than mere ability — money and family influence — in the England and in the France of the eighteenth century. . . . Fouché might have become Archbishop of Canterbury. . . . The Church under Louis XVI had not a single bishop who was not noble by birth. In England, John Potter, son of a draper, and obtaining his education as servitor at Oxford, could become Archbishop of Canterbury. Isaac Maddox, orphan and apprenticed to a pastycook, ended up as a bishop, as did Richard Watson, son of a country schoolteacher.[1]

It is just such contentions which this study undertakes to test and to evaluate.

One of the most suggestive insights offered by Tocqueville for a comparison of pre-revolutionary French and English societies was a focusing upon the degree to which the people of these societies were divided into isolated groups, which division bred suspicion, hostility, and lack of common national interests. He distinguished, for example, between the French and English aristocracies: the French nobility constituted a *caste*; that is, it was clearly, externally marked off from the rest of society by birth, so much so that even parvenu nobles lost their former ties in the middle classes and were swallowed up by the exclusiveness of privilege of the caste nobility. The English ruling class, on the contrary, constituted an undefined group with gradual demarcations so that those below the titled nobility could never quite be certain to what degree they belonged to the ruling aristocracy. In brief, the difference between social groups in the two countries was that in France everything was explicit, while in England it was subtle and unofficial. Tocqueville's contention was that the explicit divisions

[1] Alfred Cobban, *The Myth of the French Revolution* (London, H. K. Lewis & Co., 1955), p. 17.

served as greater objects of hate and eventual revolution than implicit divisions.[2]

It is fruitful to use this general frame of reference in comparatively analyzing the French and English ecclesiastical aristocrats — the bishops of the established Church. The following chapters will compare the French and English episcopates with a view towards establishing the degree to which the two groups of bishops were integrated into their respective societies and the degree to which they retained an ecclesiastical and aristocratic *caste consciousness*. First a chapter is offered by way of orienting the reader to the central issues of the Gallican episcopate's quarrel with the rest of French society. Then a study is presented of the social origins of the French, English, and Irish bishops, including an analysis of the recruitment policies of the French and British ministries. Finally, the corporate and financial organization of the French and English episcopates is presented and expanded upon in an attempt to treat the question of fiscal privilege.

[2] Alexis de Tocqueville, *L'Ancien Régime et la Révolution*, ed. by J.-P. Mayer (Paris, Gallimard, 1952-53), Vol. I, pp. 147-148.

# FRANCE: THE EPISCOPATE AND THE NATION

In presenting an analysis of the recruitment of the 18th-Century Gallican episcopate and of its corporate and financial organization, time and time again the episcopate will be shown to be in conflict and acrimonious debate with the Parlements, particularly with the Parlement of Paris. The protracted struggle between bishops and magistrates, comprising an important segment of 18th-Century French history, centered about the problem of the role of the episcopal power in society and, therein, touched directly upon its caste-like self-identification. It is the task of this chapter to orient the reader towards the central issues, theoretical and practical, of this conflict, in order that the power-position of the Gallican episcopate may be fully appreciated.

Any analysis of the theoretical and actual extent of the ecclesiastical power claimed and exercised by the French episcopate in the last hundred years of the Old Régime will invariably take for its point of departure the question of Gallicanism — the liberties of the Gallican Church. The 18th-Century bishops believed that their ecclesiastical power was held in a state of siege invested by the parliamentary proponents of secular supremacy. It was indeed the liberties of the Gallican Church which the Parlements claimed to be defending against an episcopate allegedly determined to eradicate these liberties. Yet, how had the theories of Gallicanism, formulated by the late medieval theologians in defense of the French episcopate's autonomy from Rome, come to be employed by the Parlements as weapons against the very French Church they had been designed to protect? Had the bishops abandoned Gallicanism and willingly become unquestioningly obedient to Rome, while the liberty-loving Parlements alone were left as guardians of the French Church and State? Or had the nature of Gallicanism so changed through the centuries that it survived more as a slogan than a concrete position on Church-State relations? The paradox of what was called Gallicanism being used as a weapon against an episcopate renowned for its Gallicanism — and suspect because of it in Rome — can only be resolved by investigating the actual content of Gallicanism. It is not sufficient to say with ultramontanists like De Maistre that Gallican liberties were simply the means of depriving the pope of his rightful authority,[1] with the necessary implication that the French episcopate finally acquired sufficient wisdom and humility to confess its errors and repent its disastrous pretensions. This extreme view not only condemns all non-ultramontane theories of Church-State relations but also concedes too much to the contention of the Parlements that they alone defended Gallican liberties.

A useful point of departure for gaining an understanding of Gallicanism can be found in the mistaken views of a follower of De Maistre's approach — the historian of the popes, Ludwig von Pastor. After having ascribed the religious dissension of 18th-Century France and the resultant social and political disorder to the persistence of unfortunate Gallican principles in official circles, Pastor dilated upon the wider implications of Gallicanism. He found that in the 18th Century Gallicanism was extended to non-ecclesiastical affairs so as to proclaim the sovereignty of the people, first by the Parlements and then by the Revolution.

Gallicanism, too, had prepared the ground for the doctrine of the sovereignty of the people, since according to the Gallicans, authority to govern is really vested in the universal Church, the Pope and the Bishops only exercising power in its name, so that a General Council may call the Pope to account and even depose him. To transfer this conception to the political sphere was only one step. The real supreme ruler, it was said, is the people, the King exercises authority solely by commission of the people, hence the people may call the King to account and send him to the scaffold.[2]

The conciliar theory of Church government may have "prepared the ground" for popular sovereignty, but in the 17th Century Gallicanism had undergone so profound a change that it ceased to be mere conciliarism and, indeed, had become in some measure the negation of a vital part of conciliar theory. If Pastor had been as circumspect in his use of terms as George H. Sabine, he would be less open to criticism.

[1] Joseph de Maistre, *De l'Église gallicane dans son rapport avec le souverain pontife* (Lyon-Paris, J. B. Pélagaud, 1863), p. 309 .
[2] Ludwig, Freiherr von Pastor, *The History of the Popes* (London, Kegan Paul, Trench, Trubner & Co., 1941), Vol. XXXIV trans. by Dom Ernest Graf, O.S.B., p. 419.

Sabine does find the conciliar movement an important influence in the later struggle against absolutism, but he avoids equating Gallicanism with the conciliar movement — which was precisely Pastor's error.[3] It is to the modification in the nature of Gallicanism that one must turn in order to answer adequately the primary question: who in 18th-Century France was pro-Gallican and what did such a stand imply?

The celebrated Four Gallican Articles of 1682 have often been considered expressive of the essence of the Gallican position.[4] Certainly in the 18th Century the Gallican position rested on the Four Articles, but the year 1682 was hardly the beginning of Gallicanism. The most careful student of the movement, Victor Martin, has demonstrated the innovating spirit present in the Four Articles. Articles II, III, and IV restated the old conciliar position taken at the Councils of Constance and Basle concerning the subordination of the pope to a General Council of Christendom; in these articles Gallicanism was synonymous with the conciliar theory of Church government, for Gallicanism in its primary manifestation had been nothing more than the French adaptation of the principles and decrees of the famous 15th-Century Councils.[5] The first of the Four Articles, however, not only marked an innovation in Gallican tradition, but in announcing that "... kings and sovereigns are not subject to any ecclesiastical power in temporal matters by the order of God, that they can be deposed neither directly nor indirectly by the authority of the Keys of the Church", it actually rejected an integral part of traditional Gallicanism — the theory that for certain reasons the king's subjects *could* be absolved from their oath of allegiance by a papal excommunication of the king, subject to the final authority of a General Council.[6]

At the meeting of the Estates-General of 1614-15, the Third Estate advanced the thesis that for no reason could the monarch be deposed by the ecclesiastical authority or the people's oath of allegiance be annulled. This thesis — finally embodied in the first of the Articles of 1682 — was opposed in 1614-15 by the first two Estates of the realm and was suppressed by Louis XIII. It must be understood that in op-

---

[3]  George H. Sabine, A *History of Political Theory* (New York, Henry Holt, revised edition, 1955), p. 317.
[4]  See Appendix I for a translated text of the Four Articles.
[5]  Victor Martin, *Le Gallicanisme politique et le clergé de France* (Paris, Auguste Picard, 1929), pp. 10-14. This is not to say that French scholars did not contribute heavily to the body of theory which finally found wide support at Constance; they did.
[6]  Martin, pp. 10-14; 32.

posing the Third Estate's "patriotism" in 1614-15, the clergy did not subscribe either to the theory of the *direct power* of the pope in temporal affairs developed by Boniface VIII in *Unam Sanctam* or to the theory of the *indirect power* of the pope formulated by Cardinal Bellarmine. Both these theories were in the arsenal of the ultramontanists. The first held that the Roman Pontiff had an immediate overlordship over temporal kingdoms, that in a very real sense all secular rulers were vassals of the pope. The theory of indirect power replaced the former one in the 17th Century among ultramontane controversialists; it held that the Pope had only spiritual power, but that since the welfare of the soul took precedence over the welfare of the body, the spiritual power indeed could impose penalties upon the temporal power; when the temporal power diverted men from their spiritual duties, the spiritual power might intervene — not by virtue of its temporal supremacy (as in *Unam Sanctam*), but by virtue of its superior concern for human welfare. Both these theories were in opposition to the theory of the absolute independence of temporal authority — the *regalist* position.[7]

The theory of direct power had been traditionally opposed by the Gallican Church, and the 17th-Century substitution of Bellarmine's indirect-power theory found little favor among Gallicans and was merely tolerated. There was certainly a basic difference between Bellarmine's position and that of the Gallicans: where Bellarmine held that in time of danger to the spiritual welfare of a Christian state the pope acquired a competence over temporal affairs and might intervene *directly*, that is, without any intermediary, the Gallicans offered the thesis that the pope, when intervening (which he might do!) never assumed a temporal competence but required, rather, the assistance of the sovereign power residing in the people. In a sense, then, the Gallicans were democratic where Bellarmine was theocratic.[8] Martin demonstrates that never before the 17th Century — specifically never before 1663 — had the Theological Faculty of the University of Paris entirely ruled out papal intervention in the affairs of French monarchs. The Gallicans were quick to deny the right of tyrannicide (also denied by the Council of Constance), and they disputed the vassalage of the French king, but in certain grave cases they admitted the *accidental* or cooperative power of the Church in disciplining the king.[9] It must

[7]   *Ibid.*, pp. 25-27.
[8]   *Ibid.*, p. 31.
[9]   *Ibid.*, pp. 23; 323.

be remembered that for Gallicans ecclesiastical intervention did not involve despotic papal intervention, for the actions of Rome were ultimately subject to a General Council. Furthermore, the role to be played by the people in deposing an heretical king was intended to temper ecclesiastical despotism.

The theory of the absolute independence of monarchical authority was new to the 17th Century, being a corollary of the theory of the divine right of kings. By the time of the penultimate convocation of the Estates-General by Louis XIII, the theory of divine right had been admitted by the doctors of the Sorbonne. But only the Third Estate admitted fully the implications of the new theory of kingship when it advanced the complete regalist position. In 1614-15 the king and clergy admitted the divine right of kings without concluding that monarchical authority was absolutely independent; the clergy, led by the Theological Faculty which was the molder of episcopal opinion, retained its traditional conciliarist views. However, the acceptance of a new conception of royal power along with the retention of the older view of Church-State relations became increasingly untenable. The conciliarist Gallican theory always had presupposed the participation of the sovereign people in the deposition of the king. Once the king had become sovereign by divine right, the people no longer had such a role to play. Now the Gallican theologians were compelled to decide between surrendering an offending king to the arbitrary power of the pope, or denying the applicability of an excommunication to temporal affairs. The basis for an intermediate solution had been undermined by the extirpation of popular sovereignty.[10] Thus, the regalist position which found itself accepted in the Four Articles of 1682 was part of the 17th-Century triumph of absolutism. Conciliarist Gallicanism had been anti-despotic and medieval; it had taken account of the role of the people and the intervention of a non-despotic, conciliar Church. This older view may have been democratic; but more probably it was aristocratic, in that, by *people* the important people were meant. It is not surprising that the victory of absolutism over aristocracy involved the transformation of the ecclesiastical power from the potential weapon of the anti-despots to the servant of the god-king. It is, moreover, important to recognize that the group in 1615 which was more regalist than the king was the Third Estate led by the magistrates.

[10]   *Ibid.*, pp. 324-325.

The reign of Louis XIV saw another accretion to Gallicanism which indeed fundamentally altered it. The right of the Crown to enjoy the revenues and patronage rights of vacant bishoprics, the *droit de régale*, had been traditionally recognized as applicable only to certain specific sees. Henry IV and Richelieu both had shared this view, but the Parlement of Paris in 1608 took the offensive on behalf of the secular power. Just as the Parlements — still in the ranks of the Third Estate at the Estates-General — pushed the absolute independence of the Crown farther than the king wished or found prudent, so also in the affair of the *régale* did the magistrates show themselves, if one may risk being teleological, more modern than the modernizing kings and cardinal-ministers of the 17th Century.

The two ecclesiastical assemblies of 1681 and 1682 which gave birth to the Four Articles were convoked originally to deal with the extension of the *régale*, which extension was overwhelmingly approved by the bishop-delegates. It did not escape contemporaries that these assemblies which were summoned to preserve Gallican liberties actually undermined them fundamentally. Fénelon wrote in 1688 that the Gallican liberties included the principles of the doctors of Paris which were upheld at Constance — and nothing else.[11] An anonymous piece in the Colbert papers noted with irony that if the Assembly of 1682 had truly carried out its avowed intention of preserving Gallican liberties, it would have maintained the limited application of the *droit de régale*, resisted the usurpation by secular officials of ecclesiastical power, and renewed the traditional Gallican plea for the convocation of provincial councils of the clergy to govern the Gallican Church. But the Assembly was conspicuously silent on these important questions:

What, then, do the prelates of the Assembly do on an occasion so appropriate and favorable, they who by their character are the born protectors of the right and the liberty of their Churches? ... They ally themselves to the secular power and support as much as they can the royal officials who have undertaken to destroy this very liberty.[12]

Le Camus, the bishop of Grenoble, in a letter to Chancellor Le Tellier, expressed his uneasiness over the innovations made in the name of

[11] Fénelon, "Mémoire inédit de Fénelon sur la Cour de Rome", *La Revue politique et littéraire*, 2nd series, 4th year (January 23, 1875), p. 698.

[12] "Remarques sur la déclaration de l'assemblée du clergé touchant la puissance ecclésiastique, reçue et autorisée par l'édit du roi du mois de mars 1682", quoted *in toto* in Charles Gérin, *Recherches historiques sur l'assemblée du clergé de France de 1682* (Paris, Librairie Jacques Lecoffre, 2nd edition, 1870), p. 321.

tradition. After explaining his own belief that the *droit de régale* legitimately might not be extended, he proceeded to show that even
were the extension allowed, a still more ominous consequence would
emerge:

It also seems to me grievous that the king, who acquires by the *régale* no
right other than that which the bishop, if he lived, would have [enjoyed],
helps himself to this right *beyond* the power of the bishops. I enjoy, for
example, but one vote among twenty canons, and were the bishopric [of
Grenoble fallen] into the *régale*, the king would have the rights of the
bishop and of the canons and would deprive the chapter of its rights![13]

Thus there were doubts about the purity of the Gallican Assembly's
Gallicanism and a feeling that the Church was being besieged by the
aggressive secular power. The author of a manuscript emanating from
Saint-Sulpice feared that if the regalists had their way, "... the
Church ... will become dependent on the lay judges, who up to now
have been regarded only as the most prominent within the Third
Order or Estate ..... We have nothing with which to answer the
English if they presume to inform us that we are greatly mistaken in
condemning as a heresy the right of supremacy which they recognize
in their prince." [14]

   To understand the vicissitudes of support for and opposition to the
regalist position in the 17th and 18th Centuries, it may be helpful to
subject the material to a schema. In 1615 the regalist position was
supported only by the Third Estate, which then included the magistracy; the opponents of regalism were the First and Second Estates
and the king. In 1682 officially all three estates and the monarch were
avowed regalists. In the 18th-Century disputes over so-called Jansenism and ecclesiastical jurisdiction, the Third Estate and the nobility
(the latter now led by the magistrates who had emerged from the
ranks of the bourgeoisie to become the vanguard of the aristocracy)
were regalists, even unabashed secularists where the king was too
considerate towards ecclesiastical sensibilities; the king wavered between defending his absolute power from ecclesiastical encroachment
and defending his clergy from the aggressive magistrates; the majority
of the 18th-Century bishops were evidently opposed to the regalist-
secularist position. These relationships can perhaps be reduced to the
following schema:

---

[13]   Le Camus to Le Tellier, May 30, 1681, in Gérin, pp. 150-151. Italics added.
[14]   "Observations sur le procès-verbal de l'assemblée extraordinaire des mois de
mars et de mai 1681", *ibid.*, p. 146.

|        | *Anti-regalist*             | *Pro-regalist*                              |
|--------|-----------------------------|---------------------------------------------|
|        | King                        |                                             |
| 1615   | First Estate                | Third Estate (including the magistrates)    |
|        | Second Estate               |                                             |
|        |                             | King                                        |
| 1682   |                             | First Estate                                |
|        |                             | Second Estate                               |
|        |                             | Third Estate                                |
| 18th   | First Estate (the           | King                                        |
| Century | majority of bishops)       | Second Estate (led by the magistrates)      |
|        |                             | Third Estate                                |

## POLARIZATION

| Bishops react in the direction of Rome | Magistrates move towards a secularist position |
|----------------------------------------|------------------------------------------------|

After the illusory unity of 1682, the bishops appeared to be isolated in their position of neither ultramontanism nor regalism. Before 1682 they had not stood so obviously estranged from the views of the other estates. Only the Parlements and the Third Estate had maintained what could be called a reasonably consistent position. The nobility (or at least its leadership) and the king had changed in one direction, but the bishops alone seemed to have reversed their position. This reversal could have accounted for the feeling of the Parlements that the clergy was becoming dangerously ultramontane. At one point in its war with the episcopate, the Parlement of Paris warned against the ever-present ultramontanist threat:

If the opposition which this ultramontane doctrine has suffered has rendered it less active than formerly, it always survives. How many times has it known how to show itself and carry with it revolt and division into the heart of France, *even after opposing decisions seemed to have annihilated it?* It only awaits opportunities to reappear and excite new disorders.[15]

However, neither was the position of the magistrates merely that of 1615 or 1682; it was so aggressive that even the regalism of the king seemed deficient by comparison. If the king was no longer to be limited by the Church in the guise of either pope or Council, other limits were to be forged — the so-called fundamental laws of the

[15] Remonstrance of April 7, 1737; Jules Flammermont, ed., *Remontrances du parlement de Paris au XVIII<sup>e</sup> siècle* (Paris, Imprimerie Nationale, 1888-1898), Vol. I, p. 350. Italics added.

realm as guarded and interpreted by the sovereign Parlements. These pretensions were indeed aggressive in the eyes of the bishops, for if they could acquiesce in the superiority of the lay power when in the hands of the annointed god-king of Bossuet, they found it intolerable when a body of mere lawyers-turned-noble claimed a share in the exercise of supreme secular power and pressed for what could only be considered a secular state. As Fénelon wrote in 1711:

Rome has employed an arbitrary power which troubled the peace of particular Churches. . . . One must affirm that these enterprises are greatly diminished. Now the enterprises come from the secular power, not from that of Rome. In practice, the king is more the head of the Church in France than the pope: liberties in regard to the pope, servitude towards the king. . . . Authority of the king over the Church devolves upon the lay judges: laymen dominate bishops, the Third Estate dominates the first lords.[16]

It may be unfair to seek to hold the bishops to the Articles of 1682 since it is generally agreed by contemporaries and later historians that the bishops attending the Assembly of 1682 were handpicked by the government and compelled to find for the regalist position. In a letter to Colbert, Harlay, the Solicitor-General of the Parlement of Paris, wrote that part of the difficulty in getting the Theological Faculty to accept the Four Articles lay with the nature of the Assembly: ". . . . an Assembly of the clergy whose majority would whole-heartedly change tomorrow if one permitted it." [17] Boucher, a doctor of the Theological Faculty who was exiled for his resistance to the Faculty's submission, wrote that he had been approached by several bishop-delegates imploring his aid in having the Four Articles suppressed. Gérin believes that it was not impossible that Boucher might be approached to this end, since as vicar-general of the archdiocese of Paris and the superior of the seminary of Saint-Nicolas-du-Chardonnet he was an important figure among Paris doctors and ecclesiastics. In any event, the very suggestion that the bishop-delegates would risk such an impropriety, regardless of whether true or not, demonstrates that some contemporary opinion believed the bishops to have been less than sincere in supporting the Four Articles. Martin concludes that the bishops intended only to save the king from the threat of an excommunication which Rome appeared quite likely to hurl at her Eldest Son for his aggressive extension of the *droit de régale*; they had no intention of

---

[16]    *Oeuvres de Fénelon, archevêque de Cambrai* (Paris, J.-A. Lebel, 1820-1830), Vol. XXII, p. 586.
[17]    Harlay to Colbert, June 2, 1682; Gérin, *op. cit.*, p. 387.

subordinating the Church to the State.[18] As extenuating as all this may be, the bishops in approving the Four Articles nevertheless did provide the Parlements with an effective weapon for rendering episcopal power less formidable and thereby making parliamentary Gallicanism the only legitimate form of that old and varying body of theory. The Parlements were not unreasonable in seeking to hold king and clergy to the Four Articles, and the attempts of the clergy to retreat from them seemed only to justify the rather extreme measures taken by the magistrates.

With the clergy having retreated from its position of 1682 [19] and the Parlements capitalizing on this fact, it may well be that in 18th-Century France the only Gallican in terms of the 1682 Articles was the king. Although Louis XIV, in order to placate the Papacy, had pretended to renounce the Four Articles and had had their signatories do likewise, there was in the 18th Century no retraction whatsoever. A 1766 decree of the conseil du roi concerning the acts of the Assembly of the clergy recalled:

... the unchanging principles which are contained in the laws of the kingdom, and notably in the edicts of 1682 and 1695 . . .; principles according to which it is indisputable that the Church has received from God himself a veritable authority which is subordinate to no other in the order of spiri-

---

[18]   Martin, *op. cit.*, p. 327.
[19]   The clergy's retreat was demonstrated by Le Franc de Pompignan's "Défense des actes du clergé de France" in 1765: To the Parlements' contention that the Four Articles were binding because they had been consecrated by the Assembly of 1682, he replied: "We recognize this maxim. In a profession or formula of faith it is not permitted to omit expressions adopted by the universal Church in its councils and its creeds, in order to distinguish with precision a truth which it has defined from an error which it had condemned. This is the only thing which can be called 'consecrated expressions', whose omission correctly makes suspect the faith of those who refuse to subscribe to them. However, whatever respect the Assemblies of the clergy of France since 1682 have had for the Assembly of 1682, and whatever has been their attachment to its doctrine, they have never held is authority equal to that of the universal Church or of an ecumenical council. They themselves have learned not to consider its declaration as a creed of faith. There was, therefore, no strict obligation for the Assembly of 1765, which has reasoned the same as those of 1682, to pronounce the same doctrine by absolutely the same expressions when it has employed equivalents. Nevertheless, it is not to be doubted that if the Assembly of 1765 had had the same intention as that of 1682, it would have copied literally the language as it has followed the doctrine." *Oeuvres complètes de Jean-Georges Le Franc de Pompignan, archevêque de Vienne*, ed. by abbé Migne (Paris, Chez J.-P. Migne, 1855), Vol. I, cols. 1284-1285. Thus the Four Articles were to be regarded as peculiar to the particular needs of the period in which they were pronounced. This was undoubtedly hedging!

tual affairs, having for its objective, salvation. That on the other hand, the temporal power, emanating directly from God, depends on Him alone and depends neither directly nor indirectly on any other power which exists on the earth; ... and that there is no other power which, on any pretext whatsoever, can in any case free its subjects of whatever rank, quality, or condition from the inviolable loyalty they owe to their sovereign. ... His Majesty, consequently, desires that the Four Propositions be inviolably observed in all his Estates [or States] and sustained in all the universities and by all orders, seminaries, and teaching bodies, as it is prescribed by the edict of 1682. ...[20]

## II

The survival in 18th-Century France of a system of ecclesiastical courts as an instrument of corporate independence brought the episcopate into chronic conflict with the secular legal system represented by the Parlements. Ecclesiastical courts existed in every diocese of France. The courts of the archiepiscopal sees enjoyed both immediate jurisdiction within their own territory as did any diocese and also appellate jurisdiction over their suffragan sees. Finally, the primatial sees had appellate jurisdiction over the archiepiscopal sees within their primacy; thus, the archbishop of Lyon, for example, was in addition the primate of Sens, Tours, Paris, and of all the suffragan sees dependent on them which were within the lay jurisdiction of the Parlement of Paris. The only ultimate appeal of an ecclesiastical legal decision within the ecclesiastical legal system itself was to a national council, since the laws of France did not admit the competence of any Roman tribunal.[21]

Diocesan judicial power was customarily exercised by officials of the bishop; only Flemish and Provençal bishops presided personally. These officials were grand vicars appointed solely at the pleasure of their bishops without any interference in their designation and dismissal from the secular tribunals. A royal declaration of August 17, 1700 confirmed earlier flouted legislation which had required the secular courts to refrain from interference with the free exercise of episcopal prerogatives in this area. The bishops, however, were

[20]  May 24, 1766; François-André Isambert, *et al.*, eds., *Recueil général des anciennes lois françaises* (Paris, Belin-Leprieur, 1822-1833), Vol. XXII, pp. 451-454.

[21]  *Recueil des actes, titres et mémoires concernant les affaires du clergé de France* (known hereafter as *Mémoires du clergé*) (Paris, 1768-1780), Vol. VII, cols. 310-311.

obliged to avoid doing anything more revealing when dismissing an official than merely dismissing him with thanks, for any implication that the cause of dismissal were unfitness could impel the former official to appeal to a secular court for damages.[22] Ordinarily there was but one official for the exercise of ecclesiastical jurisdiction in each diocese, located in the cathedral town; but where a diocese fell within the secular jurisdiction of more than one Parlement, the bishop was required to name officials for those parts of his diocese within the "foreign" Parlement's jurisdiction. As a result, each diocese had an *official principal* and some had, in addition, *officiaux forains*.[23] The jurisdiction of these officials was known as *contentieuse*, signifying that they exercised it in accordance with the forms prescribed by canon law and royal ordinance, and only in the ecclesiastical tribunals themselves. During visitations the bishops could not exercise any *contentious jurisdiction*, being limited to *voluntary jurisdiction* which was more informal and less enforceable; they could, however, send accused persons before their officials for investigation and trial.[24]

In summoning men before its tribunals, the episcopate was restricted virtually to competence over ecclesiastics. Civil cases against ecclesiastics were divided into those concerning either *personal* or *real* matters, while any combination of the two was deemed a *mixed* matter. Only the personal matters of ecclesiastics could be investigated and tried before the officials of the dioceses. In personal matters — those concerning only the personal conduct of an ecclesiastic — the accuser was obliged to plead in the court of the defendant, that is, in the ecclesiastical court. The accused cleric might not exercise any rights to waive his right to ecclesiastical justice, and the secular judges were bound to deliver personal cases involving clerics to the Church courts.[25] It was not uncommon, however, for two clerics involved in a litigation between themselves over personal matters to take their differences to the lay courts where justice was more speedy and judgments more definitive, since the Church court could not enforce its non-spiritual decisions upon anyone unless the secular

---

[22]   *Ibid.*, VII, cols. 297-326.
[23]   Louis de Héricourt du Vatier, *Les Loix ecclésiastiques de France dans leur ordre naturel, et une analyse des livres du droit canonique conférés avec les usages de l'église gallicane*, new edition (Neufchâtel, La Société Typographique, 1774; originally published c. 1735), Vol. I, p. 100.
[24]   *Ibid.*, I, pp. 95-97.
[25]   *Ibid.*, I, p. 157.

court of the area issued an order for compliance.[26] A cleric was subject
to ecclesiastical jurisdiction for his personal debts, but if his debts involved real property (mortgages, seigniorial rights, etc.), the case fell
under the secular judicial authority. A cleric's non-payment of wages
to his servant and evasion of the *aides* and *gabelle* were secular concerns, as were also charges brought against him in such matters divorced from the ecclesiastical life as farming and commerce. If a
cleric was sued in the person of the legal guardian of a layman
or in the role of any other proxy, he fell under secular jurisdiction. Finally, whenever the king was involved in a legal action, the
maxim held that "the king pleads in no other court but his own".[27]

In criminal cases the secular courts claimed the following qualifications on the rights of ecclesiastical tribunals:

1. Offenses were to be considered either simple, mixed or privileged cases;
in the latter two events, the enormity of the crime was such that the secular
court joined the Church court in investigating the charges and bringing in a
decision.
2. Where the alleged criminal action of an ecclesiastic was not the
principal cause of the arraignment but was incidental to it, the secular
court assumed jurisdiction.
3. If the cleric's offense was the principal cause and he was absent from
court (in contempt of court, thereby), the secular court considered the case
privileged and claimed competence.
4. If the cleric was apprehended out of his clerical garb his benefit of
clergy was forfeited.
5. Clerics committing crimes while engaged in secular pursuits, whether
these pursuits were compatible or not with their vocations, fell under lay
jurisdiction.[28]

The bishops, on the other hand, claimed that all crimes not deemed
privileged cases (that is, the so-called *délits communs*) were retained
under ecclesiastical jurisdiction, while the more serious privileged
cases were to be jointly investigated. The claims of the secular tribunals carried the day, for while cases of *common misdemeanors*
usually were delivered up to the ecclesiastical courts, the secular tribunals tended generally to ignore sharing jurisdiction over the privileged cases with the bishops' courts.[29] Several ordinances of Louis XIV
sought to ratify the provisions for joint jurisdiction, but continuing

[26]   Abbé Claude Fleury, *Institution au droit ecclésiastique* (Paris, Herissant Fils,
1767), Vol. II, p. 54.
[27]   *Mémoires du clergé*, VII, cols. 372-382; Héricourt, *op. cit.*, I, pp. 157-158.
[28]   *Ibid.*, VII, cols. 390-396.
[29]   *Ibid.*, VII, cols. 396-400.

grievances by the clergy revealed that the secular courts were assuming sole jurisdiction with impunity. The king never closed the
loophole which was the principal weapon of the secular courts — the
ubiquitous *appel comme d'abus* — which will be considered below.
It was more a commentary than a complaint when the abbé Fleury
wrote that episcopal jurisdiction was "... reduced to so narrow limits. ... It is true that they [the bishops] are no longer the masters they
[once] were to prevent litigations even between their ecclesiastics ..."[30] in secular courts.

Contemporary legal opinion held that laymen were subject to ecclesiastical tribunals solely for tithes, marriage, simony, and heresy.[31] The
secular courts did not challenge the right of the Church to declare
what constituted heresy, but they did question its jurisdiction over
anything beyond the definition and declaration of heresy. The secular
tribunals had always regarded heresy as fully under their jurisdiction
because such a heinous crime constituted *lèse-Majesté*. In 1604 the
Parlement of Paris had held that the role of ecclesiastical courts in
questions of heresy was limited to a declaratory one.[32] On the other
hand, previous edicts of Henry II and Francis II had clearly recognized the rights of the ecclesiastical power in these matters; however,
here as in other areas of government, the Parlements pursued an
aggressive policy.[33]

Royal officials could not be excommunicated for actions taken in
pursuit of their duty; before they could be so censured the Church
courts were required to appeal to Parlement or to the king. The penal-
ty for the illegal censure of royal officials was the seizure of the offending bishop's temporal goods.[34] For the crimes of blasphemy, sacri-
lege, and sorcery laymen were not subject to ecclesiastical jurisdiction, but offending clerics might be brought before secular courts
jointly sitting with Church courts for such offenses if their crimes
were considered privileged cases. The secular tribunals began to take

[30]  Fleury, *Institution* ..., II, p. 55.
[31]  *Mémoires du clergé*, VII, col. 585.
[32]  *Ibid.*, VII, col. 562.
[33]  Francis II's edict of May, 1560 read: "[We] have by our irrevocable edict left
and do leave [the question of heresy] to the prelates of our kingdom as natural
judges of this crime, and as they have formerly enjoyed it; ... forbidding our
courts of Parlement, bailiffs, seneschals, and other judges to undertake any recognition of the said crimes of heresy and to meddle in them at all, except in so
far as they may be requested by the judges of the Church to lend assistance for the
execution of their ordinances and judgements." *Mémoires du clergé*, VII, col. 580.
[34]  Héricourt, *op. cit.*, I, p. 181.

an interest in the punishment of simony in the 17th Century where before the Church had had no interference.

The jurisdiction of the Church courts over marriage was significant but by no means exclusive or uncontroverted. The ecclesiastical judge had competence over questions concerning betrothals: whether or not an engagement was binding was the question. Ordinarily, where there had been cohabitation between engaged persons, the ecclesiastical official was able to order the marriage to be celebrated: failure to comply was punishable canonically, by such means as excommunication and interdict which required no secular concurrence, and by deprivation of burial and of reception of alms and imprisonment which did require secular approval. The secular courts usually took cognizance of marriage — generally by the instrument of the *appel comme d'abus* — in questions concerning the alleged nullity of a marriage because the participants were minors, the banns had not been properly published, there had been no parental consent and no witnesses, or the local *curé* had been absent. In general, where the litigation concerned marriage as a sacrament and the invalidating impediments to marriage enumerated in canon law, the ecclesiastical courts exercised jurisdiction: they could consider appeals for annulment based on charges of bigamy, the breaking of vows of chastity, and the too proximate state of blood relationship. However, where the litigation involved the validity of the marriage of deceased persons with a view towards challenging their heirs and the disposition of family property, the secular tribunals took cognizance. The question of a legal separation was heard in lay courts since the disposal of property was involved. Although the Parlement of Besançon did hold that the ecclesiastical courts were incompetent to consider breaches of promise and could merely hear the vows of betrothal, this contention was confirmed only in the Franche-Comté. In general, then, the court which had jurisdiction over marriage was determined by whether the question under legal consideration was the vows of betrothal and the sacrament of marriage on the one hand or the civil effects of marriage on the other.[35]

It is important to note that the motives of the Parlements in 17th and 18th-Century France in questions of jurisdiction over marriage were not solely determined by their desire to make the ecclesiastical courts impotent all along the line. An enlightening article by Jacques

[35]   Fleury, *Institution* . . ., II, pp. 46-49; Héricourt, *op. cit.*, I, p. 156.

Ghestin [36] has shown that the primary concern of the magistrates in questions of marriage was social: the maintenance of parliamentary caste by the prohibition of undesirable, socially disapproved marriage alliances with inferior families. The Parlements went far beyond canon law in prohibiting the clandestine marriages of their children by enforcing strictly all the preliminary provisions before a marriage could be validly celebrated: the local *curés* of *both* partners had to be present, the banns had to be published according to specific regulations of time and place, and the members of both families were given the right to make appeals for annulment. That the Parlements' motives were not to introduce marriage solely as a civil arrangement was seen by their granting of increased power to the *curés* because the latter seemed to share roughly the same familial interests as the parents and could be more easily watched and relied upon than lay officials who more readily might cooperate in publishing the banns of those intent on misalliances. The *curés*, consequently, received a monopoly on publishing banns. On the other hand, the Parlements held that the ecclesiastical courts could have jurisdiction over pleas for the annulment of a betrothal or a marriage only if the appeals came from the married or engaged partners, while secular courts took over when the objecting appellants were the parents of the couple. The Parlements went so far as to specify those in the family who could and could not object to a betrothal or a marriage — and in a specific order of priority. They advanced far beyond Church canons on questions of seduction, holding that all marriages of minors contracted without parental consent constituted seduction and were null.

Thus, in some areas the competence of the ecclesiastical power — or at least that of the *curés* — was increased, while in others it was made impotent. But the motives of the magistrates were the maintenance of caste and not specifically the curtailment of ecclesiastical justice. In fact, however, the activities of the magistrates in marital affairs had a significance along the same lines as the other attacks on ecclesiastical power: first, the increase of secular jurisdiction over marriages was greater than the additional importance given to the *curés*; and more importantly, the increased interest of Parlements in these affairs and their successes in revising the marriage procedures for caste purposes, revealed a basically secular spirit which did not

[36] "L'Action des Parlements contre les 'mésalliances' aux XVIIe et XVIIIe siècles", *Revue historique de droit français et étranger*, Vol. XXXIV (January-March, 1956), pp. 74-110; (April-June, 1956), pp. 196-224.

hesitate to make the secular considerations paramount. In questions of marriage, therefore, the neutralization of ecclesiastical jurisdiction proceeded as evidently as in other affairs, albeit with particular peculiarities.

Two other areas where ecclesiastical justice had once played a paramount role — questions of tithes and contracts — were also being reduced to non-existence. Tithes could be claimed in an ecclesiastical court, but since possession of property was a lay matter, any question of tithes took on the appearance of a *mixed* case and ultimately was settled definitively only in the secular tribunals.[37] Laymen were not subject to the Church courts for breach of contract because as in matters of tithes and marriage, the consequences of a contract in the domain of property came to overshadow the question of oaths taken in the name of God; these questions were by nature *mixed* and the secular courts were successful in claiming full jurisdiction. Fleury noted that even contracts made between ecclesiastics before notaries were considered secular affairs.[38] *Curés* and permanent *vicaires* did enjoy the right to receive wills from their parishoners and the diocesan *notaires apostoliques* processed them; but quite clearly the role of the Church here was merely a convenience: the *curé* acted more as the local official than as a representative of ecclesiastical justice, and at any rate, since wills involved property, bequests could only be challenged in the secular tribunals.

The *appel comme d'abus* was the sole means by which the lay courts could challenge decisions of ecclesiastical courts. Anyone, including the Ministry, could file such an appeal in one of the sovereign Parlements against an ecclesiastical legal decision. If the appeal was heard, it had a "devolutive" effect but not a "suspensive" effect; that is, while the appeal was being considered by the Parlement, the ecclesiastical judgment could not be suspended from execution, but the case would devolve upon the Parlement. Only if the appellant was the Ministry itself did the appeal have a suspensive effect.[39] As Marion has observed, however, if the appeal were regarded insistently by the ecclesiastical courts as non-suspensive, the Parlements would retaliate by seizing the temporal goods of the ecclesiastical official against whom the appeal had been filed.[40] Consequently, the *appel comme d'abus*

[37]  Héricourt, *op. cit.*, I, pp. 156-157.
[38]  Fleury, *Instruction* . . ., II, p. 54.
[39]  *Mémoires du clergé*, VI, col. 239.
[40]  Marcel Marion, *Dictionnaire des institutions de la France aux XVIIe et XVIIIe siècles* (Paris, Auguste Picard, 1923), pp. 21-22.

was a foolproof loophole for the aggressive lay tribunals to employ in encroaching upon ecclesiastical jurisdiction, and they could be restrained only by the impolitic and increasingly unpopular royal intervention into parliamentary affairs. Writing about 1693, the abbé Fleury summarized the effect of the use of these *appels comme d'abus*:

... The appeals *comme d'abus* have achieved the ruin of ecclesiastical jurisdiction. According to the ordinances, this appeal should be used only for very grave matters, when the ecclesiastical judge notoriously exceeds his power or when there is a manifest enterprise against the liberties of the Gallican Church. But in practice, the *appel comme d'abus* has become very fashionable; ... It is the ordinary means which bad priests employ to maintain themselves in their benefices in spite of the bishops, or at least to tire them with endless litigation; for the Parlements always accept the appeals. On this pretext they examine the very basis of affairs and remove from ecclesiastical jurisdiction what they cannot set aside directly. There are some Parlements which people complain rarely do justice to bishops.[41]

The abuse of these appeals against abuse was so widespread that it became habitual for the clergy repeatedly to appeal to the king for redress. The resultant edict of April, 1695 attempted to codify previous declarations on the limits of ecclesiastical and secular tribunals, and it became the basis for the numerous jurisdictional squabbles of the 18th Century.

The stated purpose of the royal edict of April, 1695 [42] was to reply to the repeated representations of the Assemblies of the clergy concerning the evasion of previous royal edicts on the problem of the rival jurisdictions and "... to prevent the disorders which ... [these jurisdictional conflicts] could produce to the detriment of ecclesiastical jurisdiction, whose protectors we are...." [43] It concerned itself primarily with three areas of episcopal jurisdiction: the *droit d'institution canonique*, episcopal visitations and relations with the regular clergy, and the conflicts with the secular courts. The Edict attempted to prevent the episcopal right to institute a cleric from being so circumvented that it became purely formal. By its provisions, those provided with benefices at the hands of the pope were obliged to appear be-

---

[41] *Oeuvres de l'abbé Fleury*, "Discours X sur les libertés de l'église gallicane", (Paris, Librairie Ch. Delagrave, 1884), p. 430.

[42] Isambert, *op. cit.*, XX, pp. 243-257; Léon Mention, *Documents relatifs aux rapports du clergé avec la royauté de 1682 à 1789* (Paris, Alphonse Picard, 1893-1903), Vol. I, pp. 113-127.

[43] Isambert, *op. cit.*, XX, p. 243. In an explanatory declaration of March 29, 1696 the king observed that the 1695 Edict was designed to codify previous ordinances; that is to say, it did not innovate. *Ibid.*, XX, p. 264.

fore the bishop or his vicar-general in the region where the living was located to be examined on their qualifications, and they could not fulfill their ecclesiastical duties until they had received the ordinary's visa. Any refusal by the ecclesiastical ordinary of the indispensable visa had to be explained to the refused cleric in writing, but the secular courts might take no notice of such a refusal or make objection to any visa unless an *appel comme d'abus* were interjected, in which event the secular courts were limited to sending the offending ecclesiastic before his superior for settlement of the case. The lay tribunals, then, were enjoined from interfering with the episcopal monopoly on canonical institution of clerics, but the *appel comme d'abus* procedure was still open to them; the ambiguous wording which provided the secular courts with this ultimate weapon was the following: "... and nevertheless direct ... [the secular judges] to render such justice to those of our subjects who will have been thus refused, so that there may be no occasion of legitimate complaint." [44]

The Edict of 1695 attempted, secondly, to maintain the institution of episcopal visitations in its full force. It stated that all parish churches, even those situated within monastic communities which claimed exemptions from episcopal jurisdiction, were subject to visitations by the bishops and their vicars-general. Parish officials (for example, the lay *marguilliers* or church wardens who administered the physical plant and resources of the parish church) were ordered to execute faithfully and promptly all episcopal ordinances and to present the visitor with the accounts of income and expenditure. All the regents, preceptors, masters, and mistresses of the village schools were subject to interrogation by the visitor. The bishops and their officials were permitted to issue public admonitions (*monitoires*) in cases of grave offenses and public scandal, and the secular officials, administrative and judicial, were to order them published where the situation warrented such drastic recourse. The episcopal control of preaching was affirmed: no regular clergy might preach in their monastic churches or chapels without first appearing before the diocesan ordinary and receiving his permissive benediction; in other churches, no secular or regular clergy could preach without episcopal permission, and secular tribunals were to refrain from sanctioning any illegal preaching. No regular or secular priest might administer penance without episcopal permission, and the bishop might restrict

[44]  *Ibid.*, XX, p. 245.

such permission as to time, place, and other conditions without having to offer explanations; the only exception was to be in the case of *curés* who might administer the sacrament by virtue of their office unless specifically interdicted. The Edict was ambiguous, however, concerning the rights of bishops over the discipline of monasteries reputedly exempt from their jurisdiction, in that, it permitted episcopal visitations of both exempt and unexempt monastic communities but then qualified this permission with respect to the exempt houses of superiors of religious orders. This ambiguity was the cause of conflict in the ensuing century.[45]

It was, however, the Edict's clauses concerning the limits of secular and ecclesiastical jurisdiction which presented the picture of a royal government extremely wary about too specifically limiting either jurisdiction or permitting unrestrained encroachments of the one upon the other.

Cognizance and judgment of religious doctrine will belong to the archbishops and bishops: [we] command our courts of Parlement and all our other judges to send back [such matters] to the said prelates, to give them the assistance which they will need to execute the censures which they will be able to impose, and to proceed with the punishment of culprits, *without* prejudice to our said courts and judges to provide by other means which *they will deem proper for the correction of the scandal,* and the troubling of public order and tranquillity, and the infractions of ordinances which the said doctrine will have caused. . . . Cognizance of matters of the sacraments, vows of religion, the divine office, ecclesiastical discipline, and other purely spiritual [affairs] will belong to the judges of the Church. [We] command our officials and even our courts of Parlement to leave to them, and even to refer to them, [such] jurisdiction, without taking any notice of affairs of this nature, *if there is interjected in our said courts no appel come d'abus,* . . . *or if there is involved no question of succession or other civil effects where one would be considering the estate of deceased persons or of that of their children.* Our courts will be able to recognize or receive no other appeals against ordinances and decisions of the judges of the Church *except those which will be qualified comme d'abus.*[46]

After discussing the effective means in the hands of the secular courts for encroaching upon the ecclesiastical jurisdiction, the authors of the relevant passages in the *Mémoires du clergé* observed that the *appels comme d'abus* were left open to varying interpretations because the

---

[45]   Article 18 of the Edict of 1695 and the declaration of March 29, 1696 made it clear that the bishops were not to enjoy complete visitation rights over all exempt religious communities. *Ibid.,* XX, pp. 248; 264-265.
[46]   *Ibid.,* XX, pp. 252-253.

king and his councillors did not wish to define the scope of royal justice as precisely as that of ecclesiastical and seignorial justice lest un-
foreseen litigations in the future find the hands of royal justice tied.[47]

## III

In considering the protracted struggle between the Parlements and
the bishops in the 18th Century, the question of the motives of each
of the combatants begs for evaluation. Certainly, each party claimed
to be upholding the *status quo* and curbing the well-known aggressions of the other. Each, consequently, proclaimed itself the champion of loyalty to the king and to his prerogatives and its opponent the
truly subversive force in the nation. It became indeed embarrassing
to the lethargic monarchy of Louis XV to have the maintenance of its
regal power made the pretext for assorted aggressions, convulsions,
and near revolts. It is, then, appropriate to investigate the position,
program, and pretensions of each side in the great struggle which,
though at various times resounding with the battle cries of Gallican
Liberties, *Unigenitus, billets de confession, refus des sacrements,* appeals to a General Council, and Jansenism, was essentially the continuing struggle over the *secularization* of society.

It may be noted that secularization, from its early manifestations in
13th-Century society, through its more spectacular successes in the
era of the Reformation, down to its perhaps final victory in the 18th
Century, is not by definition irreligious. It was not always clear that
the bishops were the religious party and the magistrates the infidels.
It was not so much over faith as over the role of the Church corporately in society that the battle of secularization was waged.

There was genuine feeling in circles even outside that of the rare-
fied episcopate that the onslaught of the Parlements against the
Church was not purely defensive. The bourgeois advocate Barbier
was sympathetic to the allegation of the advocates and magistrates
that the Council of Embrun had violated Gallican Liberties after it
had been convened to discipline the unyielding Mgr. Soanen,
bishop of Senez and one of the appellants of the Bull *Unigenitus* to
a General Council.[48] Nevertheless Barbier described the advocates in
the following terms:

[47]  *Mémoires du clergé,* VII, cols. 421-422.
[48]  Jean Orcibal has written that these appellants were not pure Jansenists; they
were Gallicans of the 1682 stripe and particularly of the 1688 appeal to a Council

They believed that there was none but they who had the right in the State
by their independence to declare the great truths of the Church, without
respecting either the authority of the king, well or badly employed, or that
of the Pope, or that of all the bishops who, in a word, are reunited in the
same [anti-Jansenist] party, with the exception of four [of them].[49]

A contemporary who was more concerned with ultramontanist ag-
gression than Barbier, the marquis d'Argenson, suggested that the
Parlement of Paris was ultimately interested in favoring a type of
"presbyterianism" which would reduce the special dignities and power of the bishops to a level equal to that of simple *curés*, and also in
the proclamation of the supremacy of the king over the Church along
Anglican lines. D'Argenson explained that tactical considerations dis-
suaded the magistrates from any direct advocacy of these measures,
leading them to work more indirectly through battling against clerical
abuse in specific cases.[50]

It was clear that by Gallican liberties the magistrates meant not
the traditional conciliarism of the French Church but rather the regalist position of 1682. In condemning a thesis which claimed that
authority over the secular power did indeed reside in the Church

---

by the government of Louis XIV. (*Louis XIV contre Innocent XI. Les Appels au
future concile de 1688 et l'opinion française*, Paris, Librairie Philosophique J.
Vrin, 1949, pp. 82-83.)

[49] Barbier, *Chronique de la régence et du règne de Louis XV (1718-1763), ou
Journal de Barbier* (Paris, Charpentier, 1858), Vol. II, p. 31. Barbier cited a
contemporary song which mocked the role of the advocates as "theologians",
signifying that they were out of their element, *ibid.*, II, pp. 32-35. Several verses
of "Sur la Consultation des avocats au sujet du concile d'Embrun" follow:

1. "Du fameux concile d'Embrun
Que faut-il que l'on pense?
Tous les évêques en commun
En ont pris la défense:
Mais c'est bien affaire aux prélats!
Écoutons plutôt sur ce cas
Les avocats, les avocats,
Les avocats, les avocats de France!

4. Que de troubles ne vit-on pas
Au concile d'Éphèse?
Il fallut livrer vingt combats
Pour proscrire une thèse.
Mais falloit-il tant de fracas?
Pourquoi ne consultoit-on pas
Les avocats, les avocats,
Les avocats, les avocats de France?

8. Du troupeau soyez les pasteurs,
Dit Jésus aux apôtres,
Mais vous n'êtes pas seuls docteurs,
Mon Église en a d'autres.
Ne liez et ne déliez,
Qu'avant tout vous ne consultiez
Les avocats, les avocats,
Les avocats, les avocats de France!

9. Les avocats italiens,
Du Nord et d'Allemagne,
Ne sont pas théologiens,
Non plus que ceux d'Epagne;
Ils croient aux dogmes de foi,
Mais d'en décider c'est l'emploi
Des avocats, des avocats,
Des avocats, des avocats de France!"

[50] *Journal et mémoires du marquis d'Argenson*, ed. by E. J. B. Rathery, (Paris,
Mme Veuve Jules Renouard, 1859-1867), Vol. VII, p. 256.

conceived as a conciliar body, the Parlement of Provence held firmly that

the more the Church is superior to the Pope in the exercise of spiritual power, the more it would be dangerous to ascribe to it false attributes which would lay claim . . . to the nature and character of infallibility which it only enjoys in the defining of dogmas: discernment [of pretension] would be much more difficult than it was in the [cases of] enterprises of a single pontiff and power fallible in every respect.[51]

These parliamentary Gallican liberties led the abbé Fleury to conjure up what he called Gallican servitude, along the lines of Fénelon of Cambrai:

The great servitude of the Gallican Church: . . . it is the excessive extent of secular jurisdiction. It is no longer the ecclesiastical judge who takes cognizance of the separation of married persons . . .; it is the lay judge, on the pretext that this separation always involves property. All matters relating to benefices are considered before the lay judge. . . . Thus the bishops are deprived of cognizance over what interests them the most — the choice of worthy officials to serve the Church under them and the faithful administration of its revenue — and they are often saddened to see and powerless to prevent an incapable, unworthy priest from acquiring possession of a considerable living, because he is a more clever litigant than another — which ought to exclude him from it.[52]

Because of the close union of Church and State under the Old Régime it was often difficult to eliminate ecclesiastical implication from political positions or *vice versa*. Consequently, it must not be imagined that parliamentary support for Jansenists implied a particular theological position on the part of the magistrates, or even that 18th-Century Jansenism was theological in import. The oddly assorted 101 propositions which were condemned in the Bull *Unigenitus* were designed to serve as the touchstone of heretical Jansenism, but standing alone, many of them were inoffensive to Catholics not at all tainted with Jansenism; nor were all the propositions, strictly speaking, religious in content. In making themselves the staunchest foes of the Bull, to what exactly did the magistrates object? It was the view of

---

[51]  G. N. Nivelle, *La Constitution Unigenitus déferée à l'église universelle ou recueil général des actes d'appel interjettés au future concile général de cette constitution et des lettres pastoralis officii* . . . *avec les arrests et autres actes des Parlemens du royaume qui ont rapport à ces objets* (Cologne, 1757), Vol. III, pp. 979-980.

[52]  *Oeuvres de l'abbé Fleury*, "Discours X sur les libertés de l'église gallicane", p. 429.

informed people, cited by Barbier and corroborated by the actual remonstrances of the Parlements, that the magistrates

... are not solicitous about the fundamentals of the Constitution [*Unigenitus*]: to know what was the efficacy of the love of God, nor how many kinds of grace God has had made for those who live on this lower world. This does not concern them; it is theology. But what does irritate them in the Constitution is the 91st proposition which is condemned. ...[53]

In proposition 91 of *Unigenitus* condemnation was declared for the position that "the fear of an unjust excommunication should never prevent us from doing our duty ... One never leaves the Church even when it appears that one is expelled from it by the spitefulness of men, [provided] one is devoted to God, to Jesus Christ, and to the Church through charity."[54] Clearly there was in this proposition nothing inherent in Jansenism.[55] Instead, the condemned proposition was one of the tenets of regalism which had done battle both with the pretensions of Rome to exercise direct or indirect power over secular thrones, and with the conciliar theory of the accidental power of the Church over rulers. *Unigenitus* was an ill-conceived *pot pourri*, condemning propositions which had by interpretation seemed to aid the Jansenist position and others which had irritated Rome for centuries; these various propositions blossomed forth in *Unigenitus* as the final distillation of Jansenism. The Parlements saw the condemnation of proposition 91 as an attack upon their hallowed regalist position; they objected to other condemnations also and even opposed the very intervention of Rome into French affairs; however, proposition 91 more than any other defined for them the great struggle over secularization. In the words of the Parlement of Brittany, the condemnation of proposition 91 boded ill for the independence of the French crown and the absolute sovereignty of the king over temporal affairs. They were moved to remonstrate by

---

[53]   Barbier, *op. cit.*, II, pp. 115-116.
[54]   Mention, *op. cit.*, 11, p. 33. The text of *Unigenitus* is herein reprinted in Latin and in French.
[55]   In his "Les Idées politiques des jansénistes", *Neophilologus*, Vol. XL (January, 1956), pp. 1-18, J. A. G. Tans demonstrates the changing nature of Jansenist thought on political questions. Where regalism signified royal control over spiritual affairs, the Jansenists originally had been hostile to it; only in Quesnel's time did the Jansenists favor this implication of regalism; however, where regalism signified secular independence in temporal affairs, Jansenists had always favored it. So-called Jansenist ideas about Church government were derived from Gallicanism, in itself a varying set of tenets.

the fear . . . of seeing introduced into the kingdom the practice of accepting as sufficient juridical proofs the simple allegation of bishops, of treating as heretics those who do not hold the Church infallible in matters not revealed [in Scripture] and who do not believe they owe to these decisions the same faith as to those which are dogmatic; the dangerous consequences which have seemed to us to result from these principles, for even your sacred person, for the rights of your crown, and for our precious liberties. . . .[56]

The fear of papal excommunication was not so far-fetched. During the conflict over the extension of the *droit de régale* — the conflict which gave official birth to the regalist position — Innocent XI did excommunicate the pro-regalist archbishop of Toulouse, Mgr. de Montpezat, and he threatened like recompense for the god-king himself. In a letter to the king the pope warned:

'If you will not rescind this decree [on the *régale*] we strongly fear that you will meet with the vengeance of heaven. . . . As for us, henceforth, we shall no longer deal with this affair through letters, but we shall not fail to use the means which God has placed in our power and which, in a disorder so grave and so dangerous, we could not ignore without making ourself guilty of criminal negligence of our apostolic duty. However, we fear no danger and no uproar, as severe and horrible as it may be . . ., deriving glory from the cross of Our Lord Jesus Christ. It is with Him, no longer with us, that you will have to deal in the future . . ." [57]

One of the most recurring themes in the parliamentary war against the bishops was the so-called "system of independence" which the bishops were held to represent. Although in fact the magistrates represented nothing more than an aristocratic caste bent on preserving its privileges and extending its political power, their rhetoric created the image of a progressive force with no other interest but that of patriotism. Parliamentary patriotism was, in a sense, a form of nationalism not unconnected with the revolutionary nationalism which saw the people as one in the symbol of the *patrie* or the Republic.[58] The

[56]   A. Le Moy, *Remontrances du Parlement de Bretagne au XVIIIe siècle*. Textes inédits précédés d'une introduction (Angers, Imprimerie Burdin, 1909), pp. 41-44. The Parlement of Normandy opposed *Unigenitus* because it struck at the independence of the secular power. Floquet, *Histoire du parlement de Normandie* (Rouen, Edouard Frère 1840-42), Vol. VI, p. 255; remonstrance of May 17, 1730.
[57]   Innocent XI to Louis XIV, December 29, 1679; quoted in Georges Guitton, S. J., *Le Père de la Chaize, confesseur de Louis XIV* (Paris, Beauchesne, 1959), Vol. I, p. 68. Martin also feels that the excommunication of Louis XIV was imminent in this period; *op. cit.*, p. 327.
[58]   For a discussion of pre-1789 French nationalism and the role which the Parlements played in its development, see Robert R. Palmer, "The National Idea

Parlement of Paris orated as if it believed that all Frenchmen should be equally subject to the laws of France — that is, to the king ruling in accordance with the fundamental law, which was in the guardianship of the magistracy. The magistrates, notwithstanding the divisive character of their legal privileges and social exclusiveness, professed to oppose all divisive elements in the nation: whether Huguenots who were somehow un-French and conjured up memories of civil wars and rebellion; or Jesuits who could never be French because they were blind followers of an Italian prince; or non-believers who weakened the influence of religion and encouraged civil disobedience and social disorder; [59] or bishops who under the influence of Jesuitical pretensions constituted a danger to the unity of the State. In the face of such overwhelming potential and actual danger to the unity of the nation, the Parlements alone were able to preserve the nation because they, in fact, represented the nation.

In assailing the "system of independence" of the Church, the Parlement of Paris' Grand Remonstrance of April 9, 1753 on the continuing *refus des sacrements* to alleged Jansenists so fundamentally attacked the traditional image the Church had of its social role that the Assembly of the Clergy felt it necessary to reply to the charges in detail. The remonstrance first proceeded to sever the clergy from the rest of the king's subjects in order to create between them an unbridgeable chasm; it explained the uniquely clerical "system of independence":

The desire for independence, Sire, is born with all men; but it is not the same with ecclesiastics as with the rest of your subjects. The latter find nothing either in their estate or in their functions which does not call them to the law of a just obedience — no pretext of creating limits to it, no object which arouses in them this love of independence which they have sacrificed for ever. They deem themselves fortunate to enjoy peacefully all their rights under the protection of Your Majesty, and to have influence only through their intimate union with all the bodies of the State.

With the ecclesiastics, however, the practice of exercising a sacred power which they do not derive from the sovereign; that of perpetually receiving hommage, so much more profound because they are the ministers of divinity itself and the oracles of truth; the ability they have to form a powerful,

in France Before the Revolution", *Journal of the History of Ideas*, Vol. I (January, 1940), pp. 95-111.
[59] This argument is demonstrated for the Parlement of Toulouse by David D. Bien, *The Calas Affair. Persecution, Toleration, and Heresy in Eighteenth-Century Toulouse* (Princeton, University Press, 1960).

rich, and distinguished order within the State; finally, the union between them and a foreign power, joined by common views and interests — what sources of dangers and temptations for men![60]

After having dubbed the ecclesiastical community virtually an alien body within the body politic, a *status in statu*, the remonstrance then proceeded to describe with ominous implications for the rights of the king and the nation the consequences of the ecclesiastical "system of independence".

More enterprising or less repressed at certain times, the ecclesiastics have been seen to proceed from independence to usurpation, to become the arbiters of your subjects, the judges of magistrates, even the sovereigns of sovereigns. More vulnerable in some other epochs, they have at least always refused to perform the duties of subjects; abusing the respect due to religion, they have usurped in favor of an imposing title an almost universal domain. External and public functions, temporal goods, personal conduct, and even crimes against the State of which some of them have been guilty — everything has become a spiritual matter, entirely independent of secular jurisdiction, in the end, entirely subject to the judgment of the Church alone or of their individual consciences.... Fortunate that these ecclesiastics have never succeeded in suggesting to the sovereign himself that the sacrifice of his authority [would be] an hommage due to religion.[61]

All the pretensions of the episcopate to power and independence the not irreligious Parlement ascribed to its deviation from a more primitive Christianity. The magistrates' remonstrance cited the abbé Fleury's *Ecclesiastical History* to demonstrate that once the bishops had been merely bishops, "but soon *the bishops of France, having become lords and admitted to a share of government, believed that they might enjoy as bishops what they only enjoyed as lords* and pretended [the right] to judge kings publicly".[62] Tracing the history of ecclesiastical usurpations of secular authority, the remonstrance held that only a vigilant Parlement, the "born contradictors" of all ecclesiastical enterprises,[63] had saved royal authority — which was all the more reason for opposing the condemnation of the 91st proposition of *Unigenitus*, a condemnation clearly designed to make resistance to such usurpation nearly impossible. In a fit of righteous exasperation the Parlement of Paris demanded the end of ecclesiastical independence:

[60]  Flammermont, *op. cit.*, I, pp. 530-531.
[61]  *Ibid.*, I, pp. 531; 535.
[62]  *Ibid.*, I, p. 532.
[63]  Remonstrance of September 3, 1731; *ibid.*, I, p. 274.

... It is at last time that ... [justice] exert its rights upon all citizens [ci-toyens] indiscriminately because they are all indiscriminately its subjects. It was never more essential to repress rigorously those who aspire to create within the State an independent state by means of spiritualizing everything they wish to usurp.[64]

In defining what it considered the legitimate extent of ecclesiastical authority, the Parlement of Paris made precise distinctions:

We shall, Sire, never confuse two things which should always be distin-guished: the one which involves the inner administration of the sacraments and which is reserved to the ecclesiastical power; the other which concerns the general policing of the kingdom, the tranquillity of peoples, and which belongs essentially to the power of the sovereign.[65] If it could be said that your Parlement was in no way competent to oversee a matter so vital to your peoples, it would be to dispute in a sense even Your Majesty's right to do so.[66]

... The ministers of the Church are accountable to the king and, in a case of abuse, to the court under his authority, ... for all which could, in the exer-cise of the power which they hold directly from God, injure public tranquil-lity, the laws, and the maxims of the kingdom.[67]

For adherents of the conciliar form of Church government the ul-timate authority in the Church was a General Council, and as con-ciliarists the magistrates agreed. However, the Parlement of Paris went beyond this position by contending that since a General Council could not alter doctrine legitimately, some higher authority would have to be empowered to examine the bases for its doctrinal pronouncement, for in a concrete case the Parlement did not believe a General Council infallible. That higher authority turned out to be the supreme authority of the French sovereign who, according to the fundamental laws of France, had to concur in all the laws of the Church which were to bind his subjects. The decrees of the Council of Trent had not been received in France. Nor had even the popular decrees of Constance and Basle been received *in toto*; rather, the Assembly of Bourges held by Charles VIII had determined which of the conciliar decrees were to be accepted into French law. Finally, if the secular power was *de facto* the supreme authority over the French Church, the Parlement of Paris found it quite consistent in

---

[64] *Ibid.*, II, p. 151.
[65] Such matters as *refus des sacrements* to alleged Jansenists would and did disturb public order; hence they came under secular jurisdiction.
[66] Flammermont, *op. cit.*, I, pp. 309-310.
[67] Mention, *op cit.*, II, p. 70

1737 to claim the right to investigate whether any Church pronounce-
ments really had the approval of the *whole Church* and could therefore be admitted into France.[68] In its remonstrance of April 7, 1737
the Parlement of Paris stated its position on secular supremacy with
definitiveness:

Our fathers have always maintained as we shall always maintain after them
that . . . even in connection with ecclesiastical affairs, far from the authority
of our kings being regarded as foreign or impotent, the inspection and
concurrence of the royal authority was always useful and necessary.

The kings cannot make doctrine but they *can*

. . . examine the truth of the facts on everything that is passed on at the
time of a [dogmatic] decision, before recognizing it and permitting its execution and promulgation in their States, to see that there is nothing which
injures the purity of the former canons, that the right of bishops as necessary judges of doctrine [69] and the liberty of suffrage has been fully preserved,
or that in what emanates from the power or the suffrage of the bishops,
there is nothing glossed over with the name of doctrine and religion which
harms the maxims of the kingdom and tends to disrupt public tranquillity
or to encroach upon the inalienable rights of sovereignty.[70]

What the Parlement was groping for was some ultimate authority with
which to check the potential and real despotism of the Church. It had
the *appels comme d'abus* as ". . . an invincible rampart for blocking
the enterprises of the ecclesiastical power against the legitimate and
immutable rights of royal authority. . . ." [71] It felt that there was inherent danger in the statement of the 1765 Assembly of the clergy
that

the laws of the Church can be qualified only by the same authority which
has pronounced them. These qualifications pertain even to the law; they

[68]   Flammermont, *op cit.*, I, pp. 334-337. For a convennient summary of the
Paris Parlement's theories of lay supremacy even in ecclesiastical affaires, see F.
Bassieux, "Théorie des libertés gallicanes du parlement de Paris au XVIIIe siècle",
*Nouvelle Revue historique de droit français et étranger*, Vol. XXX (1906), pp.
330-350.
[59]   It is evident that the Parlement even claimed to be defending episcopal rights,
presumably against Roman encroachment. Although the bishops viewed the
problem and the source of encroachment differently, the Parlement was sincere
in defending episcopal rights *as it understood them*. The theory of the mutual
fate of episcopal and parliamentary Gallicanism was summarized by Chancellor
d'Aguesseau: "There is a connection so narrow between the rights of the episcopate and the fundamental maxims of our liberties, that one could not strike the
least blow against the one without causing real injury to the other . . ." *Oeuvres
de d'Aguesseau* (Paris, Chez Napoléon Chaix, 1865), II, p. 264.
[70]   Flammermont, *op. cit.*, I, p. 336.
[71]   *Ibid.*, I, p. 267.

determine the kind of submission which is due to it and it is for the Church alone to determine its character and extent.

To this manifestation of ecclesiastical independence the Parlement remonstrated:

It is to the Church undoubtedly, Sire, that the definition of faith belongs; but if, on the pretext of defining faith, things are proposed which are foreign to dogma or contrary to the peace of the State, then it will be false to claim that it is for the Church alone to determine the character and extent of the laws which it pronounces.[72]

Because the ecclesiastical power was usurped and usurping power it could not be entrusted with self-restraint. The demands for *billets de confession* and the persecution of so-called Jansenists only confirmed the Parlement in the conviction that the lay power must discipline the Church.

The Parlement of Provence seems to have advanced in its advocacy of secular control of the Church even farther than the Parlement of Paris. The Provençal magistrates were Catholic, but they feared the power of a Church governed by a single head with irresponsible, absolute authority; their ideal was a national Church subject to the king and to the law, having only those relations with Rome which were indispensable for the unity of the Faith. The Provençal magistrates were later to find the realization of their concept of the French Church and its relations with Rome in the Civil Constitution of the Clergy, albeit under a national government and social order totally distasteful to them.

The Provençal magistrates enunciated a theory of Church-State relations which denied all independence to the former; according to them, only the State was truly sovereign. The Church was not sovereign because it was not absolute: it obeyed a divine Legislator and could not alter the laws it had received from Him; it could not *make law*; its constitution was immutable and its original law omnipotent. On the other hand, lay power was absolute: it had the right to subject men even to unjust laws and arbitrary institutions; it could alter its constitution or suspend it when necessary.[73] Consequently, the

---

[72] *Ibid.*, II, p. 606.
[73] This view of sovereignty as absolute power — even to the point of altering the fundamental law — seems to have been considerably more absolutist than the views of the Parlement of Paris concerning the inviolability of the fundamental law. According to Roger Bickart, these fundamental laws were seen by the Parlement of Paris as constituting the contract between king and nation, and they

State was superior to the Church in authority; if the State oppressed
the Church, the latter had recourse only to prayers and tears, but not
to resistance. It was the Church which had submitted to the State
when, in return for protection, it had rendered the State an account
of its dogmas, rites, rules, and activities; the State was only subject
to God; it was "the most sublime power".[74] The touchstone, then, of
the Provençal magistrates' position was: "the public interest should
override religious interest".[75]

The 18th-Century French episcopate took the stand that its rights
and jurisdiction were being usurped by the secular tribunals and that
the magistrates' position was aggressive, intending to destroy the
venerable doctrine of the *two swords*. The General Assembly, the
united voice of the bishops, claimed that this ancient doctrine was
held in too much respect for the magistrates blatantly to attack it and,
consequently, they were forced to undermine it more subtly. Of the
Parlements and the prevailing theory of the two swords the Assembly
declared:

They appear to adopt it; but they evade it and actually combat it by
restrictions which confound the rights of the two powers. They attribute to
the secular authority cognizance over everything which in spiritual affairs
has a real connection with the temporal. Spread by a pile of writings, this
maxim delivers even the fundamentals of religion up to the princes of the
earth and to their officials. . . . There is indeed nothing so divine and so
sacred which they do not refer indirectly to the tribunal of the secular
power.[76]

It was by this means that the magistrates allegedly came to claim
cognizance over all religious affairs, such as the refusal of sacraments,
which concerned external matters and public tranquillity. The bishops
concluded that since most spiritual endeavors had external manifestations, there would be left no ecclesiastical authority over which the
secular power could not exert its prior rights — a situation which they

---

could legitimately be violated only when the king failed to fulfill his contractual
obligations. *Les Parlements et la notion de souveraineté nationale au XVIIIᵉ siècle*
(Paris, Félix Alcan, 1932), pp. 66-67. In the later 18th Century the Parlement of
Paris did accuse the government of risking a rupture of the bonds of society
(*ibid.*, pp. 259-260).
[74] P.-Albert Robert, *Les Remontrances et arrêtés du parlement de Provence au
XVIIIIᵉ siècle* (Paris, Arthur Rousseau, 1912), pp. 461-467; 472.
[75] *Ibid.*, p. 476.
[76] *Collection des procès-verbaux des assemblées générales du clergé de France
depuis l'année 1560* (known hereafter as *Procès-Verbaux*) (Paris, Imprimerie de
Guillaume Desprez, 1767-80), VII, Part I, pièces justificatives, col. 174).

felt was as perverse as the ultramontane theory of the superiority of the ecclesiastical power.[77]

In opposing what they considered the onslaught of the magistrates against their legitimate power, the bishops held up the menace of the perversion of religion and, like the Parlements, the curtailment of the rights of the king. The Assembly warned that "... if spiritual matters are subjected to the decisions of the magistrates; if everything exterior is in their competence, there is, Sire, no longer in your kingdom any Church or any episcopate".[78] During the General Assembly of 1730 the bishop of Boulogne conjured up the specter of a parliamentary-*curé* coalition to destroy the episcopal office.[79] His efforts resulted in a remonstrance to the king on the consequences of such a coalition:

The independence and revolt of the *curés* are openly protected, the most sacred rights of the bishops are contested, and their ministry is rendered useless; laymen constitute themselves judges of doctrine, and what is still more distressing, the spirit of schism is gradually introduced into your States. These, Sire, are the sad and ominous results of the continual usurpations of the secular tribunals upon the spiritual authority.[80]

The *appel comme d'abus* was described in this remonstrance as "the most monstrous of all abuses" because it "... renders ... the episcopal ministry absolutely useless".[81] With characteristic hyperbole the bishop of Carcassonne, in a letter to Cardinal Fleury quoted in the *Nouvelles ecclésiastiques* of March 27, 1728, expressed the fear that because of the assaults of the magistrates, religion was in more grave danger than it had ever been before in France.[82]

Just as the Parlements unfailingly asserted that their actions were designed to defend royal authority against ecclesiastical encroachment, so also did the bishops warn the king, in terms similar to the famous condemnation of Presbyterianism given by James I of England, that "... when one injures ... [ecclesiastical jurisdiction], the tribunals can acquire [more] rights; but Your Majesty loses his. ..."[83] The General Assembly of 1755 was so stung by the Parlement of

---

[77]  *Ibid.*, VIII, Part I, pièces justificatives, cols. 175-176.
[78]  *Ibid.*, VIII, Part II, pièces justificatives, col. 370.
[79]  *Ibid.*, VII, cols. 1082-1084.
[80]  *Ibid.*, VII, col. 1092. Remonstrance of September 12, 1730.
[81]  *Ibid.*, VII, col. 1095.
[82]  *Nouvelles ecclésiastiques, ou mémoires à l'histoire de la Constitution Unigenitus* (Paris, March 27, 1728), p. 40.
[83]  *Procès-Verbaux,* VIII, Part II, pièces justificatives, col. 369.

Paris' condemnation of its "system of independence", that it con-
descended to make an accusation-by-accusation reply. To the "odious
distinction" which the parliamentary remonstrance had drawn between
the loyalty of ecclesiastical and lay subjects the bishops were particularly
sensitive. To the parliamentary thesis of the dangers of ecclesiastical
independence the bishops opposed their concept of how the union of
Church and State preserved the secular power:

Only religion can purify and strengthen for ever the sacrifice which men
make of their natural love of independence to a legitimate power. It is the
firmest rampart of sovereign authority and the most powerful restraint on
every kind of revolt; . . . it causes obedience to be loved by consecrating
authority; and by this doctrine it renders the ministry of its pastors as useful to the State as it is necessary for the salvation of souls.[84]

To the Parlement's devotion to patriotism, ". . . so much vaunted in
our days, but so little understood . . .", the bishops offered their conception of true patriotism: a spirit ". . . which leads all the bodies of a
State to enjoy their respective rights and to conserve them peacefully
under the common protection of their sovereign".[85] Nor was the separate corporate existence of the clergy deemed divisive, for what was
more beneficial to the common weal than each order working in its
own way for the common good! Thus, it was by emphasizing the
benefits accruing to the State from its union with the Church that the
bishops sought to justify their special status and power. No doubt
the Parlements intended in their defense of the secular power to enjoy
both the benefits of an established Church and the effective subordination of that Church to the supreme power of the king and his
Parlements.

The bishop's vehement opposition to the parliamentary contention
that external religious affairs such as the refusal of sacraments fell
under secular jurisdiction was actually more rigid and pretentious
than their position in 1682. In a written defense of the *droit de régale,*
dated February 3, 1682 and delivered to Innocent XI, the clergy had
claimed that a change in discipline — in externals — did not constitute
a change in faith. The extension of the *régale* was ". . . a matter of
discipline which, changeable according to time and place, is suscep-
tible to compromise. . . . ." More importantly, the clergy had claimed
that a higher consideration than the *régale* motivated their acquiescence in the royal policy:

[84]   *Ibid.,* VIII, Part I, pièces justificatives, col. 162.
[85]   *Ibid.*

And even when the Canons strictly interpreted would be opposed to this surrender [of power to the king], we would not have permitted [such an interpretation], because the peace of the Church would have obligated us; for charity being the fullness of the law, one satisfies the law when one does what charity dictates.[86]

This higher consideration could have served as the basis for avoiding the refusal of sacraments; it was indeed the parliamentary excuse for intervention. But public tranquillity in the mid 18th Century was not as important to the bishops as the maintenance of their every prerogative. In this sense the bishops could be seen as aggressive.

The year 1755 was a significant one in the changing lines of the episcopal defense against the Parlements. The debates of the General Assembly of that year revealed that the bishop-delegates were divided over the question of refusing the sacraments to alleged Jansenists. There was general agreement that *notorious* opponents of *Unigenitus* should be refused the sacraments, but what exactly constituted notorious opposition was disputed. Divided into two almost equal parts between rigid *théatins* and more lenient *feuillants*,[87] the episcopate, heretofore jealous of its Gallican liberties, appealed to Rome and received in reply the first of the modern encyclicals, the *Ex omnibus* of Benedict XIV.[88] In a letter from the Assembly to the bishops of France, the bishop-delegates offered this solace:

It would have been very satisfying for us to have happier events to announce to you; but if they have not corresponded to our efforts and our hope, we at least have the consolation of seeing us all reunited in the same sentiments of deference to the Holy See. . . .[89]

The general desire of the Assembly for unity with which more effectively to defend the episcopate against parliamentary critics, who had always found a few members of the episcopate — those suspected of Jansenism — favorable to the Parlements, led the bishops to seek strength in Rome. In order not to appear to be fleeing to Rome too precipitously, the bishops, while finding their ultimate strength there,

---

[86]  Mention, *op. cit.*, I, pp. 10-11; 20. All in italics.
[87]  The *feuillants* were those bishops who owed their preferment to the incumbent minister of ecclesiastical affairs (the holder of the *feuille des bénéfices*), Cardinal de la Rochefoucauld; the *théatins* were those who had been preferred by the previous minister of the *feuille*, Boyer, who had been a member of the Theatine Order.
[88]  Paul Nau, "A l'Origine des encycliques modernes: un épisode de la lutte des évêques et des parlements, 1755-1756", *Revue historique de droit français et étranger*, 4th series, Vol. XXXIV (April-June, 1956), p. 247.
[89]  *Procès-Verbaux*, VIII, Part. I, pièces justificatives, col. 195.

did slightly qualify their newly-found ultramontanism — but only slightly.[90] The importance of 1755, however, was the episcopal appeal to Rome and the resultant unity of all bishops, moderates and extremists, behind *Ex omnibus*, which was itself a moderate papal pronouncement received from the hands of the so-called "Jansenist" Pope Benedict XIV. Regretfully but nevertheless deliberately, when faced with hostile Parlements, a vacillating king, and its own disunity, the episcopate sought strength in a Roman encyclical.[91]

When one labels the royal position in the episcopal-parliamentary conflict *vacillating*, it is at the risk of not appreciating fully the difficulty of assuming an effective royal posture. On the one hand the king was conscious of the increasingly revolutionary demands and pretensions of his Parlements. On the other hand, however, the king was a Gallican of the 1682 variety, and the full force of the Four Articles had never been actually denied in practice.[92] He was wary of upsetting the balance too much in favor of the episcopate. The officially imposed silence on the question of *Unigenitus* was generally understood to be more favorable to the Parlements than to the episcopate. One of the more recurring demands which the General Assemblies made in their periodic *cahiers* presented to the king was for the convocation of provincial councils to deal with ecclesiastical discipline. Except for the disastrous Council of Embrun which deposed a *notorious* Jansenist bishop, no provincial councils were permitted. The royal replies to such requests always revealed a hesitation to open up

[90]  The feeble qualification read: "Each prelate has declared that he intends in no way by the unanimous recourse to our Holy Father the Pope to call into question truths already decided, which are contained in the different articles [of the *feuillants* and *théatins*]: each of them has moreover added that in awaiting the decision of the Holy See, he will continue to conform his behavior to the dictates of his conscience, to the usages of his church, and to the principles contained in the articles to which he has adhered." *Ibid.*, VIII, Part I, cols. 558-559, partially quoted in Nau, *loc. cit.*, p. 236.

[91]  Nau concerns himself primarily with the development of the encyclical form of papal pronouncement; but he does show that this document which carried somewhat less authority than a duly registered Bull was fully accepted by the bishops in 1756; the modern ultramontanism of Catholic episcopates surely was foreshadowed.

[92]  As late as 1770 the Four Articles were still law. Cardinal de Bernis informed the Court of Rome: "The kings of France will never renounce for any part of their domains the *droit de régale*, nor the teaching of the four propositions of the Assembly of the clergy of 1682. These two points are part of the fundamental maxims of this kingdom ..." De Bernis to Clement XIV, February 25, 1770; *Archives du ministère des affaires étrangères*, Correspondance Politique, Rome, Vol. 851, folios 177-178.

this channel for an ecclesiastical counterattack.[93] It was precisely the bishops' contention that lack of discipline demanded such councils immediately, but the king was never more than vague — probably a sign of evading an unpleasant decision in either direction.

It was not erroneous for both the Parlements and the bishops to agree that the main weapon of the one and the main obstacle of the other was the *appel comme d'abus*. The Royal Council, in revoking to itself cases in which such an appeal had been interjected, more often than not decided against the appellant and in favor of the Church. Such a solution was, however, a hollow victory for the bishops, indeed a dangerous victory, since it made episcopal rights dependent not on their just claims as much as on the seemingly arbitrary and increasingly unpopular intervention of the government in the judicial affairs of the Parlements.[94] The abbé Fleury lamented that the royal councillors were laymen imbued with the same secularizing principles as the magistrates, resulting in a theoretical, if not always actual, advantage for the parliamentary position in questions of ecclesiastical jurisdiction.[95]

The government never favorably replied to the bishops' requests that the *appeal comme d'abus* procedure be reformed; it merely reiterated the full force of the equivocal Edict of 1695. The royal declaration of August 18, 1732 voiced indignation at rumors that the government intended to abolish the *appel come d'abus* — " a means so necessary for obstructing the course of every reciprocal undertaking against the rights of the priesthood or those of the empire".[96] About as far as the king would go in dealing with the appeal controversy was to reassert ominously this reciprocal nature of the *appel comme d'abus*:

The magistrates who are charged with sustaining . . . [the rights] of the king should always remember that the conservation of the rights of the spiritual authority does not constitute less a part of the maxims of France than that of the rights of the temporal authority, and that according to our customs

---

[93] *Procès-Verbaux*, VII, p.j., cols. 461-462; VIII, p.j., col. 372.
[94] Robert R. Palmer has written that royal absolutism as "arbiter between irreconcilables" continued to be popular in many quarters, e.g., with Voltaire. Nevertheless, the denunciations of absolutism seemed to have had a louder ring. In either case, royal intervention did the bishops no ultimate good. (*The Age of the Democratic Revolution*, Princeton, University Press, 1959, I, p. 92.)
[95] *Oeuvres de l'abbé Fleury*, "Discours X sur les libertés de l'église gallicane", p. 430.
[96] Isambert, *op. cit.*, XXI, pp. 375-376.

the means of the *appel comme d'abus* is equally available to the two sides against any undertaking against one kind of power or the other.[97]

The royal desire for a balance between these rival claimants to power and prestige was difficult of accomplishment, as is any such middle-of-the-road equilibrium. Success required initiative and intelligence, but the government of Louis XV could only react defensively. As such, it was incompetent to deal with a fundamental political and social conflict and could only appear vacillating — an encouragement to the Parlements to continue their attacks on episcopal power and a sign for the bishops that Rome might be the least of several possible servitudes.

It is with this important segment of 18th-Century French history ever in view that we should turn to the recruitment of the Gallican episcopate and to its social and institutional history.

[97]   Flammermont, *op. cit.*, I, pp. 356-357; royal reply to the Parlement's remonstrance of April 6, 1737.

II

# FRANCE: THE RECRUITMENT OF THE BISHOPS

In his autobiographical account of the last years of the Old Régime and the ensuing emigration, J. M. Augeard, the private secretary to the late Queen Marie-Antoinette, narrated an incident occurring among the *émigrés* in Germany. At a dinner attended by Prince Charles of Lorraine, the guests were read a manuscript by a Suabian nobleman entitled "Lettre d'un gentilhomme à son voisin le baron de Flachs-landen" which concerned itself with the causes of the Revolution in France. Among the topics treated in the manuscript was the social composition of the former French episcopate; the following sharp contrast was drawn:

In every century the gateway to bishoprics has not ceased to be accessible to every class of the ecclesiastical estate, since if one made a bishopric-by-bishopric account of the subjects who have possessed these sees, one would find that until this century more than three-quarters of them were from the bourgeoisie. Why does one find only a single example of this in the reigns of Louis XV and Louis XVI — in the person of the bishop of Senez? The bishops and the ministers of ecclesiastical affairs are not ashamed to say that bishoprics are made only for men of quality — and this in a religion which preaches modesty, equality, and humility! [1]

Such a view of the prevailing 18th-Century trends in the nomination of men to the Gallican episcopate identified a perceptible social phenomenon in terms of an idyllic contrast between the past and the present. A far less idyllic juxtaposition of the two periods in question, the reign of Louis XIV and those of his next two successors, but one equally mordant and far more conspiratorial has been bequeathed to us by a lady of the court of Louis XVI, Mme Campan. After offering her comments on the Ségur law of 1781 which liquidated the

[1] *Mémoires secrets de J. M. Augeard, secrétaire des commandements de la Reine Marie Antoinette* (Paris, Henri Plon, 1866), pp. 345-346. The "Lettre" is dated July, 1795; the phrase "ministers of ecclesiastical affairs" is a free translation of "ministres de la feuille" which will be explained below.

attempt to foster a *noblesse militaire* and effectively closed the higher
military ranks to members of the ignoble classes, Mme Campan added:

Another decision of the Court, one which could not be announced by edict,
was that in the future all ecclesiastical endowments, from the most modest
priory to the richest abbeys, would be the appanage of the nobility. . . . I
obtained from the queen support for the request of a *curé* friend of mine
who was seeking a priory near to his benefice and intended to retire there;
I obtained this boon for him. Upon my return from the waters, the abbé
[de Vermond, adviser to the minister of ecclesiastical affairs] learned of it
and came to tell me very severely that I would be acting in a manner completely contrary to the wishes of the king if I again obtained such boons;
that in the future the endowments of the Church were to be uniquely destined for the support of the poor nobility; that such was the interest of the
State and that a plebeian priest lucky to have a good benefice should
remain a *curé*.[2]

It was more than literary convenience which led Mme Campan to
couple these two developments of noble monopolization of high
position in Church and military, for contemporaries who viewed these
developments did regard them as part of a larger social movement. The
*cahiers de doléances* of the Third Estate of the bailliage Saint-Sau-
veur-le-Vicomte reflected an overall concern with the nobility's assault upon the positions of prestige and power in the nation:

The high nobility or the Court nobility absorbes all the places and all the
favors of the Court; it seems that all dignities, as much ecclesiastical as
military, constitute a part of its patrimony, and that under the name of pensions and gratuities it owns a portion of the revenue of the State. It is not
personal merit, it is not the services rendered to the State and to the Nation
which cause places and favors to be bestowed; it is influence. A great
name makes an archbishop, a bishop, or an abbé; rarely does merit place
the marshal's baton into the hands of a soldier.[3]

These 18th-Century views of the changing course of episcopal appointments have been cited and repeated in works too numerous to
enumerate. While there have been differences in their estimates of
how many bishops at any given time actually had non-noble social

[2] Mme Campan, *Mémoires sur la vie privée de Marie-Antoinette, Reine de France et de Navarre* (ed. by Barrière), (Paris, Baudouin Frères, 4th edition, 1823), Vol. I, pp. 237-238. Partially quoted in abbé Augustin Sicard, *L'Ancien Clergé de France: les évêques avant la Révolution* (Paris, Librairie Victor Le-coffre, 5th edition, 1912), p. 8.
[3] *Archives Parlementaires de 1787 à 1860* (Paris, Librairie Administrative de Paul Dupont), 1st series, Vol. III, p. 67. Partially quoted in A. Denys-Buirette, *Les Questions religieuses dans les cahiers de 1789* (Paris, E. de Boccard, 1919), p. 302.

origins, and certain individual bishops have been variously classified, basic agreement has remained that 18th-Century France saw the exclusion of plebeians from the Gallican episcopate. It is the task of this chapter to examine the state of the French bishoprics in the period 1682-1790 and the method of nominating ecclesiastics to them; to offer a statistical analysis of the social composition of the episcopate; and finally to explore the reactions engendered by the established system.

I

Just as the civil organization of the domains of the king of France and Navarre, being the product of a slow, organic growth, was an irrational one, so also was the ecclesiastical organization of the nation markedly unrelated to such rational factors of organization as population and geography. The 130 bishoprics of France,[4] divided into twenty ecclesiastical provinces, retained in the 18th Century virtually the same geographic limits by which they had been defined in Roman Gaul of the 4th Century. A few admittedly approximate population figures can help to emphasize the unequal distribution of the French bishoprics. Employing the findings of the second report of the Comité de Revision of the Constituent Assembly in 1790 which estimated the total French population of that year at 26½ million,[5] one finds the following geographic relationships: in the Northwest, Northeast, West, and Center of the kingdom there was one diocese for approximately every 300,000 people; in the Southwest and the Southeast there was one diocese for every 110,000 people. Avoiding such a rational division of the kingdom into six geographic sections in favor of the old division into provinces and generalities, one is confronted with inequalities in the population-bisphopric ratio which are even more glaring. Using this time the 1785 estimates of Neckar who placed the total population at a figure of 25 million,[6] one meets the following diversity:

[4]   The total of 130 sees is arrived at by excluding the five dioceses located in the papal enclaves within France, the five Corsican sees acquired late in the 18th Century, and the sees of Tournai and Ypres acquired in the latter 17th Century and lost in the Peace of Utrecht.
[5]   Paul Boiteau, État de la France en 1789 (Paris, Librairie Guillaumin, 2nd edition, 1889), pp. 8-10.
[6]   E. Levasseur, La Population Française (Paris, Arthur Rousseau, 1889), Vol. I, p. 218.

| | |
|---|---|
| Province of Languedoc: | 1 diocese for every 75,000 people |
| Province of Provence: | 1 diocese for every 60,000 people |
| Province of Brittany: | 1 diocese for every 250,000 people |
| Generality of Paris: | 1 diocese for every 350,000 people |
| Generality of Tours: | 1 diocese for every 450,000 people |
| Generality of Lyon: | 1 diocese for 635,000 people |

Consonent with the unequal distribution of bishoprics among the population, the various sees were of unequal size. The number of parishes in a given diocese varied from as much as 1388 for the archdiocese of Rouen, through the dioceses of Chartres, Limoges, Besançon, Clermont, and Bourges which had each between 800 and 900 parishes, down to the comparatively miniature dioceses of the South with fewer than thirty-five each: Digne, Apt, Agde, Marseille, Toulon, Vence, and Grasse.[7]

A more decisive source of inequality between bishoprics — more decisive in the quest for nominations and translations to and from bishoprics — lay in the unequal revenues of the different sees. There were indeed wide gulfs between episcopal wealth and poverty. Comparing revenues from the mid 18th Century, one finds that they varied from as little as the 1,000 livres of the almost nominal see of Bethléem [8] and the 10,000 livres or less of the sees of Vence, Saint-Paul-Trois-Châteaux, Belley, and Saint-Pol-de-Léon, all the way up to the more than 100,000-livre incomes of the sees of Cambrai, Metz, Paris, Strasbourg, Narbonne, Albi, Auch, Rouen, and Toulouse.[9]

Size and wealth were not the only factors in the invidious comparison of bishoprics. Various sees had attached to them certain temporal and spiritual dignities. The bishops of Paris, Beauvais, Reims, Langres, Laon, Noyon, and Châlons-sur-Marne were Peers of France with precedence over all nobles not of the blood royal; they enjoyed the right to sit in the sovereign Parlements. The sees which had been annexed to France at the expense of the Holy Roman Empire retained imperial dignities: thus the bishops of Strasbourg, Metz, Cambrai, Besançon, Belley, Toul, and Verdun were no less than sovereign princes of the Empire. Most of the provincial estates in the *pays d'états* were

---

[7] *Almanach royal* (Paris, 1715), pp. 35-39. For the sake of accuracy, these figures have been checked against the 1755 and 1789 Almanachs.

[8] The see of Bethléem was not merely a titular see for bishops *in partibus infidelium*; it was located in the Hôpital de Pantenère near Clamecy in Burgundy and, unlike titular sees, had a regular endowment.

[9] For a list of episcopal revenues see Appendix II.

presided over by bishops *ex officio*: the Estates of Languedoc by the archbishop of Narbonne, Provence by the archbishop of Aix, Burgundy by the bishop of Autun, Artois by the bishop of Arras, Foix by the bishop of Pamiers, and Béarn by the bishop of Lescar.[10] Finally, other bishoprics carried titles of count, baron, and prince which were more than nominal, placing into the hands of the bishops seignorial rights.

A glittering example of the French bishops' temporal style of life is provided by the following excerpt from an 18th-Century manuscript:

There are not in every diocese fixed honorific duties which the nobility of the diocese is obliged to perform for the bishops at the time of their entry. But in certain dioceses there are particular duties attached to the fiefs which depend on the demesne of the bishopric. M. d'Olive ... writes that when the bishop-count of Cahors makes his first entry into his episcopal city, the baron de Cessac is obliged to go before him outside the city, to place his foot upon the ground, to salute him bareheaded and without a coat, with his right foot and leg bare and in a slipper; and after having saluted him, he takes the bishop's mule by the reins, goes to the cathedral church and from there to the episcopal palace, where he stops to wait on the bishop's table during his dinner. After having satisfied this requirement, the mule and the dinner are offered to him.[11]

In an age of very worldly ecclesiasticalism these temporal advantages incorporated into certain bishoprics undoubtedly carried more weight than more exclusively spiritual prerogatives. The latter sort, however, had their own attractions for the seekers of prestige. In a spiritual context, the most desirable see was that of Reims, for its archbishop had the right to perform the indispensable rite of consecrating the Most Christian King. A number of sees claimed the prerogatives and dignities of primatial sees — a position above that of a mere archbishopric. Owing to the Gallo-Roman origins of primatial titles, however, these high pretensions overlapped. If the archbishop of Lyon was the primate of the Gauls and of Germany, and the archbishop of Reims the *légat-né* of the pope and the primate of Gaul and Belgium, what was left to the poor archbishop of Vienne but to insist that, after all, he was the *primate of primates*! [12]

[10] *Correspondance administrative sous le règne de Louis XIV* (Paris, Imprimerie Nationale, 1850-55), Vol. I, pp. 7; 322, 418; 559; 603.

[11] "Des Droits honorifiques que la noblesse doit aux évêques à l'entrée dans leur diocèses", Bibliothèque nationale, fonds français, MSS. 6458, folios 47-48.

[12] Marcel Marion, *Dictionnaire des institutions de la France aux XVIIe et XVIIIe siècles* (Paris, Auguste Picard, 1923), pp. 177-178.

This striving for distinctions, ecclesiastical and secular, quite readily led to conflicts over which *grand seigneur ecclesiastique* had which titles and prerogatives, the vanity of which was handsomely demonstrated by a letter of the archbishop of Reims, Mgr. de Rohan-Guémené, to the king concerning the contested use of his titles at the sessions of the provincial assembly of the clergy. Three bishops opposed the archbishop's use of the title of prince in the official procès-verbal of the session.

. . . The bishops of Laon and Châlons [-sur-Marne] and the deputy of M. the bishop of Noyon declared in a formal protest "that they do not recognize . . . that the lord archbishop may use the title of prince in any acts drawn up in common with them, which use would, they believe, injure the dignity of the episcopate with which they are honored and would be contrary to the practices of the province, even of those of other provinces, and of the general assemblies of the clergy." . . . The archbishop of Reims could produce a great number of titles and acts to show that the persons of his house may legally use the title of prince and that they have always enjoyed in the kingdom the prerogatives attached to the rank of a foreign prince. . . . [The complaining bishops] say . . . that if they recognized that the archbishop of Reims might assume the title of prince in their common proceedings, they would injure the dignity of the episcopate with which they are invested. The archbishop of Reims is not less persuaded than these prelates of the dignity and excellence of the episcopate, . . . but one has never thought to harm its preeminence when joining to the title of archbishop or bishop those which one possesses either by his birth, his offices, or his property. M. the archbishop of Vienne of the house of Bouillon, M. the archbishop of Besançon of the house of Monaco, M. the bishop of Bayeux of the house of Lorraine all take the title of prince. The archbishop of Aix uses the name of Vintimille of the counts de Marseille-Dulau; M. the bishop of Metz that of the duke of Coislin, Peer of France; M. the bishop of Luçon that of comte de Bussy-Rabutin; M. the bishop of Châlons [-sur-Marne] does not forget in his titles that of first almoner of the queen.[13]

## II

Since Francis I's Concordat with Rome in 1516 the right to nominate bishops in France had been a function of the royal prerogative. In the period of our concern, 1682-1790, all ecclesiastical nominations in the prerogative of the king, whether to bishoprics or abbeys *in commen-*

[13] The archbishop of Reims to the king, 1728. *Archives du ministère des affaires étrangères* (Mémoires et Documents, Fonds France), Vol. 1261, folios 56-62. Hereafter *AAE*.

*dam,* or to other benefices which had fallen into his patronage, were made through the regularized ministry of government known as the ministry of the *feuille des bénéfices.* The titular head of the *feuille des bénéfices* was the minister of ecclesiastical affairs, responsible for making recommendations to the king on ecclesiastical appointments and for receiving and disposing of the numerous seekers after Church preferment.[14]

The ministers of the *feuille* were themselves always clerics. Louis XIV relied on his Jesuit confessors to exercise this area of his prerogative; the names of the Pères de la Chaize and Letellier dominated the disposition of benefices in the later years of his reign. The reaction against the long rule of Louis XIV which manifested itself under the Orléanist Regency included among its features an attempt to diminish the power of the royal confessor over ecclesiastical appointments; the ministry of the *feuille* was replaced by a *conseil de conscience* under the presidency of the archbishop of Paris, the devious and difficult Cardinal de Noailles. The *conseil* soon collapsed with the rest of the polysynodal structure of government which characterized the early Regency, and the waxing opposition of the Regent to the pro-Jansenist and anti-*Unigenitus* sentiment which he had initially patronized resulted in the removal of the unreliable Noailles from any decisive role in Church preferment. In the latter years of the sway of Philippe d'Orléans an advisory role over ecclesiastical appointments was bestowed upon a *chambre ecclésiastique* whose membership included the Cardinals de Rohan and de Bissy, Bishop Massillon of Clermont, and the former bishop of Fréjus (and future Cardinal) Fleury; the minister of the *feuille* was at the same time the abbé de Thésut. After the death of the Regent the predominant voice in

---

[14] The *feuille* was exactly what its name implies: a page listing vacant benefices and the clerics who were newly named to them. Examples can be found in the Bibliothèque nationale, fonds français, MSS. 20969, and in *AAE*, Mémoires et Documents, Fonds France, Vol. 1234, folios 197-231. That the titular head of the *feuille des bénéfices* was the recognized dispenser of ecclesiastical patronage is clear from a mémoire of the Maison du Roi dated in 1784. The Secretary of State for the Maison du Roi, the baron de Breteuil, had received a request from a certain abbé de Novy to be allowed to exchange his two benefices for a pension. It was decided that since the abbé was not demanding a benefice, but rather was offering to surrender two, and since the pension he sought was not to be paid from the revenues of a bishopric or from those of an abbey, the minister of the *feuille* could have no interest in the affair. *Archives nationales* (hereafter *AN*), 01 595, no. 251. Similar evidence of the specific role of the minister of the *feuille* is offered in a letter of the minister of the *feuille,* Marbeuf, to Breteuil, April 30, 1788; *AN* 01 595, no. 474.

Church affairs passed to Fleury who, after a short interlude, became
in all but title the first minister of the king. When the Jesuit confessors of Louis XV renounced in 1725 all interest in the disposal of
benefices in order to deflect away from themselves the hostility inevitably directed towards whoever was wielding such provocative
authority,[15] Fleury no longer had even the titular rivalry of the royal
confessors to interfere with his administration of ecclesiastical preferment. His successors in the ministry of the feuille were all bishops
or former bishops: Boyer of Mirepoix (1743-55); Cardinal de la
Rochefoucauld (1755-57); Jarente de la Bruyère of Digne and
Orléans (1757-71); Cardinal de la Roche-Aymon (1771-77); Marbeuf
of Autun (1777-1788); and Le Franc de Pompignan of Vienne at the
outbreak of the Revolution.[16]

These ministers of the *feuille des bénéfices* were the *titular* dis-
pensers of ecclesiastical livings and favors. Their actual power depended upon the credit they had with the king and the strength of
the rivals who challenged their position at Court. As virtual first
minister of the king, Fleury was no less supreme in dispensing benefices than in conducting the other affairs of state. Less powerful ecclesiastical ministers had to contend with numerous favorites: the
reputedly occult and terrible sway of Père de la Chaize over Louis
XIV was sometimes successfully countered by the machinations of
Mme de Maintenon and Harlay de Champvallon, the archbishop of
Paris. The titular members of the Regent's *chambre ecclésiastique* had
a very limited role; he dispensed benefices himself with the advice of
the abbé de Thésut, and the influence of Cardinal Dubois was undoubtedly great.[17] The Regent's many vices have been written about
at length; but perhaps ignored among them is the sin of nepotism. He
pressured various French bishops and the papal court to provide
benefices for his illegitimate son, the abbé de Saint-Albin, who
quickly succeeded to the sees of Laon and Cambrai.[18] The Regent
reportedly justified his nomination of a second unworthy successor to

---

[15]    Sicard, p. 496.
[16]    Documentation of the role of Roche-Aymon, Marbeuf, and Le Franc de
Pompignan may be found in the following manuscript sources: *AAE*, Correspondance politique, Rome, Vol. 885, folio 45; *AN*, 01 473; pp. 219 and 378; and
*AAE*, Correspondance politique, Rome, Vol. 911, folio 97.
[17]    *AAE*, Mémoires et Documents, Fonds France, Vol. 1233, folio 235; Vol. 1234,
folio 218; Vol. 1236, folio 61.
[18]    *AAE*, Mémoires et Documents, Fonds France, Vol. 1247, folios 174-175; 181-
183; 189-190.

the esteemed Fénelon, Dubois having been the first, with this pun:
" 'Les Jansénistes ne se plaindront, car je viens de tout donner à la
grâce, rien au mérite'." [19]

The entire method of selecting the leadership of the Gallican
Church through the minister of the *feuille* and the resultant flattery
and intrigue were to be devastatingly indicted by Mirabeau before the
Constituent Assembly. Replying to the objections of the ecclesiastical
deputies to the election of bishops under the Civil Constitution of
the Clergy, the deputy of the Third Estate of Aix-en-Provence spoke
as the personification of a century or more of indignation:

... Some seek to insinuate that religion will be lost if it is the choice of the
people which bestows ecclesiastical office. For our bishops know, as does
all France, to what odious corruption the majority of them are obligated for
the character which they now display with so much daring against the wisdom of your laws. There are certainly several of them who would have to
blush too much to see uncovered on the great day the obscure and in-
decent intrigues which have brought about their vocation to the episcopate.
And in conscience the clergy cannot conceal just what was the administration of the *feuille des bénéfices*.[20]

So powerful was the position of the minister of the *feuille* that even
when he exercised less than the monopolistic control attributed to
him by disappointed applicants, he was the sun in the horizon of the
horde of cormorant office seekers. François Hébert, the *curé* of the
royal parish of Versailles during the latter part of the reign of Louis
XIV, offered his impressions of the bishops' flight to Court:

Several of them only rarely resided in their dioceses, because intending to
obtain richer ones, there was nothing that they did not do to acquire them.
One saw them vilely paying court to the father-confessor or even to the
courtiers whom they knew to be in favor, and ... to ladies whose disso-
luteness they should have rebuked, had they desired to fulfill their obligations.[21]

It was a vital need of ecclesiastical office hunters to keep abreast of
the shifting influence of various ministers and courtiers lest they be
caught courting impotent patrons. In the later years of Fleury's
ministry he sought advice on ecclesiastical appointments from the

[19]   Quoted in Sicard, p. 496.
[20]   *Archives Parlementaires*, 1st series, Vol. XXI (Nov. 26, 1790), p. 11.
[21]   François Hébert, *Mémoires du curé de Versailles (1686-1704)* (Paris, Les
Éditions de France, 1927), p. 20.

abbé Couturier, the superior-general of the seminary and congregation of Saint-Sulpice. In recounting his student days at Saint-Sulpice, the abbé Baston depicted the effect which the discovery of the Cardinal-Minister's gray eminence had had on the ambitious:

When the noble and powerful families — those who had pretensions to the episcopal mitre or at least to the parasitic mitre of abbeys *in commendam* — perceived that the channel of favors of this sort was at Saint-Sulpice, they hastened to send there those of their children whom they intended for the service and the riches of the altar. The great seminary was found filled with men of the highest distinction; one saw even princes there.[22]

The different ministers of the *feuille* acquired different reputations according to the use which they made of their sensitive position. Père de la Chaize was reputed by some to have successfully withstood the more scandalous place seekers, the impenetrable barrier to flatterers, degenerates, hypocrites, and

> Ces Abbés de nom seulement,
> Aspirant à la prélature,
> Qui, par leur brillante figure,
> Sont du Clergé l'inutile ornement,
> Ces ignorans polis qui ne connaissent guères
> Ni l'Écriture, ni les Pères,
> S'imaginant bien acheter
> Par des soins concertés, par des douceurs flatteuses
> Qu'un ridicule excès rend presque injurieuses,
> Ce que par les vertus ils devraient mériter.[23]

Perhaps one of the most pathetic scenes in all the trafficking in benefices — the more pitiful because of the eminent individual involved — was the strenuous endeavor of the dying Bossuet of Meaux to procure at any cost a bishopric for his unqualified nephew, only to be disappointed by the opposition of La Chaize.[24] Since no minister of the *feuille* could escape disappointing the vengeful, the witty, or the idealistic, none escaped biting criticism: certainly no exception was made of La Chaize. A letter of Fénelon designed for the king re-

---

[22]  *Mémoires de l'abbé Baston,* ed. by abbé Julien Loth and Ch. Verger (Paris, Alphonse Picard, 1897-99), Vol. I, pp. 172-173. Fleury named the abbé Couturier to screen ecclesiastical aspirants for him; AAE, Mémoires et Documents, Fonds France, Vol. 1525, folios 200-201.

[23]  Quoted from Boyer's "Caractères des prédicateurs, des prétendants aux dignités ecclésiastiques", 1695, by Georges Guitton, S. J., *Le Père de la Chaize, confesseur de Louis XIV* (Paris, Beauchesne, 1959), Vol. I, pp. 207-208.

[24]  *Ibid.,* I, pp. 201-206.

flected the former's indignation that a single royal confessor should be entrusted with all the power to make bishops — especially a confessor whom he deemed ". . . the dupe of all who flatter him. . . ." [25]

In a considerably different vein was the opinion of La Chaize entertained by the fastidious duc de Saint-Simon. He praised the royal confessor for his good judgment and contrasted him with Bishop Godet des Marais of Chartres, the rival for ecclesiastical influence intruded into Court by Mme de Maintenon: where Saint-Simon viewed the confessor as moderate towards the Jansenists and dedicated to ecclesiastical peace, he found the influence of Godet des Marais tending towards the population of the episcopate with men of neither birth nor moderation. According to this self-appointed guardian of an unadulterated nobility, Godet des Marais ". . . infested the episcopate with stubborn, ultramontanist ignoramuses, dirty beards from Saint-Sulpice, and persons all of low estate and lesser talent — which has since been only too much emulated".[26] Unquestionably, for Saint-Simon *insignificant persons* defined those of a social origin less unstained and an ecclesiastical politics less anti-Roman than his own. He attacked Letellier's administration of the *feuille* in terms identical to those employed for Godet des Marais; but when the *conseil de conscience* under the presidency of the appellant Noailles was substituted, Saint-Simon praised it as the last hope of those hostile to papal encroachment.[27] He evidently believed that the disposal of ecclesiastical benefices should be the means of maintaining the high nobility and limiting ultramontanist partisanship within the Gallican Church. As a slow but sure means of purging the episcopate of undesirable elements, however, the judicious use of the *feuille des bénéfices* was a two-edged sword. If the *conseil de conscience* had been the means of reacting against the use made of the authority to bestow benefices under the last confessor of Louis XIV, the *chambre ecclésiastique* later in the Regency was viewed by Mathieu Marais, an advocate in the Parlement of Paris, as a painless means of obliterating opposition to *Unigenitus* — ". . . a good expedient for rendering useless all the promises made to the appellants, whom, if one does not

[25]  *Correspondance de Fénelon, archevêque de Cambrai* (Paris, Ferra Jeune, 1827-29), Vol. II, p. 342. Fénelon's letter probably was never shown to the king, but rather to the duc de Chevreuse. E. Levesque, "Fénelon et les candidats à l'épiscopat", *Bulletin de littérature ecclésiastique*, Vol. XXIII (1922), p. 182.
[26]  *Mémoires de Saint-Simon*, ed. by A. de Boislisle (Paris, Librairie Hachette, 1879-1928), Vol. VII, p. 179.
[27]  *Ibid.*, XXIX, pp. 59-62.

harm, one will not favor, and they will be allowed to die without benefices".[28]

Those seeking ecclesiastical preferment had to take cognizance of this change in the Regent's outlook on Jansenism and relations with Rome. In both parts of his "reign" *Unigenitus* dominated ecclesiastical affairs. In 1719 it was still possible for benefice hunters to offer to the Regent their staunch opposition to Roman encroachments. In seeking a benefice for his brother, the advocate-general of the Parlement of Besançon summarized his case:

I add, Monseigneur, that since I have had the honor of being advocate-general in the Parlement of a province which has an infinite predilection for ultramontane principles, I have neglected nothing in opposing the flood of error at every opportunity which presented itself. Monsieur the duc de Noailles and Monsieur le Guerchois could also inform Your Royal Highness that the zeal with which I have defended our [Gallican] liberties has brought down upon me in this province all kinds of vexations. It is in this situation that I entreat you, Monseigneur, to grant my brother the benefice which has just become vacant. . . .[29]

In a similar vein, the *président à mortier* of the same Parlement of Besançon listed the reasons in favor of a benefice for his son:

The happiness which I have had in raising first with Monsieur our *premier président* the standard for the execution of the wishes of Your Royal Highness, the support of the rights of the Crown against the court of Rome and the rejection of ultramontane principles; the services of more than forty years of my late father, first advocate-general, and my own services as *président à mortier*; those of my eldest son, counsellor, and of my son-in-law, also counsellor; and of my two dead brothers, captains of cavalry in the service of the king, form the basis of my aspirations.

When the president Filain's son was given the coveted abbey, the ultramontanists in the Franche-Comté felt the blow. Evidently, the Regent had yielded to Filain's filial inclinations in order to have his support in the Parlement.[30]

As the Regent's policy changed, however, correspondents sought fit

[28]   *Journal et mémoires de Mathieu Marais, avocat au Parlement de Paris, sur la Régence et le Règne de Louis XV (1715-1737)* (Paris, Firmin Didot Frères, 1863-68), Vol. I, pp. 486-487.
[29]   Letter of M. Michotey to the Regent, July 18, 1719; *AAE*, Mémoires et Documents, Fonds France, Vol. 1237, folios 354-355.
[30]   Filain to the Regent, June 25, 1719; *AAE*, Mémoires et Documents, Fonds France, Vol. 1237, folios 282-283. Premier Président Boisot to the abbé de Thésut, October 7, 1719; *AAE*, Mémoires et Documents, Fonds France, Vol. 1582, folios 239-241. Filain to the Regent, August 20, 1720; *AAE*, Mémoires et Documents, Fonds France, Vol. 1582, folios 281-282.

to note that their protégés thought it sufficient "... to follow the pope and not to advance more quickly than he" and shared the views of His Royal Highness which "... lead equally to the tranquillity of the kingdom and to the good of religion ...".[31]

The advocate Marais had feared a policy which was transformed by Cardinal Fleury into a system for the religious pacification of the nation. His nominations to the bishops' bench were founded on a careful selection of aspirants: a review of their theological position to discover the modicum of orthodoxy he required for the enforcement of *Unigenitus* and a scrutiny of their past conduct to find the love of religious peace. To achieve his aim of eliminating the divisive Jansenists the Cardinal-Minister sought for the episcopate men who had accepted *Unigenitus* but lacked the additional ardor to persecute the misguided zealots of Jansenism. He would seek to destroy the Jansenists by a policy of neglecting them.[32] Perhaps typical of Fleury's attitude was his praise for Souillac of Lodève and his handling of an outbreak of Jansenist *convulsions* in his diocese; he wrote to the bishop:

I can only applaud the conduct which you, Monsieur, have followed in the pretended miracle. ... You have very wisely avoided an uproar, taking the precautions necessary to oppose the progress of a fanaticism which is only too contagious ... One could not be too attentive in suppressing with silence these sorts of temptations. ...[33]

[31]   The bishop of La Rochelle to a Cardinal in Paris (either Dubois, Rohan, or Bissy), November 15, 1721; *AAE*, Mémoires et Documents, Fonds France, Vol. 1247, folios 72-73. In this letter the bishop of La Rochelle appears as a moderate supporter of the bull, but his willingness to follow Rome was enough to make him a fanatic in Saint-Simon's eyes. (Armand Jean, *Les Évêques et les archevêques de France depuis 1682 jusqu'à 1801*, Paris, Alphonse Picard, 1891, p. 149.) By 1722 applicants were assuring the abbé de Thésut that their protégés had" ... never been appellants and had always been in agreement with the views of the holy father the pope." *AAE*, Mémoires et Documents, Fonds France, Vol. 1254, folio 160.

[32]   The marquis d'Argenson without hesitation ascribed the policy of exclusion directed against Jansenists to his own recommendations that Jansenism be made a liability in the struggle for place. While he disapproved of the preferment of nobles to the highest positions in the Church as an improper use of royal patronage, he did approve using patronage to "... reconcile the priesthood to the empire, to exercise royal supremacy over the Church, stopping where political authority ends and spiritual authority begins, to support the Parlements, and to repress every undertaking which would proceed too quickly or too far". *Journal et mémoires du marquis d'Argenson*, ed. by E. J. B. Rathery (Paris, Mme Ve. Jules Renouard, 1859-67), Vol. III, pp. 49-50; Vol. IV, pp. 214-215.

[33]   Fleury to Souillac, October 1, 1735; quoted in Émile Appolis, "A Travers le XVIIIe Siècle catholique. Entre jansénistes et constitutionnaires: un tiers parti",

Fleury's appreciation of Souillac was all the more gratifying to him since he had previously had grave doubts about the advisability of promoting him to the see of Lodève. Fleury's concern for that modicum of orthodoxy was revealed by the following pre-episcopal letter of Souillac to the Cardinal:

As I have had no part in the overtures made on my behalf to Your Eminence, Monseigneur, I have not been hurt by the scant success which they have had; but I canot fail to be hurt when I learn, Monseigneur, that Your Eminence retains an idea of my doctrine which I had believed completely destroyed by my very precise declaration of belief, by the interest taken in me, Monseigneur, by persons the least suspected of favoring Jansenism, and by the redoubled testimony of my own bishop who indeed desired to be my bond with Your Eminence.

Far from refuting these very favorable proofs of my vindication, Monseigneur, my whole conduct in civil society and in the exercise of the ecclesiastical ministry has demonstrated my integrity and even my jealousy for the reputation which I require.

I have not, Monseigneur, received a soul so abject as to be capable of being the hateful person of which one wishes to have me suspected. I have said repeatedly on all occasions that I condemn with the Church the five [Jansenist] propositions, that I believe it justified to demand an interior belief of dogmatic facts, and that I regard and receive the constitution *Unigenitus* as a dogmatic law of this same Church, which every believer must obey. I do not have the reputation of being a dishonest man, and I dare to inform Your Eminence, Monseigneur, that in three or four dioceses where my ministry has taken me, there is no man of honor who has not believed my word until the moment when Your Eminence considered it his duty to make sufficiently public his continuing doubts about my way of thinking. It is this, Monseigneur, which leads me to take the liberty of recourse to the justice and charity of Your Eminence in the bitterness and simplicity of my heart.[34]

Fleury's policy was essentially political and pragmatic. In manifesting greater concern for public order than for the intricacies of ecclesiastical controversies, he resembled strikingly the figure of the anti-enthusiastic Walpole, his British counterpart. A 1789 critic of the ecclesiastical abuses of the Old Régime in fact did evoke the memory of Sir Robert, a memory still apparently living, in scorning the use of

*Annales: Économies, sociétés, civilisations*, Vol. VI (April-June, 1951), p. 159. Other evidences of Fleury's moderation may be found in the following: Fleury to the bishop of Châlon-sur-Saône, July 22, 1739. *AAE*, Mémoires et Documents, Fonds France, Vol. 1496, folios 214-215. Fleury to the bishop of Orléans, July 14, 1731, *AAE*, Mémoires et Documents, Fonds France, Vol. 1671, folios 35-36.
[34]   Souillac to Fleury, February 19, 1732, *AAE*, Mémoires et Documents, Fonds France, Vol. 1644, folios 179-181.

the ecclesiastical patronage of the Crown for political advantage.[35] This comparison of Fleury to Walpole is a fertile one. In 1742 the Cardinal received a mémoire from Etienne de Silhouette, the future Controller-General of Finance, suggesting that in solving her ecclesiastical problems France emulate England. Fleury's reaction is not known, but the Silhouette recommendations seem to have been much along the same lines he was following:

The remedy is the establishment of an act by which the State assures itself that all who fill public posts, whether civil or religious, conform to the dominant religion; it is, in other words, the requirement of either an oath or the signing of a formulary. . . . I know that I must expect to bear the brunt of a violent attack on the part of the party which has made itself only too popular and whose total credit is founded upon self-deception and bigotry. But I have reason to hope that this storm will pass away of itself when it will be seen that the requirement of signing a formulary, limited as I propose to persons who wish to occupy public offices, does not attack the liberty of conscience and that it is entirely free from all reproach of persecution. That is, I believe, the sole means of rendering useless all the artifices of a party extremely skilled in taking advantage of them. Every sect deprived of the honors of the State, even if it were based on the truth, can make little progress in this corrupt century. We have an obvious example of this in the Catholics of Holland and England. . . .[36]

Thus was recommended nothing less than a Test Act to bar Jansenist nonconformists from civil and ecclesiastical employment. In controlling the *feuille des bénéfices* Cardinal Fleury was enforcing just such an act, albeit unofficially.

Fleury's attitude towards the Jansenist difficulties was not formed in an ecclesiastical vacuum, independent of broad, political considerations. As merely one of several members of the *chambre ecclésiastique* he had worked to restrain the persecuting proclivities of the Cardinals de Rohan and de Bissy. When he received the post of minister of the *feuille* under the general ministry of the duc de Bourbon, Fleury did find it possible to separate ecclesiastical from general affairs, and to pursue the appellants relentlessly. It was of major importance, however, that upon becoming virtual first minister after the duc de Bourbon's resignation he concluded that he could not direct ecclesiastical and political affairs along conflicting lines. Fleury was forced by his

[35] Abbé Laurent, *Essai sur la réforme du clergé par un vicaire de campagne, docteur de Sorbonne* (Paris, Durand, 1789), pp. 216-217, Bib. nat. Ld4. 5982.
[36] "Dissertations sur l'union de la religion, de la morale et de la politique", January 18, 1742; AAE, Mémoires et Documents, Fonds France, Vol. 1326, folios 10-13.

position of responsibility to integrate ecclesiastical policy into the whole of state policy; from this union of both responsibilities in the same hands was born the policy characteristic of Fleury: firm, but non-persecuting opposition to the Jansenists.[37]

To say that Fleury's policies were political and pragmatic is to describe them as secular. What better source of approval than from the essentially secular abbé (later Cardinal) de Bernis? In spite of Bernis' own pique at Fleury's refusal to favor him with a desirable preferment in the Church.[38] he had sufficient grace to grant the first minister this much in his administration of the *feuille des bénéfices*:

The ministry of the Cardinal de Fleury had almost destroyed Jansenism in France. The convulsions had already thrown a great ridicule upon this party; the famous writers who had defended it were dead; there remained no more than a single suspected bishop; besides he had one foot in the grave. From then on it was only a question of placing in the Church persons of a sound doctrine and opposing scorn and silence to the vain efforts of that expiring faction. Everything was finished: the Church and the State would have enjoyed a lasting tranquillity.[39]

Perhaps the least disguised secular interpretation of the administration of the *feuille des bénéfices* as advocated by Bernis and d'Argenson and practiced by Fleury was that of the abbé de Véri who suggested that Loménie de Brienne be given charge of its administration. Loménie de Brienne was his choice because he had the talent to use the post to decrease the religious fanaticism which was diminishing public respect for Church, King, and Parlement alike. The reputed

[37] Georges Hardy, *Le Cardinal de Fleury et le mouvement janséniste* (Paris, Librairie Ancienne Honoré Champion, 1925), pp. 39-40. A tribute to the firmness of Fleury's policy was given by *Nouvelles ecclésiastiques* which recognized what his administration of the *feuille* signified: " '... the execution of his scheme destructive of all good in the kingdom ...' " (*ibid.*, p. 326). The Jansenists were especially unhappy about the naming of Vintimille to succeed Noailles as archbishop of Paris; see *Nouvelles ecclésiastiques, ou mémoires pour servir à l'histoire ecclésiastique* (Paris, September 30, 1729), article II.

[38] Bernis' disappointment was reflected in his opinion that Fleury was induced by his confidant, the abbé Couturier, to name decidedly mediocre men to the episcopate. *Mémoires et lettres de François-Joachim de Pierre Cardinal de Bernis (1715-1758)* (Paris, E. Plon, 1878), Vol. I, p. 25.

[39] *Ibid.*, I, pp. 82-83. For other contemporary praise of Fleury's success see: R. P. de Neuville, *Oraison funèbre de S. E. Monseigneur le Cardinal de Fleury, ministre d'état, &c., prononcée au service fait par ordre du roi, dans l'église de Paris, le 25. mai, 1743* (Paris, Chez Coignard et Guerin, 1743), p. 51. Abbé Jean-Bruno de Ranchon, *Histoire de André Hercule Cardinal de Fleury, principal ministre* (1758, 2 vols., Bibliothèque nationale, nouvelles acquisitions françaises), MSS. 2076-2077, Vol. I, pp. 446-447.

atheism of his candidate struck the abbé de Véri as no disqualification: "... Of what importance is the secret of his thoughts if his conduct in the direction of public affairs is good." [40]

Fleury's successor in the ecclesiastical department, Boyer, a former Theatine monk and bishop of Mirepoix, had the two-edged reputation of having abandoned the policy of a *politique* for that of an ardent champion of ultramontanism. It was by contrasting Boyer with Fleury that Bernis sought to discredit the former: he considered Boyer's direction of affairs to be despotically and fanatically monkish, stirring up the dying ashes of Jansenism and permitting its partisans to find succor in the sovereign Parlements. [41] Indeed, when in 1755 the bishops attending the General Assembly of the Clergy found themselves divided over the question of depriving "notorious" Jansenists of the sacraments of the Church, it was the corps of bishops who owed their elevation to the ministry of Boyer — the *théatins* — which assumed the more intractable pose. Voltaire's assessment of Boyer was, not surprisingly, very much like Bernis' — that of a man who used his authority to promote fanatics who proceeded to come into conflict with the Parlements. [42]

By far the worst press of any of the ministers of the *feuille des bénéfices* was enjoyed by Jarente de la Bruyère, bishop of Digne and Orléans. In his conspiratorial interpretation of the French Revolution *à la philosophie*, the abbé Proyart was unrestrained in his judgment of Jarente:

To the Boyer's and to the Fleury's who had deserved so well of the clergy during their ministries succeeded a bishop of Orléans whose residence at Court was to be for the Church of France the epoch of its saddest humiliation. Only with difficulty would one imagine a more monstrous contrast: the person who ought to have fixed upon himself the public esteem, as the first spokesman near the throne of a Power to which the powers of the earth

---

[40] *Journal de l'abbé de Véri*, ed. by baron Johan de Witte (Paris, Librairie Plon, 1933), Vol. I, pp. 199-200. The marquis d'Argenson also viewed the ministry of ecclesiastical affairs as essentially no different from any other department of government: "It would certainly not be necessary to place an ecclesiastic in charge. One should follow the maxim of the other departments which forbids entrusting a military man with the [ministry of] war or a naval officer with the [ministry of] marine..." *Journal et mémoires du marquis d'Argenson*, IV, p. 215.

[41] *Mémoires et lettres de ... Bernis*, I, pp. 82-83.

[42] Voltaire. *Histoire du Parlement*, in *Oeuvres complètes de Voltaire* (Paris, Garnier Frères, 1877-85), Vol. XVI, p. 79. His scorn knew no bounds; he described Boyer as one "... qui signait toujours *l'ane évêque de Mirepoix*, au lieu de signer *l'anc.*; il croyait mettre l'abréviation d'*ancien*, et il signait son nom tout au long". *Oeuvres complètes*, XL, p. 452.

render hommage, was seen grovelling vilely before a dishonorable woman [Mme de Pompadour], and in days of impiety opposing the daring assaults of Jansenism and the magistrature with only the compromises of cowardice. Great was the scandal; but it was enormous and seemed complete when he, who by virtue of office and estate was a man of religion at Court and entrusted with making it seem venerable, revealed himself as the equal of the most vicious courtiers; when he who was delegated in the name of the Church to enlighten the government on the choice of first pastors and the disposal of a sacred patrimony, was seen circulating shamefully in the society of mountebanks and dragging the pastoral dignity down into the degradation and debauchery of their licentiousness.[43]

In a lighter vein, Bachaumont related an episode during which the duc de Choiseul, patron of Jarente, had two actresses impersonate two covetous abbés who asked the minister of the *feuille* for Church preferment. Jarente's reaction, according to Bachaumont's scandal-mongering account, was cool until he heard that the two unknown clerics were relatives of Choiseul; thereupon, his unfriendly demeanor changed: "The heart of the bishop of Orléans melted, no doubt with sympathy; he promises wonders, and by way of high favor could not restrain himself from embracing those two lovable ecclesiastics. . . ." [44]

The complete odium cast upon Jarente has moved a modern biographer of the bishop-minister to seek to exonerate him — albeit not on the basis of the high-minded criteria of outraged clerics and moralists. According to Louis d'Illiers, Jarente was appointed to what was essentially a political post; his assignment was to name to the bench of bishops men with temperaments and convictions which would work for conciliation between the magistrates and the episcopate. Jarente was selected by Mme de Pompadour and the duc de Choiseul because they were impressed with his diocesan record at Digne — a record marked by moderation and restraint in the midst of flaming ecclesiastical and jurisdictional controversy; and they intended him as an antidote to the hard-bitten and inflammatory policy of Boyer. Judged by these standards, Jarente was a success: he shared his patrons' distaste for ecclesiastical enthusiasm; when they fell from power he followed. D'Illiers has concluded that if the Dauphin had been justified in lamenting, "M. de Jarente has chosen too many per-

[43]   Abbé Liévain Bonaventure Proyart, *Louis XVI détroné avant d'être roi* (Liége-Brussels, new edition, 1814; original edition, London and Hamburg, 1800), pp. 317-318; partially quoted in Sicard, p. 504.
[44]   Bachaumont, *Mémoires secrets pour servir à l'histoire de la république des lettres en France* (London, John Adamson, 1777), Vol. IV, August 13, 1769, p. 335.

sons like himself", the latter had undoubtedly found that only in such passionless and worldly ecclesiastics could he discover the type of men he was commissioned to elevate to the bench of bishops.[45] Like the defense of Fleury's policy, this defense of Jarente is a secular one; it is decidedly in the tradition of Voltaire, who writing to d'Alembert to reassure him that Diderot would not be refused membership in the Académie française, remarked that Diderot needed to fear the opposition of neither Mme de Pompadour, the duc de Choiseul, nor the bishop of Orléans; the bishop of Orléans "will not speak against him as had the *mage* Yebor [i.e., Boyer]. . . ."[46]

## III

Having noted the reputed 18th-Century trend towards the monopolization of high ecclesiastical office in the hands of the nobility, and having examined the office of the *feuille des bénéfices*, through which any such monopolization would have operated, we can proceed to a statistical analysis of the 18th-Century episcopate, determining its social composition and the trends prevailing within its recruitment. Table I presents a breakdown of the French bishops in the period 1682-1790 into three categories: nobles, *roturiers*, and those of un-

TABLE I

*Three-Period Breakdown of All Bishops*

*1682-1790*

| Period | Number of Bishops | Noble | | Roturier | | Undifferentiated | |
|---|---|---|---|---|---|---|---|
| | | # | % | # | % | # | % |
| 1682-1700 | 194 | 170 | 88 | 16 | 8 | 8 | 4 |
| 1700-1774 | 240 | 200 | 83 | 9 | 4 | 31 | 13 |
| 1774-1790 | 192 | 173 | 90 | 2 | 1 | 17 | 9 |
| Totals | 626 | 543 | 87 | 27 | 4 | 56 | 9 |

[45] Louis d'Illiers, *Deux Prélats d'ancien régime, les Jarente* (Monoco, Editions du Rocher, 1948), pp. 31-32. The words of the Dauphin, father of Louis XVI, are also cited in Sicard, p. 504.
[46] *Oeuvres complètes de Voltaire*, XL, p. 452; Voltaire to d'Alembert, July 9, 1760.

known origins — the latter group being made up of those bishops whose membership in either the nobility or the commonalty I have not been able to identify with any accuracy. Table I also depicts the contrast between the social origins of those bishops in office in the years 1682-1700 with those in office during the period 1774-90.

Table II divides the contingent of noble bishops according to type of nobility. *Sword* nobles were those bishops whose families were reputed members of the Second Estate by virtue primarily of their chiv-

TABLE II

*Three-Period Breakdown of Noble Bishops*

*(Origin of Nobility)*

| Period | Number of Noble Bishops | Sword Origin | | Robe | | Administrative | | Cloche | | Undifferentiated Nobles | |
|---|---|---|---|---|---|---|---|---|---|---|---|
| | | # | % | % | # | # | % | # | % | # | % |
| 1682-1700 | 170 | 83 | 49 | 38 | 22 | 23 | 14 | 2 | 1 | 24 | 14 |
| 1700-1774 | 200 | 137 | 69 | 31 | 16 | 9 | 5 | — | — | 23 | 12 |
| 1774-1790 | 173 | 130 | 75 | 14 | 8 | 2 | 1 | — | — | 27 | 16 |
| Totals | 543 | 350 | 64 | 83 | 15 | 34 | 6 | 2 | .4 | 74 | 14 |

alric origins. *Robe* nobles were those whose families had acquired noble status through magisterial office in the Parlements and sovereign courts. *Administrative* nobles were those whose families had achieved noble status through a variety of administrative posts which conferred either immediate or gradual nobility; such posts included those of the offices of *secrétaire du roi* and *maître des requêtes*, those of the *bureaux des finances*, and various governorships, posts of *grand baillif*, and the like. Nobles of the *cloche* were those ennobled through municipal office, while the *undifferentiated* nobles were those who were unquestionably noble and whose families can often be found in the genealogies but whose precise source of nobility cannot be clearly given. Some sword families were also active parliamentarians, holding high office in the Parlements, but these have been treated as sword nobles because their parliamentary activities post-dated their chivalric origins. Table III supplements Table II with a breakdown according to approximate length of noble status, while Tables IV and V follow the same classification as the first two tables as they divide the data into twelve unequal periods corresponding to a particular minister of the *feuille des bénéfices* or committee of ecclesiastical advisers.[47]

It has long been suspected, though without statistical study, that the French nobility by the end of the Old Régime had established a near monopoly of high Church office, as of military and naval office. The above tables reveal, however, that not only were commoners quite effectively barred from the episcopate towards the end of the 18th Century, but that commoners did not have great success in this quest even in the allegedly golden age of Louis XIV. The period 1682-1700 does not appear to have been one highly favorably to the episcopal ambitions of the Third Estate: only 8% of the bishops were commoners. Indeed, the years 1774-1790, when only 1% of the bishops were commoners, were even less favorable to the Third Estate. In real numbers, there was a decline from 16 commoner bishops in 1682-1700 to only 2 in 1774-1790. The noble monopoly over the episcopate was an eyesore just before the Revolution: but it had already existed in the late 17th Century, and it became all the more irritating when the thin ranks of non-noble bishops were not replenished. It was during the second half of the reign of Louis XV that the nobles achieved their virtually complete possession of episcopal office. Dur-

---

[47] Genealogical information has been gathered from the following sources:

J. Bluche, *L'Origine des magistrats du parlement de Paris au XVIII<sup>e</sup> siècle* (Paris, Au Siège de la Fédération, 1956).

François Alexandre Aubert de la Chesnaye-Desbois, *Dictionnaire de la Noblesse* (Paris, Schlesinger, 3rd ed., 1863-76), 19 vols.

*Gallia christiana in provincias ecclesiasticas distributa qua series et historia archiepiscoporum, episcoporum et abbatum* (Paris, V. Palme, 1856-99), 16 vols.

Jean Chrétien Ferdinand Hoefer, *Nouvelle Biographie générale depuis les temps les plus reculés jusqu'à nos jours* (Paris, Firmin Didot Frères, 1855-66), 46 vols.

Honoré Fisquet, *La France pontificale* (Paris, E. Repos, 1864-73), 21 vols.

Louis-Pierre d'Hozier, *Armorial général de la France* (Paris, 1738-1872), 7 vols.

Armand Jean, *Les Évêques et les archevêques de France depuis 1682 jusqu'à 1801* (Paris, Alphonse Picard, 1891).

P.-Louis Lainé, *Archives généalogiques et historiques de la noblesse de France* (Paris, Lainé, 1828-50), 11 vols.

J. F. and L. G. Michaud, *Biographie universelle ancienne et moderne* (Paris, A. Thoisnier Desplaces, 2nd edition, 1843-65), 45 vols.

Louis Moréri, *Le Grand Dictionnaire historique* (Basle, Jean Louis Brandmuller, new edition, 1740), 6 vols.; *Supplement* (Basle, Jean Christ, 1743-45), 3 vols.

TABLE III

## Three-Period Breakdown of Noble Bishops
### (Age of Gentility)

| Period | Number of Noble Bishops | Over 200 Years | | 100-200 Years | | Under 100 Years | | ? |
|---|---|---|---|---|---|---|---|---|
| | | # | % | # | % | # | % | % |
| 1682-1700 | 170 | 86 | 51 | 24 | 14 | 21 | 12 | 23 |
| 1700-1774 | 200 | 119 | 60 | 18 | 9 | 12 | 6 | 25 |
| 1774-1790 | 173 | 137 | 79 | 6 | 3 | 2 | 1 | 17 |
| Totals | 543 | 342 | 63 | 48 | 9 | 35 | 6 | 22 |

TABLE IV

## Breakdown of All Bishops According to Ministers of the
### "Feuille Des Bénéfices"

| Period | | Number of Bishops | Noble | | Roturier | | Undifferentiated | |
|---|---|---|---|---|---|---|---|---|
| | | | # | % | # | % | # | % |
| Before 1682 | | 124 | 108 | 87 | 10 | 8 | 6 | 5 |
| La Chaize | 1682-1708 | 113 | 101 | 89 | 6 | 5 | 6 | 5 |
| Le Tellier | 1709-1715 | 31 | 23 | 74 | 3 | 10 | 5 | 16 |
| Conseil de Conscience | 1715-1718 | 14 | 12 | 86 | 1 | 7 | 1 | 7 |
| Chambre ecclésiastique | 1718-1723 | 36 | 30 | 83 | 2 | 6 | 4 | 11 |
| Fleury | 1723-1742 | 100 | 87 | 87 | 3 | 3 | 10 | 10 |
| Boyer | 1743-1755 | 55 | 45 | 82 | — | — | 10 | 18 |
| La Rochefoucauld | 1755-1757 | 6 | 5 | 83 | — | — | 1 | 17 |
| Jarente | 1757-1770 | 59 | 54 | 92 | — | — | 5 | 8 |
| La Roche-Aymon | 1771-1777 | 38 | 34 | 89 | 1 | 3 | 3 | 8 |
| Marbeuf | 1777-1788 | 46 | 41 | 89 | — | — | 5 | 11 |
| Le Franc de Pompignan | 1789-1790 | 4 | 3 | 75 | 1 | 25 | — | — |

TABLE V

Breakdown of Noble Bishops According to Ministers of the
"Feuille des Bénéfices" (Origin of Nobility)

| Period | | Number of Noble Bishops | Sword | | Robe | | Administrative | | Cloche | | Undifferentiated | |
|---|---|---|---|---|---|---|---|---|---|---|---|---|
| | | | # | % | # | % | # | % | # | % | # | % |
| Before 1682 | | 108 | 55 | 51 | 21 | 19 | 17 | 16 | 1 | 1 | 14 | 13 |
| La Chaize | 1682-1708 | 101 | 50 | 50 | 25 | 25 | 10 | 10 | 1 | 1 | 15 | 14 |
| Le Tellier | 1709-1715 | 23 | 14 | 61 | 5 | 22 | — | — | — | — | 4 | 17 |
| Conseil de Conscience | 1715-1718 | 12 | 10 | 83 | 2 | 17 | — | — | — | — | — | — |
| Chambre ecclésiastique | 1718-1723 | 30 | 25 | 83 | 1 | 3 | 4 | 13 | — | — | — | — |
| Fleury | 1723-1742 | 87 | 56 | 64 | 16 | 18 | 1 | 1 | — | — | 14 | 16 |
| Boyer | 1743-1755 | 45 | 31 | 69 | 5 | 11 | 1 | 2 | — | — | 8 | 18 |
| LaRoche-foucauld | 1755-1757 | 5 | 5 | 100 | — | — | — | — | — | — | — | — |
| Jarente | 1757-1770 | 54 | 46 | 85 | 3 | 6 | — | — | — | — | 5 | 9 |
| LaRoche-Aymon | 1771-1777 | 34 | 22 | 65 | 5 | 15 | 1 | 3 | — | — | 6 | 17 |
| Marbeuf | 1777-1788 | 41 | 35 | 85 | — | — | — | — | — | — | 6 | 15 |
| LeFranc de Pompignan | 1789-1790 | 3 | 1 | 34 | — | — | — | — | — | — | 2 | 66 |

ing the years 1743-1770 no ecclesiastics were nominated to bishoprics whom I have been able to classify as plebeian. In the last two decades before the Revolution only two commoners received episcopal office: one, Beauvais of Senez, whose elevation aroused the indignation of the aristocrats; [48] and Asseline of Boulogne, who was preferred during the Revolution itself — the last nomination to the episcopate before the Civil Constitution of the Clergy completely revolutionized the Church of the Old Régime.

These statistics also show that another trend in the preferment of men to the Gallican episcopate during the course of the 18th Century was one towards the preference for nobles whose origins were in the nobility of the sword rather than for those from families whose gentility had arisen from magisterial or administrative office. The

[48] Abbé Augustin Sicard, *L'Ancien Clergé de France: les évêques avant la Révolution*, p. 7.

real difference between 1682-1700 on the one hand and 1774-1790 on the other lay not as much in the increase of noble bishops as in the great increase in bishops from the *sword* nobility; 49% of noble bishops in the earlier period came from sword families, as against 75% in the later period. Correspondingly, the contingent of bishops from the robe nobility fell in importance, from 22% of the noble bishops in the earlier period to 8% in the later years; in the case of bishops from administrative noble families, the decline was from 14% to 1%.

If in the course of the 18th Century the ministers of the *feuille des bénéfices* simply continued rather than initiated an overwhelming preference for noblemen for the episcopal dignity, they did nevertheless reveal a perceptible change in the sort of nobility they preferred. Churchmen of magisterial and administrative nobility found it increasingly difficult to become bishops. The decline on the episcopal bench of the sons of men who had become noble through administrative office may perhaps be explained by the fact that the most honorable and useful offices which in the 17th Century had conferred noble status upon commoners, in the 18th Century came to be transmitted in families already noble, thereby becoming closed off to commoners.[49] It was still not difficult for commoners to acquire noble status through the purchase of other offices — useless ones such as those of *secrétaire du roi* and *maître des requêtes* — through usurpations, and for a time through the *noblesse militaire*. But the sons of those thus ennobled were not made bishops in the latter part of the 18th Century. Thus, if we look upon those bishops from the administrative nobility in the late 17th Century as relatively new to nobility, their absence in the late 18th Century is an indication that the episcopate was increasingly the domain of the aristocracy of birth. Successful noble social aggressiveness was evident in the episcopate as well as in the military and the royal administration. In the late 17th Century the sons of the Colbert, Le Tellier, and Desmaretz families, ennobled through their administrative labors, were elevated to bishoprics; as mere bourgeois they would have had more difficulty. In the late 18th Century, wealthy bourgeois continued to win ennoblement through venality of office, but they were less likely to be found in the high administrative posts of the royal government, and their sons rarely received bishoprics — either as bourgeois in origin or as the sons of administrative noblemen.

[49] Henri Carré, *La Noblesse de France et l'opinion publique au XVIIIᵉ siècle* (Paris, Librairie Ancienne Honoré Champion, 1920), p. 8.

But what of the relative exclusion of the sons of the nobility of the robe from the episcopate? If the robe nobility was increasingly assuming the institutional leadership of the resurgent aristocracy, and if the invidious distinctions between robe and sword were losing their virulence, why should the robe nobility have lost its former access to high ecclesiastical office? It could not have been that the robe bishops were concealed under the trappings of chivalric origin fabricated according to the needs of rising aristocratic sensibilities — not if the prevailing trend was in the direction of eliminating these invidious distinctions within the nobility. Franklin L. Ford has noted that to counter the disdain of sword noblemen like Saint-Simon and the Regency dukes and peers, the magistrates manufactured pretensions of their own: the magistrates' usual claim was that the administration of justice was as valid a source of nobility as military service; their more extravagant pretensions held that in administering justice the magistrates exercised the most noble of the powers of the medieval kings — far above the mere bearing of arms.[50] Such arrogant magistrates would hardly fabricate the trappings of a not-at-all superior chivalry. In any case, the available genealogical materials often do offer a basis for determining whether a particular noble house was of magisterial origin, regardless of the aristocratic eminence and elegance which it may have enjoyed in the 18th Century. All this is to say that the changing ratio of sword to robe families depicted by the above tables was not a function of the changing self-identification of noble families, but the result of an objective change in the recruitment of bishops.

To account for the marked reduction in the proportion of noble bishops who belonged to the magisterial nobility recourse must be had to the protracted 18th-Century struggles between the bishops and the magistrates over the issues of Jansenism, Gallicism, and ecclesiastical vs. secular jurisdiction. We know that certain ministers of the *feuille des bénéfices* like Boyer zealously favored the controversial *Unigenitus*, while the less "monkish" Fleury sought to make Jansenism a bar to ecclesiastical preferment. It was more than coincidental that robe representation in the episcopate began to diminish during the ministry of Père Letellier, the period of the promulgation of *Unigenitus*. What, then, accounted for the changing complexion of the noble majority of the episcopate was the evident fact that in the

[50]   Franklin L. Ford, *Robe and Sword: The Regrouping of the French Aristocracy After Louis XIV* (Cambridge, Harvard University Press, 1953), p. 72.

Parlements and the magisterial families the Jansenists and appellants found perhaps their most vocal and most effective support — their institutional support. Individual exceptions allowed, as a whole the magisterial nobility would not have appeared to the Fleury's,[51] and especially not to the Boyer's, as a good recruiting ground for bishops who would reliably follow the ecclesiastical policy laid down by the régime; less favorable then the robe nobility to the appellant position — at least institutionally, collectively — the sword nobility was a better source of dependable prelates. The contingent of bishops opposed to official ecclesiasticalism — numbering perhaps thirteen in 1727 [52] — was effectively reduced to virtual extinction when its leadership was undermined and its ranks not replenished. The decline of robe bishops was the result of this policy.

The use of the Crown's patronage to pacify the Parlements, a suggestion of d'Argenson, was never tried, except perhaps in the period when the Regent was tolerant of opponents of *Unigenitus*.[53] The failure to seek an appeasement of the *robins*, as suggested by the following mémoire in the files of the Foreign Ministry, served to harden the antagonism between Parlement and Church.

The Parlement of Paris gradually must be completely won over; certainly not in order to have it betray ... the common weal or to introduce ultramontanism into France (for what could it imagine that the ministers and bishops would gain by that?) but rather in order to make it stop entertaining

[51]    For Fleury's views on the Parlements, see Appendix III.
[52]    Twelve bishops in 1727 protested against the condemnation of Soanen by the Council of Embrun. Hardy, p. 93.
[53]    Although the Regent was for a time more tolerant of appellants than either Louis XIV or Fleury, he probably placated the magistrates with only lesser benefices. Table V does not show that the Regency was a period of greater nomination of bishops of robe origin. It is undeniable that in general the robe nobility's access to the episcopate was restricted because of governmental suspicion of its orthodoxy. The converse, however, was not necessarily true—that in the early Regency a tolerant Philippe d'Orléans would name men from the robe families to the episcopate because of their pro-Jansenism. The reaction against Louis XIV's long reign included a scorn for his willingness to be served by officials of low origin. The Regency was the reaction on the part of the great peers; the polysynodal structure of government was designed to give the aristocracy more actual power. Indeed, the Regent was known as an aristocrat; his rule saw a period of frantic solicitations for place, civil and ecclesiastical, by a nobility which believed its advocate was at last in power. (See *AAE*, Mémoires et Documents, Fonds France, Vols. 1233, fol. 15; 1234, fol. 10; 1237, fols. 228-229; 1238, fol. 9; 1243; fols. 88-90, 120-121; 1248, fols. 21, 24, 41; 1582, fols. 99-100.) In short, Jansenism was never a motive for naming certain individuals to bishoprics. And under Fleury and his successors doctrinal orthodoxy was a necessary but not sufficient condition for prospective prelates.

this very illusion and cease supporting rebels. There are so many ways to accomplish this: by the trifling matter of the places which you grant, by the benefices and indults of which you dispose, by several pensions, and by a regular policy which makes men who think themselves all too independent fear the Court and hope for its favor.[54]

The refusal to take such advice seriously was all the more strange in view of the frequent use of the *feuille des bénéfices* for political advantage. The Breton estates were a fountain of chronic opposition to the Crown. All the nobles of the province attended at will and tranquillity was usually at a premium. The government strove to tame the Breton nobility on the one hand by limiting membership in the Second Estate to older nobles who enjoyed a certain wealth and in the First Estate to a fixed number of ecclesiastics; [55] and on the other hand by using the *feuille* to develop within the First Estate a loyal contingent capable of calming the exuberant nobility.[56] This policy met very mixed reactions. The comte de Puisaye saw special royal treatment of ecclesiastical appointments in Brittany as a sign of the retention of ancient "liberties" and praised a system which named bishops almost always according to the wishes of the Estates ("no matter whether it were with a view towards conciliating their deliberations or for another reason entirely"); he felt that the Breton prelates were less influenced by court intrigue and its corrupting influence.[57] On the other hand, a member of the Breton nobility earlier in the century found that the government's policy was making the Estates ineffective:

The Order of the Church followed its ordinary path, sustained by the example of its presidents. It viewed the most solid interests of the assembly as a foreign and indifferent matter; or having no part in it they could be as obliging as the [royal] commissioners demand. This way could procure them some advantage or at least many comforts; and the other way of doing good seemed of no use to them. Furthermore, the nobility wished to have itself walk side-by-side and have the same sitting with them, that is, with the bishops; but a rash audacity overwhelmed them and made them swear

---

54 "Considerations politiques sur l'état présent des anticonstitutionnaires", June, 1733, *AAE*, Mémoires et Documents, Fonds France, Vol. 1283, folios 196-211.
55 *AAE*, Mémoires et Documents, Fonds France, Vol. 1522, folios 370-381.
56 Letter of Malesherbes, Secretary of State for the Maison du Roi, to Cardinal de la Roche-Aymon, March 24, 1776, *AN*, 01 472, p. 92. Armand Rebillon, *Les États de Bretagne de 1661 à 1789* (Rennes, Imprimeries Réunies, 1932), p. 108.
57 Comte Joseph de Puisaye, *Mémoires, qui pourrent servir à l'histoire du parti royaliste françois durant la dernière révolution* (London, E. Harding, 1803-06), Vol. III, p. 403.

that they would never be their friends during all of the session — a humble and generous ground for abandoning what they owed to their flock. To sacrifice a whole people is quite worthy of the ministers of the altars.[58]

The self-satisfied testimony of the comte de Puisaye differed startlingly from the resentment of Jacquelot de Boisrouvray, and their views of what the government's policy indeed accomplished were not identical; nevertheless, the government was consciously considering its relations with the Estates in naming bishops and other ecclesiastics to the sees of the province.

Thus there was a willingness to use the *feuille des bénéfices* to win over the nobility of the Estates, but not the Parlements. The latter's resentment was reflected in the protracted struggle between the bishops and the magistrates, and also in the magistrates' attitude towards the Concordat which had given Francis I and his successors the right to name bishops. A Foreign Affairs Ministry mémoire drawn up at the time of the second Assembly of Notables concerning the changes to be wrought by an Estates General spoke of the magistrates' desire to abolish the Concordat, differentiating between their strong opposition to the arrangement and the alleged approval of the rest of the nobility. Referring to the Parlement of Paris, the mémoire read:

... I shall note that the most fanatical opponents of royal authority are incensed that it has this beautiful prerogative which subdues the high nobility and obliges it to submit its right and its wishes. They would be fascinated to see the elections to the great benefices reestablished. They include especially malcontents and bad subjects to whom it has been impossible to give any benefices. But I also add that the most sensible part, the largest in France and consequently the part which will dominate at the Estates General, loves the king's prerogative to award places, benefices, and honors, and these advantages are the foundation of a monarchy; for one doesn't love a monarch for his beautiful eyes or his fine appearance, but because he governs his kingdom with justice and kindness and is beneficent. Strip the king of France of the means of giving favors and you will strip royalty.[59]

In a remarkably perceptive work entitled *Histoire de l'esprit révolutionnaire des nobles en France, sous les soixante-huit rois de la mo-*

---

[58] Jacquelot de Boisrouvray, *Journal inédit d'un député de l'ordre de la noblesse aux États de Bretagne pendant la Régence (1717-1724)*, ed. by G. de Closmadeuc, *Archives de Bretagne*, Vol. XIII (1905), p. 204.

[59] "Mémoire sur les intérêts du Souverain Pontif relativement aux États Généraux", 1788, AAE, Mémoires et Documents, Fonds France, Vol. 1404, folios 179-192. The mémoire was too optimistic about the strength of the supporters of the Concordat but correct about the Parlement's hostility.

*narchie*,[60] Giraud wrote perceptively of the effect of the struggle over *Unigenitus* upon the French nobility:

The bull *Unigenitus* suddenly occupied the imagination of the mitered nobility. This Roman decree gave birth to the French *formulaire*, and the latter divided into two irreconcilable parties the whole episcopal body. As all of it considered itself in the noble caste, by common principles, by equality of privileges, and by fortune, there was equally a schism in the body of the nobility of the sword and in that of the nobility of the robe. Thus did disunity intrude itself into the whole nobility of *France*. The king Louis XV found himself placed between the army of *acceptants* and the army of *appellants*. The number of neutrals was the smallest because good sense never offers the charm of a faction.[61]

For Giraud, then, the significant split within the nobility — and this internal split is important in understanding the struggles between bishops and magistrates throughout the 18th Century — was not between those of sword and robe origins *per se*; the significant split was between those of whatever noble origins who took the pro-*Unigenitus* side and those who appealed against it. Because the robe nobles provided an institutionalized means of fighting the bull, and because they consequently met greater obstacles in entering the episcopate, the intra-noble division and strife came to reassemble a struggle between bishops and magistrates. It is at this point that we may with Giraud divide the nobility of France into a "noblesse de robe" and a "noblesse en camail".[62]

## IV

To the nobility the increasingly exclusive hold which its members acquired over the bishoprics of the nation was easily justified. The places of prestige and wealth within the Gallican Church were viewed by the nobles as means for providing for their excess offspring, recouping family fortunes, and generally aiding the clan. The duc de Saint-Simon as one of the leading advocates of aristocratic proprietor-

[60]  Paris, Baudouin Frères, 1818, 2 vols. in one. This work's chief claim to notice is its thesis: the "modern" view that the French Revolution was begun as a revolt of the aristocracy which thereby taught the obedient bourgeoisie how to rebel. The book is an indictment of the disloyal nobility from the Frankish period up to 1789. Rather than fall into the temptation to label its thesis "modern", we should perhaps note that modern historians have come to see the Revolution and its causes more like some very perceptive contemporaries.

[61]  *Ibid.*, II, p. 300.

[62]  *Ibid.*, II, p. 302.

ship over the highest livings in the Church described in great detail
the family policy of the La Rochefoucauld's. For that noble house, as
for many others, the Church was more than a religious necessity:

The ducs de la Rochefoucauld had for a long time been accustomed to
desire among them only one heir to receive all the property and wealth
of the father; to marry off neither daughters nor younger sons, whom they
considered worthless; and to throw them into the Order of Malta or the
Church. The first duc de la Rochefoucauld made his second and fourth
sons priests: the elder died as bishop of Lectoure; the other was content
with abbeys; the second [of these] was a chevalier of the Order of Malta.
Of the six daughters whom he had, four were abbesses, the last one a nun.
The third one, tougher than the others, absolutely desired a husband; they
did not want to give her any.[63]

Talleyrand was one of the unwanted noble children whose ecclesiastical career was deemed "more favorable for the advancement of the
family". He lamented in his *Mémoires* that among the nobility the individual — even the yet unborn — was subordinated to the welfare of
the clan.[64] The duc des Cars was also destined for the Church; because, unlike Talleyrand, he escaped this unwanted vocation, he was
able to enumerate its proffered attractions with less bitterness. The
duc des Cars depicted how his mother had coaxed him into entering
the seminary to prepare for an ecclesiastical career:

She gave me the sweetest and most attractive description of this seminary
life at Paris, in the midst of my family. She showed me pensions from abbeys first raining down in abundance, soon followed by rich priories and
great abbeys. I would be almoner to the king, agent of the clergy [an office filled by the General Assembly], later at the age of thirty a bishop, and
finally the richest in my family! [65]

Had he remained in the seminary, the duke would have undoubtedly
climbed just such a ladder of preferment.

The foundation, then, of the nobility's temporal interest in the
Church was its use in maintaining the nobility in its accustomed

---

[63]   *Mémoires de Saint-Simon*, XXIII, p. 227; also cited in Sicard, pp. 13-14. The
"tough" daughter finally got her man!
[64]   *Mémoires du prince de Talleyrand* (Paris, Les Éditions Henri Javal, 1953),
Vol. I, p. 53. A recent article by Louis S. Greenbaum, "Talleyrand and His
Uncle: the Genesis of a Clerical Career", *The Journal of Modern History*, Vol.
XXIX (September, 1957), pp. 226-236, seeks to revise the accepted idea that
Talleyrand's Church career was decreed by his parents with a discussion of the
strong influence of his uncle, the archbishop of Reims.
[65]   *Mémoires du duc des Cars* (Paris, Librairie Plon, 1890), Vol. I, p. 8; cited
in Sicard, p. 18.

social and economic position. This prevailing system found perhaps its most devastating critic in the Jesuit moralist, Bourdaloue, towards the end of the reign of Louis XIV. According to his description,

"Hardly . . . has this child been born than the Church becomes his portion; and one can say of him, although in a perverted sense, what is written of Isaiah, that from his mother's womb he is destined for the altar. The younger son hasn't the advantage of primogeniture; without seeing whether God calls him or will accept him, one offers him up. . . . It is enough that he be the younger son of his house to have no doubt that he is thereby called to the formidable functions of a pastor of souls. If the face of things were to change, his vocation would likewise change; while he has an elder brother, it will remain. . . . [If] this elder son has in birth not been sufficiently endowed by nature and lacks certain qualities for upholding the glory of his name, without regard for God's view of him, one contemplates degrading him, so to speak, by relegating him to the rank of the younger son who is substituted for him; to accomplish this one extorts a forced consent, one uses deceit and violence, caresses and threats. . . . If out of the several children who comprise the same family there is one more contemptible than the others, it is always he to whom the honors of the Church are reserved. If he is disgraced, malformed, or if he doesn't enjoy the affection of his father and mother, he must be made into a clergyman." [66]

Discounting the possible disdain of a Jesuit for the secular and beneficed clergy, one can nevertheless derive from Bourdaloue's indignant critique the impression of a widespread opinion among the nobility that the Church existed for the care of the noble class no less vitally than for other purposes.

It was, however, no mere rationalization of the services a wealthy Church rendered the nobility which aristocrats employed to justify their monopoly of its higher offices. Since the clergy was the First Estate of the realm, the only possible source of its leadership appeared to them to be in the nobility. It was held essential for the good of the provinces that bishops be men of high birth.[67] Just as the appointment of plebeians to high secular office was scorned by the aristocrats as the creation of so many royal servants, so also was the nomination of plebeian bishops equated with royal preference for subservient flunkies.[68] The very survival of the episcopate as anything more than

[66] Quoted in Sicard, p. 15; pieced together from two sermons "Sur l'Ambition" and "Sur le Devoir des pères par rapport à la vocation de leurs enfants", *Oeuvres de Bourdaloue* (Paris, Firmin Didot Frères, 1840), Vol. I, pp. 262-263; 496.

[67] The archbishop of Narbonne to the Regent, August 26, 1720, *AAE*, Mémoires et Documents, Fonds France, Vol. 1243, folios 136-137.

[68] There is evidence that in 1721 the government was considering the establishment of an academy in which the sons of the nobility and the sons of ". . . those

the ecclesiastical lackeys of the government was held by the noble propagandists to be at stake.[69] As minister of the *feuille* Boyer reputedly excused his delay in providing a poor relation of the Cardinal de la Rochefoucauld with a bishopric with a self-evident, " 'Yes, I know the abbé de la Rochefoucauld; but so fair a merit requires a great see.' "[70] The abbé Proyart's praise for Boyer's alleged success in ignoring the solicitations of unworthy candidates and their families and court partisans was liberal indeed, but he was honest enough to concede the prejudices by which Boyer conducted business.

Although personally alien to the nobility, it had nonetheless been among the nobility that this prelate had labored to discover proper persons to sit in the ranks of first pastors — persuaded as he was that joined to the humble and sublime virtues of the apostolate, a distinguished birth ordinarily gave them still more eminence and character; always at least more of that outward dignity useful to a first pastor, in that he must both win the respect of his colleagues and sustain the interests of religion in the circle of great persons or treat with them in the government.[71]

In similar fashion, after having denied virtually every charge of simony and irregularity levelled against Marbeuf during his ministry, his biographer was compelled to admit a certain lack of firmness. To the charge that Marbeuf refused to nominate the abbé d'Aviau to a bishopric because he had received no proof of his family's ancient lineage the biographer can only reply: "Perhaps in regard to this candidate, so worthy of eulogies, the minister of the *feuille* yielded a little to the spirit of the century in which he lived." [72]

The belief that the nobility should have the highest places in the Church reserved for it did not solve the problem of which of the many

---

whom the services of war have granted the same prerogatives ..." would be educated ". . . such that this school may become in due course a source of chosen men, so much more worthy of the most eminent places in the Church and of the first offices, political and military, that their education will always repay us with the piety, the virtue, and the courage with which they will sustain with glory the interest of religion, the preservation of our laws, and the fame of our arms ..." "Projet d'établissement d'une académie royale, pour l'éducation de la noblesse de France, en forme d'édit ...", December 31, 1721; AAE, Mémoires et Documents, Fonds France, Vol. 1247, folios 124-133.

[69]    Sicard, p. 6.
[70]    *Ibid.*, pp. 23-24.
[71]    Proyart, pp. 316-317; cited also in Sicard, p. 7.
[72]    Abbé Charles Monternot, *Yves-Alexandre de Marbeuf, ministre de la feuille des bénéfices, archevêque de Lyon (1734-1799)* (Lyon, H. Lardanchet, 1911), pp. 36-37.

qualified noble families were to be succored and which forced to await the next episcopal demise. The competition between rival claimants was fierce indeed; even a pliant minister of the *feuille* was faced with more noble appeals than his sympathetic heart could answer.[73] The ecclesiastical career of the eventual bishop of Avranches, Godart de Belbeuf, offers an illustration of the difficulties of even well situated noble houses. The future prelate's brother, the marquis de Belbeuf and procurator-general of the Parlement of Rouen, was seeking to have him made vicar-general of Pontoise in the archdiocese of Rouen: the marquis received this piece of advice from Nicolay, the bishop of Verdun and superior of the hopeful abbé de Belbeuf:

If Monsieur the bishop of Orléans [Jarente] . . . sometimes followed my suggestions, Monsieur your brother would have long ago been established and placed, . . . but I have no actual credit with this minister. All I can do is to support, to animate the zeal of Monsieur the prince de Tingry who seems to me to be greatly attached to you and truly to wish prosperity to your brother. It is necessary that on your part you also devote yourself to these activities and that you seize the opportunities which can be favorable.[74]

When the ambition of the abbé de Belbeuf and that of his brother had advanced to the quest for a bishopric, the going was not without disappointments. The marquis received an explanation for the delay from Montmorency-Longuy:

You know that this prelate [Jarente] makes many pretty promises and for their realization one must press him still further. He only made me this objection, that it was only a short while ago that M. your brother acquired the living which he holds.[75]

Finally, the marquis was informed that the death of the bishop of Tarbes had placed into the hands of the minister of the *feuille* ". . . a place agreeable and rich enough for someone who would not fear to travel two hundred leagues. . . ." His correspondent, the bishop of Lescar, added: "Make up your mind! Speak firmly! You

---

[73] At the death of the bishop of Tarbes in 1717 we have a striking example of the fierce competition for this see on the part of numerous abbés and their highly placed patrons; AAE, Mémoire et Documents, Fonds France, Vol. 1228, folio 215.
[74] Em. Sévestre, ed., *Les Idées gallicanes et royalistes du haut clergé à la fin de l'ancien régime, d'après la correspondance et les papiers inédits de Pierre-Augustin Godart de Belbeuf, évêque d'Avranches (1762-1803)* (Paris, Alphonse Picard, 1917), pp. 29-30; letter of Nicolay to the marquis de Belbeuf, May 1, 1766.
[75] Montmorency-Longuy to the marquis de Belbeuf, no date; *ibid.*, p. 44.

are offering a good candidate and you support a just request with good services rendered." [76] When the abbé de Belbeuf finally got his bishopric of Avranches, the minister of the *feuille* wrote him: "I thought that this place would be doubly agreeable to you in that it leaves you in the midst of your family." [77]

Thus was the competition within the qualified Second Estate for the positions of leadership in the First Estate an active one. Saint-Simon wrote of the fierce rivalry for ecclesiastical preferment between the houses of La Tour-d'Auvergne and Noailles; in the middle of a struggle for a recently vacated see the former clan accused the latter of formerly having been its mere retainers, upon which the Noailles' had their genealogies published and reviewed for all to see the history of rebellion and heresy in the family closet of the La Tour-d'Auvergne family.[78] This was the "fury of genealogy" of which a pamphlet of 1789 lamented.[79]

An increasingly employed device for acquiring bishoprics was for aristocratic clerics to obtain the post of grand vicar from an episcopal relative. The abbé Baston distinguished these dutiless grand vicars from the working grand vicars who actually administered the dioceses of overworked or non-resident prelates, but who could expect little

[76]   De Noé to the marquis de Belbeuf, February 18, 1769; *ibid.*, p. 45.
[77]   La Roche-Aymon to Bishop Godart de Belbeuf, January 16, 1774; *ibid.*, pp. 44-45.
[78]   Sicard, p. 25.
[79]   *Ibid.*, p. 31. With competition within the nobility for ecclesiastical place so keen, more than more birth was needed. We are assured by a pamphleteer of 1789 that "to be a bishop today one must be a gentleman. Something more is still necessary; nobility left to itself is not sufficient. One sees nobles who join their titles to many talents and who remain in the *roturier* class of the Church. One must bolster his name with intrigues and with influence: these are the means of reaching the episcopate." *Tableau moral du clergé de France, sur la fin du dix-huitième siècle, ou le clergé françois, avant les États-Généraux, et ce qu'il doit devenir après* (s.l., April 1789), p. 2. There is a letter in the papers of the Ecclesiastical Committee of the Constituent Assembly relating the career of a certain abbé Perreau who held a bishopric *in partibus* and had been designated, during the reign of Louis XVI, to be the first bishop of Martinique. He became the victim of intrigue and never received his bishopric. The unnamed correspondent, undoubtedly a cleric, who informed the Committee of Perreau's career went on to relate that the abbé in vain had pleaded with M. de Maurepas that a bishopric *in partibus* served him not at all in pursuing his religious objective in the Carribean; he claimed ". . . it was much more natural and more just to give him a see in France; that his birth, besides, which was then an essential attribute, called him to it as all the others; since there had been in his family many relatives of his name who had occupied sees in France, one among others named to the bishopric of Metz and died Cardinal-bishop of Viterbo . . ." But apparently he didn't have the necessary Court connections. *AN*, Dxix, 24, no. 374.

recompense.[80] The process of reaching a bishopric could take this form: first, the study of a minimum of theology at an institution such as Saint-Sulpice; then, further study at the Sorbonne for a doctorate in theology; finally, the winning of a post of grand vicar, the passport to higher things; most bishops in the latter 18th Century had previously been grand vicars. Some prelates had a great many more grand vicars then were required for any occupational purposes in their dioceses: these posts provided kinsmen and other worthy noble clerics with the required "work experience" which reforming opinion deemed necessary in a bishop-elect. In this manner, the best intentions of reforming the episcopate merely caused a change of technique in the exercise of abusive practices; according to *Nouvelles ecclésiastiques* in 1780:

With the best intentions in the world, the late king had been persuaded to name to bishoprics only ecclesiastics who were already grand vicars, who thereby could be considered to have performed the duties of the priesthood and could in fact be placed at the head of a diocese. Thence, so many young priests who, believing they had the right by birth to aspire to the episcopate, hastened right after their ordination to acquire the title of grand vicar. Many bishops had the kindness to accede to their desires, without it being required that these young abbés leave Paris and the Court, perform any duty of the holy ministry, or learn the duties of the office to which they had called themselves.[81]

If only grand vicars were to be made bishops, and if bishops could alone name grand vicars, even a well-meaning minister of the *feuille* would have had his horizon of choice limited by the cooptative interests of the incumbent episcopate. Familial self-perpetuation was the potential result of good intention.[82] A pamphlet appearing sometime in the last decade before the Revolution denounced the "pious" decision of the king to make only grand vicars into bishops as a pious fraud:

[80]  *Mémoires de l'abbé Baston*, II, pp. 379-380; quoted also in Sicard, p. 320.
[81]  Quoted in Sicard, p. 319.
[82]  The naming of coadjutors also perpetuated certain families in the episcopate. The Bishop of Saint-Flour's last earthly concerns were for his family; writing to Fleury he noted: "Here I am today in the forty-ninth year of the episcopate; my age, my infirmities, and my rank as dean of the bishops of the kingdom require that I be given assistance. The favorable testimonies which I have been given concerning the conduct of Monsieur the abbé de la Fare d'Alais, my nephew and godson, vicar general of Monseigneur the bishop of Langres, make me bold to request him as my coadjutor. What a joy for me and what satisfaction, if before dying I could see ... my flock in the hands of a nephew who will not be less zealous for the Church and the State than my family and I have been and will be." Bishop of Saint-Flour to Cardinal Fleury, January 11, 1742; *AAE*, Mémoires et Documents, Fonds France, Vol. 1487, folios 74-75.

through the new policy the king more than ever would become the captive of a small group of willful men.[83]

So valid was the bitter judgment of a 1789 pamphlet that plebeian lineage had become a "second original sin" that when one of the only two plebeians given bishoprics in the period 1743-90 was recommended, his partisans were compelled to overcome great opposition and to work feverishly to justify such a rash nomination. The abbé de Beauvais [84] finally won the see of Senez because of strong support from influential circles. He had in his favor his experience as a preacher before the Court, the Académie française, and the General Assembly of the Clergy; his post of grand vicar in the diocese of Noyon; and his recommendation by the Mesdames de France, the daughters of Louis XV. Still, it was only through the active solicitations of his supporters that anything at all was accomplished.

One of the abbé de Beauvais' partisans, Bishop Bazin de Besons of Carcassonne, wrote to the daughters of the king: " 'Mesdames, recognize that a man who, like M. de Beauvais, belongs by his merits to the Bossuet's, the Bourdaloue's, the Massillon's, the Fléchier's, and the Mascaron's, can dispute with the most noble families of the kingdom.' " And in writing to the Cardinal de la Roche-Aymon the bishop of Carcassonne made the cause of the abbé de Beauvais his own: " 'Monseigneur, if I believed that nobility was the principal quality required for the episcopate, I would trample on my crosier and renounce the high dignity with which I am vested.' " [85]

Himself thwarted in his ecclesiastical ambitions because of his base origins, the abbé Maury [86] spoke bitterly about the struggle required to elevate the abbé de Beauvais to the episcopate; he described the new bishop of Senez as " '... one of those prelates whom a blind prejudice perhaps presumes to degrade but whom it yet honors without intending it by calling them *men of fortune*, whereas they are on the contrary the only bishops for whom fortune has done nothing' ".[87]

These strenuous efforts to insure that the promotion of the abbé de Beauvais would not be obstructed by the aristocrats offered a dis-

---

[83]   *Sur l'Ascendant aristocratique de la noblesse dans le clergé* (s.l., 178-), Bibliothèque nationale, Lb39 1213, p. 17.
[84]   With him as with many other bourgeois the particle *de* was a recent, unauthorized addition to a plebeian surname.
[85]   Sicard, p. 7.
[86]   Xavier Raduget, "La Carrière politique de l'abbé Maury de 1786 à 1791", *Revue d'histoire de l'église de France*, Vol. III (1912), p. 508.
[87]   Sicard, p. 8.

heartening commentary on the prevailing climate of opinion in influential circles. The only other plebeian preferred to the episcopate after 1743, Asseline of Boulogne, had the "advantage" of a revolutionary ferment and a minister of the *feuille*, Le Franc de Pompignan, who, not obsessed with aristocratic integrity, could respond intelligently to it. But it was too late.

We have seen that a continuing theme in the criticism levelled against the ecclesiastical policy of the government in the latter 18th Century was that of deviation from the policy of Louis XIV.[88] The pamphlet cited above, *Sur l'Ascendant aristocratique de la noblesse dans le clergé*, offered an interpretation of the changing ecclesiastical policy consistent with the *thèse nobiliaire*. Recognizing the transformation of the magistracy into an aristocratic caste and its assimilation to the nobility of the sword, the author of this pamphlet set out to demonstrate that "... the present ascendancy of the nobility within the clergy, far from belonging to the monarchy, has really all the characteristics of *aristocracism*".[89] He found that in contrast to former kings and their ministers who had used wealth to crush the proud nobility, the monarchs and ministers of the 18th Century were inclined "... to consider the riches of the Church as a resource earmarked for the nobility, because they nourish the poorest, and in accumulating them one uses them to restore the brilliance of great families impoverished by the misfortunes of the army and the luxury of the Courts. This policy bends the laws of the Church to those of the monarchy".[90]

---

[88] The testimony of Talleyrand serves as well as any to document this theme: "In the Church and the episcopate, the most lucrative dignities had become the almost exclusive portion of the noble class. In this respect, the principles invariably followed by Louis XIV were abandoned." *Mémoires du prince de Talleyrand*, I, p. 109. The writer Mercier implied that it was by way of repaying the nobility for its services that the king gave it all the high Church positions in the later 18th Century; this would have signified not so much an abandonment of Louis XIV's belief that the nobility must be rendered merely ornamental, as a recognition by the government that the nobility was becoming increasingly disaffected and had to be rewon by the Crown: "To whom do they give the bishoprics? To the nobles. The great abbeys? To the nobles. All the great livings? To the nobility. What, it is necessary to be a gentleman to serve God! No. But in that way the Court attaches to itself the nobility; and it pays for military services, as for other less important services, with the wealth of the Church." L. S. Mercier, *Tableau de Paris* (Amsterdam, 1783-89), Vol. IV, p. 145 (1783).

[89] *Sur l'Ascendant ...*, p. 10; all in italics. The author claims that in using the word *aristocracisme* for *aristocratie* he intends to connote a question more of pretension than of actual power.

[90] *Ibid.*, pp. 9-10.

Continuing, the author of this tract accepted the three estates of the realm as the system upon which national unity depended. However, he found that the aristocratic ascendancy threatened the status quo:

If one of the three Orders, the first, for example, was continually represented by the members of the second — that is, if the children of the nobles exclusively comprised the higher clergy — there would actually remain only two Orders; one Order would possess two votes for its own point of view, and that would leave only one Order. The Third Estate would comprise only the subjects of the aristocracy, and the monarch would be only the head; he would be no more than a man of the nobility.[91]

In this manner the work of eight centuries would have been undone. Once more royal authority would be threatened. Louis XIV — again that idyllic note — had always been able to honor the nobility without becoming a mere tool in its hands; he named plebeians as well as nobles to the bench of bishops. Any reversal of this sage policy boded ill for the survival of royal authority:

If the choice of men and the distribution of favors no longer corresponded to the particular inclinations and the distinctive spirit of the sovereign; if he had always made up his mind according to the plaudits of the surrounding nobility; if the members of the Second Order of the State assumed an exclusive right to the honors of the First Estate, you would recognize no longer royal authority, but the exercise and the habit of aristocratic power. The habit and the power! Don't forget that in time these things become mingled. . . .[92]

The author warned that the time had arrived for the king to reassume his exclusive right to name bishops — and to name them from all estates — for the present century was one in which "all the years are marked by exclusive gifts, for ever granted to the strongest and lost to the weakest".[93]

In the *cahiers de doléances* of 1789 the Concordat of Francis I was only specifically singled out as the root of the abuses in nominating men to the Gallican episcopate by a minority of the *cahiers* of the Third Estate. Neither the peasantry, the nobility, nor the clergy to any significant extent demanded a root-and-branch reform of the existing system of preferment. Their suggestions usually concerned the utilization of the existing system for more desirable ends. A frequent suggestion was that "real" pastoral experience be a pre-requisite for

[91]   *Ibid.*, pp. 10-11.
[92]   *Ibid.*, p. 25.
[93]   *Ibid.*, pp. 25-26.

elevation to the hierarchy of the Church: the Third Estate of a Provençal *sénéchaussée* recommended as a pre-requisite twenty years of diocesan service; a Breton parish *cahier* sought to have each bishop serve for four years as a simple *curé*. There was some feeling that bishops should come from the provinces in which they were given sees; the clergy of Troyes petitioned: "The king will be entreated in nominating bishops to have regard less for birth than for virtues and merit, and to choose as often as possible ecclesiastics born in the province of the vacant see and experienced in the pastoral ministry." [94] Even pleas that ecclesiastical careers be opened to talent were often modest: the Third Estate of Aval sought to have one-half of the benefices in royal patronage opened to the plebeian classes, while the clergy of the *bailliage* of Amont were content to seek one-fourth of them for non-noble clerics.[95]

Where the abolition of the Concordat was sought, the former practice of elections was idealized. The Third Estate of the *sénéchaussée* of Rennes believed that two and one-half centuries of " 'corruption, intrigue, and despotism' " in the making of bishops were enough, but it demanded more than a mere restoration; it demanded that the election of bishops be based on " '... the principle of an entire and complete national representation....' " [96] Implicit in whatever mistrust of the Concordat there existed was the feeling expressed in a pamphlet written under the name Francheville: that the restoration of episcopal elections was necessary because even the best intentioned of kings — and Louis XVI was nothing less — could not select qualified men for the hierarchy of the Gallican Church; for only the ambitious and the intriguing came to his notice, while the virtuous and worthy ecclesiastics remained unknown in the provinces. A well-intentioned minister of the *feuille des bénéfices* could do no better.[97]

---

[94]   A. Denys-Buirette, pp. 308, 323.
[95]   *Archives parlementaires*, 1st series, Vol. I, p. 759; Vol. II, p. 145.
[96]   Denys-Buirette, p. 445.
[97]   Francheville, *Lettre à M. le curé de . . ., député aux États Généraux, sur les principaux abus qu'il faut réformer dans la Cour de Rome, et dans le clergé de France* (Cosmopolis, 1789), Bibliothèque nationale Lb 39 7131, pp. 32-33.

# III

## ENGLAND: THE CHURCH ESTABLISHMENT AND
## THE RECRUITMENT OF BISHOPS

In pre-reform England, the period from the restoration of 1660 until the fundamental reforms of the 1830's which marked the end of the Old Régime, the familiar pattern obtained of the throne-altar alliance characteristic of all the European states, monarchical or republican. If one were to emphasize those features of the relationship of the English ecclesiastical establishment to the monarchy which were uniquely English, one would have to note particularly the fact that the English conviction of "no bishop, no king" was more than a pious platitude or a piece of special pleading. In England, "no bishop, no king" was an experience and a fact. Where in other European states the established Churches were held up to be the indispensable support of the throne and the teacher of civil obedience and morality, without which authority would collapse and strife and anarchy prevail, in England this view was, in addition, the product of the nation's 17th-Century experience. Regardless of whether one interprets the English Civil War as the revolution of a progressive bourgeoisie and landed gentry or as the last desperate rising of the "Elizabethans", regardless of whether the Parliamentary party fought for constitutional, religious, or economic liberty,[1] certain undeniable

---

[1] Even so formidable an exponent of a teleological, economic interpretation of the English Civil War as Christopher Hill has sufficiently broadened his horizons to admit: ". . . Questions of religion and church government should not be 'left behind the door'. We must have a better explanation of their importance for contemporaries than the theory that Puritanism helps landowners to balance their income and expenditure, or encourages the bourgeoisie to grind the faces of the poor . . . Religion was the idiom in which the men of the seventeenth century thought. One does not need to accept the idiom, or to take it at its face value, to see that it cannot be ignored or rejected as a simple reflex of economic needs. Any adequate interpretation of the English Revolution must give full place to questions of religion and church government, must help us to grasp the political and social implications of theological heresy." *Puritanism and Revolution. Studies in Interpretation of the English Revolution of the 17th Century* (London, Secker & Warburg, 1958), p. 29.

facts remain. The established Church of England did fall with established monarchy; the years 1660-62 did see the restoration of the
Church no less than of the monarchy. Charles I had viewed his own
choice of death rather than ecclesiastical innovation as the choice
of martyrdom; in an unsanctimonious sense he had perished truly
as the King Charles the Martyr of the Anglican liturgy. For twenty
years the Church and the monarchy had consoled each other in
sorrow; in 1660 they returned to exalt each other in victory. The
Church and the monarchy were one another's indispensable corner-
stone.

Since the Church and the monarchy were in the national experience
the necessary complements of one another, the twenty-seven bishoprics of the established Church could never be filled on grounds totally
divorced from the exigencies of politics. Theological, social, and
other factors certainly were major considerations in the nomination of
men to the leadership of the Church, but in a kingdom whose monarch
was seen to depend on the Church of which he was the supreme head,
the political welfare of the nation dictated the ecclesiastical policies
which were to be pursued. Since the period under consideration, 1660-
1836, was one during which Parliamentary supremacy was evolving,
the political importance of an episcopate which sat and voted in the
House of Lords and which was influential in the managing of elections
to the House of Commons naturally did grow; the specifically political
role of the Anglican episcopate merits treatment separate from the
discussion of its recruitment. However, in a consideration of the recruitment policy of the government the fact of the tried and tested Church-
State alliance always intrudes to recall the political basis for episcopal
appointments. The episcopate thereby emerges as a body in the middle of the political life of the nation.

The period from the Restoration to the Revolution, the second
revolution of the century, was marked by the unusually united position taken by the Anglican clergy. The king and the Church had
been restored, and the prosperity of both demanded recognition of
the principles of indefeasible divine right and passive obedience.
When these principles of monarchy were joined to the series of laws
against non-conformists which bore the label "Clarendon Code", the
security of Church and State appeared to be founded on rock. Despite occasional fears of the Catholic proclivities of Charles II and a
disquietude caused by the prospect of the accession to the throne of
the already Catholic Duke of York, the Restoration era was one in

which the Anglican clergy needed to have very few doubts about the health of the Church-State alliance. The immediate danger of Popery, real and imagined, was met by the Test Act.

It was the reign of James II and the resultant Revolution which subverted the previous Church-State alliance. By commitment and by policy, James II did not provide the churchmen with the security they demanded as the price of their support of the monarchy. He severed the previous union of the principles of passive obedience with those of the paramount safety of the Church *as established*. No longer did the one imply and sustain the other. The dilemma posed by James was one between a passive obedience which would permit the king to endanger the Church at will and a concern for the safety of the Church which would render passive obedience impossible. The Glorious Revolution was by obvious semantic juggling for the sake of "tender consciences" able to pretend that James had ceased to be king, while for unabashed proponents of Exclusion and Parliamentary supremacy no such pretense was needed. The imperative to decide between obedience and resistance — incumbent on all in public life — was particularly importunate for the churchmen since they above all had preached passive obedience and divine right. The Revolution of 1688, then, split the churchmen into those who placed passive obedience even above what they knew to be the safety of the Church, and those who accepted a compromise with principle in order to save the Church as established. The former were the non-jurors, and having by their decision removed themselves from any possibility of ecclesiastical preferment, they vanish into insignificance in any treatment of the public importance of the 18th-Century Church. The juring clergy were united in their allegiance to the new monarchs, but divided over the issues of high and low churchmanship which in the reigns of William III and Anne came to have great political significance. The high churchmen were considered Tories, the low or latitudinarian churchmen Whigs.[2]

In the reigns of William III and Anne the government found the

---

[2] The work of Sir Lewis B. Namier has shown that in 18th-Century politics after 1715 the terms Whig and Tory had lost their political meaning and may fruitfully be used only to distinguish views on Church dogma and government and on Church-State relations. In his view, Whig denoted low church and Tory high church. (See *Monarchy and the Party System*, Oxford, Clarendon Press, 1952, p. 24.) Following these definitions, when we treat the so-called Church-Whig alliance under the early Hanoverians, we shall have to define the man who was a Church Whig as essentially a Tory in Church government who supported the

source of high ecclesiastical personnel in the ranks of the juring clergy. If the government of King William preferred those known as latitudinarians, Queen Anne usually sought bishops among high churchmen. The high church position in the last years of the Stuart monarchs was not characterized so much by the ritualism and emphasis on Catholic tradition which have since become its distinguishing marks. It was in this period centered more around the simple desire to abolish the Toleration Act and to restore the principles of passive obedience and divine right which its protagonists had been forced to violate by the challenge of James II. The Tory electoral victory of 1710 was founded on the great electoral support for the cause of Dr. Henry Sacheverell. The impeachment by the House of Lords in 1709 of this paradigm of high churchmanship was based on four counts, and they may be considered fundamental to the unabashed extreme high church position. Sacheverell was found guilty of: preaching against the Revolution of 1688 by questioning the right of a people to resist an evil king; opposing the toleration of Protestant dissenters as defined by act of king-in-Parliament; charging that the Church was in danger from the State; and deeming the Queen's Whig ministry destructive of the Constitution.

In contrast, the low church position was one of willingness for moderate alterations in the essentially neo-Laudian organization of the Church and avoidance of theological disputes. A sympathetic, restrained, and unquestionably beautiful description of latitudinarianism had been offered by one of its episcopal proponents, Bishop Burnet of Salisbury, before his elevation to the episcopate:

They declared against superstition on the one hand, and enthusiasm on the other. They loved the constitution of the church, and the liturgy, and could well live under them: but they did not think it unlawful to live under another form. They wished that things might have been carried with more moderation. And they continued to keep a good correspondence with those who had differed from them in opinion, and allowed a great freedom both in philosophy and in divinity: from whence they were called men of latitude. And upon this man of narrower thoughts and fiercer tempers fastened upon them the name of Latitudinarians.[3]

The low church party felt that the safety of its position and of the

---

Parliamentary ministries of the period 1715-36. If Whig denoted low church, the Church Whig was no true Whig.
[3] *Bishop Burnet's History of His Own Time* (Oxford, University Press, 2nd edition, 1833), Vol. I, p. 342.

Toleration Act which it supported lay in the maintenance of the Protestant Succession. Between the extreme high churchmen on the one hand and the latitudinarian party on the other were the mass of churchmen who found in Queen Anne the orthodoxy and Protestantism alone able to guarantee the safety of the Church as established.

The successful institution of the Hanoverian dynasty in 1715 removed all Jacobites from the possibility of ecclesiastical preferment. Loyalty to the Hanoverian dynasty was the *sine qua non* of office, civil, military, or ecclesiastical. Consequently, the so-called Jacobite clergy, that is, those who were not non-jurors but whose support of the new dynasty was uncertain, were ostracized as long as the cause of defending the Hanoverian dynasty against a Stuart restoration could be waved as a bloody shirt by ministerial politicians — until the latter part of George II's reign, after the defeat of the Young Pretender in 1745. The clergy that remained after the ostracism of the juring Jacobites provided the personnel for high ecclesiastical livings. If the politicians of the reigns of the first two Georges could best be labelled "ins" and "outs" rather than Whigs and Tories, the clergy eligible for ecclesiastical office could be designated as loyal Whigs and loyal Tories: the loyal Whigs being those enthusiastic for the new dynasty, the loyal Tories those high churchmen acquiescent in the new dynasty. The disloyal Tories were those whose acceptance of the Hanoverian settlement was something less than minimal, while to their right were the dwindling non-jurors who had not even accepted the accession of Queen Anne; both these latter groups were ineligible for high Church office.

## II

The twenty-seven episcopal sees of the Church of England in the pre-reform years 1660-1836 were filled by the king's nomination of bishops. In the medieval period, the pretensions and interests of the English monarchs and the Roman pontiffs had coincided to reduce to a mere formality the venerable right of the cathedral chapters to elect their own bishops. By the 14th Century the real power to nominate bishops had become a royal prerogative and the power to accept bishops a papal prerogative. After the Tudor breach with Rome the monarch had been left with full control over the selection of bishops:

according to Tudor legislation, the Crown was to fill an episcopal vacancy by sending a *congé d'eslire* to its cathedral clergy with the name of the cleric who was to be "elected"; if after twelve days the clergy had failed to obey the electoral instructions, the Crown could appoint its candidate by simple letters patent.[4]

These English bishoprics in the patronage of the king varied greatly in size and in wealth. The ecclesiastical census taken in 1676 to ascertain the number of conformists to and dissenters from the established Church revealed the unequal distribution of the dioceses among the Anglican population. Counting all Anglicans over the age of sixteen, the census takers found that the number of conformists in the dioceses of the province of Canterbury — the southern province comprising all but five of the English sees — varied from as little as roughly 28,000 in the dioceses of Rochester and Bangor, and 30-40,000 in the dioceses of Ely, Worcester, Oxford, and Llandaff, to 215,000 in the diocese of Lincoln and 263,000 in the diocese of London.[5]

Using the general population figures of the official census of 1801 when the Industrial Revolution was significantly altering both the total number and the distribution of the British population, we find more striking differences between the old dioceses. Out of a total population for England and Wales of 8,900,000, the sees of Bangor, Ely, and Carlisle comprised areas which had populations of 90,000, 89,000, and 80,000, respectively. At the upper reaches, the sees of York, London, and Chester had populations, respectively, of 839,000, 1,093,000, and 1,103,000.[6] Similarly, the number of benefices within each diocese varied greatly: from 24 in the small see of Sodor and Man, 98 in Rochester, 124 in Bangor, and 127 in Carlisle; to the vast sees of York, Norwich, and Lincoln with benefices numbering, respectively, 913, 1,046, and 1,259.[7]

---

[4]  S. L. Ollard and Gordon Crosse, eds., *A Dictionary of English Church History* (London, A. R. Mowbray, 2nd edition, 1919), pp. 58-59.
[5]  *Calendar of State Papers Domestic*, 1693, pp. 448-450; given in *English Historical Documents 1660-1714*, ed. by Andrew Browning (New York, Oxford University Press, 1953), pp. 413-414.
[6]  *Comparative Account of the Population of Great Britain in the Years 1801, 1811, 1821, 1831*, By Order of the House of Commons, October 19, 1831, pp. 407-408.
[7]  *The Clerical Guide and Ecclesiastical Directory, ... compiled from the report of the commissioners appointed "to inquire into the Established Church in England and Wales" and presented to both houses of Parliament in June 1835 ...* (London, J. G. & F. Rivington, new edition, 1836).

The most reliable data for evaluating the gross inequalities in the revenues of the English dioceses are provided by the reports of the ecclesiastical commissioners in the 1830's. The report presented to the Parliament of 1835 revealed the following diversity in the net revenue of the dioceses: annual revenues ranged from the low points of £ 924 for Llandaff, £ 1,459 for Rochester, and £ 1,897 for St. David's; to the high incomes of the dioceses of Ely with £ 11,105, Winchester with £ 11,151, York with £ 12,629, London with £ 13,929, Durham with £ 19,066, and the primatial see of Canterbury with an annual net income of £ 19,182. Thus, at the time of the reform of the ecclesiastical establishment, eleven of the twenty-seven English sees enjoyed revenues of 20% or less than the revenue of the richest see of Canterbury. Inequalities would seem to have been even greater earlier in our period: fairly reliable figures for the year 1762 reveal that fifteen sees, more than half of the total number, were valued at 20% or less than Canterbury; figures for 1680 show that eighteen sees or two-thirds of the total were valued at 20% or less than Canterbury.[8]

The selection of bishops in the restoration period of Charles II was dictated primarily by the need to strengthen the restored monarchy with the unquestioning obedience of the people led by a thankful Church and clergy. While the return of Laudian principles concerning the economic power of the Church and its independence of Parliament had been made impossible by changing political, economic, and social realities,[9] the Laudian personnel did return to fill the many

[8] The 1835 figures are to be found in *The Clerical Guide and Ecclesiastical Directory* . . ., Table I. The 1762 figures come from a document in John Fortescue, ed., *The Correspondence of King George the Third* (London, Macmillan, 1927), Vol. I, pp. 33-44. The 1680 estimates derive from "A Book of the Valuations of all Ecclesiastical Preferments in England and Wales", 1680, given in *English Historical Documents 1660-1714*, pp. 418-419.

[9] A controversy in historical interpretation has arisen between R. S. Bosher on the one hand, and H. R. Trevor-Roper and Christopher Hill on the other, over the question of indeed what kind of Restoration 1660 was for the Anglican Church. Hill and Trevor-Roper — Hill, *Economic Problems of the Church, From Archbishop Whitgift to the Long Parliament* (Oxford, Clarendon Press, 1956), pp. 348-352; Trevor-Roper, *Archbishop Laud 1573-1645* (London, Macmillan, 1940), pp. 429-436 — contend that the essence of Laudianism was the revival of the economic, social, and political power of the medieval Church — a restoration of all that the Reformation had overturned except papal supremacy. Bosher's view is that Laudianism was restored in 1662 in the anti-calvinist theology of the Church of England and in the successful legislation against dissenters: it was in his view a victory of the branch of the Church which is now generally designated

episcopal vacancies. The Anglican bishops who had remained in England during the Cromwellian period were suspect in the eyes of the returned exiles; the former had allegedly compromised the Anglican position either through acquiescence in many of the policies of the revolutionaries or through want of enthusiasm in bearing witness to the truth of the persecuted Church. The survivors among the non-emigrating Anglican bishops were for the most part denied translation, while the vacancies were filled by those ecclesiastics who, if they had not been Laudians in the period when Charles I, Laud, and Strafford had ruled the nation with an iron hand, had nevertheless imbibed their principles with the lees of the bitterness of exile, abortive conspiracy, and the neglect of foreign allies. Laymen and clerics previously hostile to the admittedly reactionary ecclesiastical policy of Laud beat their breasts in recognition of the meaning of the king's decollation and vowed a stern hand against ecclesiastical dissent. The Clarendon Code created the first official Protestant non-conformity in England. All the important sees were filled by Laudian enemies of the Great Rebellion. As a symbol of restoration, the primacy of Canterbury was entrusted to the feeble Juxon who, though incapable of any active role in either Church or State, was deemed a proper link with the past now restored. The real primate over ecclesiastical policy was Sheldon, bishop of London and Juxon's successor at Canterbury.[10] Thus, in Charles II's reign the stabilizing needs of a restored establishment dictated the choice of bishops for the Church; the rewards claimed by deserving exiles and the irrepressible suspicion of the collaborationist clergy insured the creation of an episcopate devoted

Anglo-Catholic. Robert S. Bosher, *The Making of the Restoration Settlement. The Influence of the Laudians 1649-1662* (Westminster, Dacre Press, 1951), pp. 278-283. Thus, Bosher stresses the religious meaning of Laudianism, Hill and Trevor-Roper the interpretation of Laudianism as a form of medieval ecclesiasticism. It seems to me that Bosher's view is essentially the modern secularist view that religion is something apart from everyday public and private life; the other two historians share a view of the meaning of the Church closer to the 17th Century and closer still to the Middle Ages; thus, Hill and Trevor-Roper view the so-called victory of Laudianism as the executed archbishop himself would have viewed it. Laud would not have been able to celebrate 1660 in the modern terms of Bosher. It is my view that the Restoration of the Church saw the restoration of forms and personnel from the pre-revolutionary period, but that the essence of Laudianism as a revival of a medieval social order quite obviously saw no restoration in England.
[10] Norman Sykes, *From Sheldon to Secker. Aspects of English Church History 1660-1768* (Cambridge, University Press, 1959), pp. 6-9; R. S. Bosher, *op. cit.*, p. 183.

to the maxims of the passive obedience of the subject and the divine right of the ruler.

In undermining the passive obedience of the subject through a successful revolution and the divine right of kings through a kingmaking Parliament, the Revolution of 1688 altered the basis upon which bishops were named. The support of the Church for the monarchy could no longer take the form characteristic of the reign of Charles II. Henceforth, as the king depended upon Parliament for his title and for his government — the Triennial Act of 1694 having made illegal both prolonged Parliaments and uncalled Parliaments — the Church's support manifested itself through the support given to the ministry by the episcopal corps in the House of Lords and by the bishops' intervention in Parliamentary elections; and the careful disposal of benefices was a means of winning support in the House of Commons from politicians seeking ecclesiastical benefices for kinsmen and retainers. If the Church and State were irrevocably tied politically, the growth of Parliamentary life made the dispensation of ecclesiastical benefices more political than ever before.

William III did owe his successful seizure of the Crown to a combination of Whigs and Tories. But only the Whigs — the low church conformists and the Protestant non-conformists — had "called for an Orange" with any enthusiasm, while the juring Tories had acquiesced in a painful necessity. Furthermore, only the Whigs supported those continental military adventures which were uppermost in King William's mind: he had indeed come to the throne not to save England but more effectively to wage his international war against the power of Louis XIV. Lukewarm in devotion to his candidacy and isolationist in foreign affairs when a "blue water" policy was not deemed sufficient, the Tories did not appear to King William able to provide churchmen sympathetic to his policies. Theologically, King William was a dissenter from the Church of which he had become the head, and he approved whole-heartedly latitudinarian attempts to make the established Church flexible enough for the accommodation or "comprehension" of dissenters. Thus, King William was a Whig and he preferred Whig politicians and Whig prelates. Where, however, the catering to Tories in Church and State seemed politically profitable there was no hesitation on his part to try to win their support.

Intrinsically uninterested in what the more clerically minded deemed the safety of the Church, King William gave a large share of authority over ecclesiastical appointments to his wife, the co-sovereign Queen Mary II. His long absence on the continental battlefields and in his Dutch domains made her participation necessary. At her death in 1694 he established an ecclesiastical commission for the dispensation of benefices in the royal patronage. Originally composed of the prelates of the sees of Canterbury, York, Salisbury, Worcester, Ely, and Norwich, the commission was officially empowered to recommend ecclesiastics for the English bishoprics and to other livings worth more than £ 20 in the official and medieval record books which might fall vacant during the king's presence in England; during his absence, the commission was free to dispose, in his name, of all benefices in the royal patronage above the old £ 20 level except bishoprics, deaneries, most prebendaries, canonries, and professorships. Other benefices were to be filled by transmitting to him their recommendations.[11] The commission, then, was designed to serve as a means of ordering the disposal of benefices, the king being abroad much of the time. It was also intended to spare the Secretaries of State the solicitations of the needy and the greedy: all requests and correspondence concerning the disposal of ecclesiastical livings were to pass first through the critical consideration of the ecclesiastical commission whose resultant recommendations would provide a better basis for royal action.[12] These provisions, however, were violated by their very maker, the king. Gilbert Burnet, one of the commissioners, conceived of the commission as an effective means of enlightened ecclesiastical policy and deplored its perversion. He warned the Primate: " 'We are under much obloquy already, and I am sure we will become justly so if we are only to skreen the recommendations of a lewd Court.' " [13] The members of the commission were not compatible — another source of difficulty. The primate of York was a member primarily because of his high station; as a Tory, however, his influence was distasteful both to King William and to Tenison and Burnet, the chief Whigs on the commission. In practice, Sharp of York was generally bypassed. The other commissioners sought to promote sound Whigs to the bench of bishops. The king coupled this policy with the political requirement to bribe Parliamentary Tories

---

[11] Edward Cardwell, ed., *Documentary Annals of the Reformed Church of England* (Oxford, University Press, 1844), Vol. II, pp. 403-408.
[12] Edward Carpenter, *Thomas Tenison, Archbishop of Canterbury. His Life and Times* (London, S.P.C.K., 1948), p. 172.
[13] Burnet to Tenison, May 25, 1700; quoted in *ibid.*, pp. 174-175.

into supporting his foreign policy and granting him the required funds. Political expediency in conflict with ecclesiastical politics rendered the ecclesiastical commission no more than a convenience; it initiated very few successful important nominations.

If the reign of the Whiggish King William saw the domination of ecclesiastical policy by the low church, Whig party, the succeeding reign of Queen Anne marked the reemergence of the high church, Tory faction under a monarch fundamentally a partisan of the Church interest. Until high church sentiment revealed its full vitality among the mass of the lower clergy and a good part of the laity with the Sacheverell Affair of 1709-1710, promoting the formation of a distinctly Tory ministry, Anne had been forced to accept Whig ministers during most of the years before 1710. The Whigs were in their ecclesiastical preference for latitudinarianism and their toleration of dissent highly obnoxious to this orthodox and typically Stuart queen. In the non-ecclesiastical area — if there indeed could be an actual differentiation between the two — the Whig position on the maintenance of the succession in the family of the electoral house of Hanover was not compatible with the queen's dislike of that offshoot of the Stuart line and her hope to see her half-brother, the Pretender, return as a Protestant king to the land of his birth and brief sojourn. It was only the Whig strength in Parliament and the need for Whig support in the successful prosecution of the military policy of her Duke of Marlborough which led the queen to accept — and rather condescendingly, at that — the tutelage of the Whig lords.

Personally hostile to King William, the queen contemplated his population of the bishops' bench with staunch Whigs with repugnance. The ranks of the lower clergy were still Tory, often Jacobite, and the political and ecclesiastical division created within the clerical corps by the ecclesiastical policy of the Whigs revealed itself threateningly in the convocation disputes between the upper house of Whig bishops and the lower house of Tory clergy. The first survival of the previous reign's ecclesiastical policy to fall into disuse was the ecclesiastical commission; misused and ignored as it had often been by King William and his ministers, it had still been for the Tories a symbol of the Church in danger from "Presbyterians" masquerading in the copes and mitres of bishops. To replace the commission of Whig advisers Queen Anne relied on Archbishop Sharp of York whose advice on the nomination of bishops was that of a man very much of her political and theological stripe. The high churchmanship of

Sharp was largely ecclesiastical and appealed to Anne's concern for the maintenance of orthodoxy and prelacy, while the high church-manship of Harlay and St. John, the Tory leaders and later the lords Oxford and Bolingbroke, respectively, was political and appealed to her sentiment in favor of a Protestant and Stuart restoration in the person of "James III".[14]

The queen pursued a policy of accepting Whig ministers supported by the Whig majority in Parliament while she preferred many Tories to episcopal rank. The Whig Junto acutely felt the political injustice of such a policy since it denied them some of the most lucrative rewards of power while laying upon them the responsibility for government and the successful prosecution of the continental war. The Queen protested to her Duke of Marlborough, to whom Whig dissatisfaction had been communicated, that she properly had named bishops for the welfare of the Church and not according to the dictates of the Whig politicians; and she expressed a non-partisan desire to have in her ecclesiastical service able men of all political persuasions.[15] The insincerity of her protestations of non-partisanship was soon revealed, however, when after the Tory electoral victory of 1710 no more Whigs were elevated to the episcopate.

First the influence of Harlay, a moderate Tory, worked for the elevation of moderate Tory clerics; then the influence of the Jacobite St. John preferred to the episcopate such outright opponents of the Protestant Succession as Atterbury. Norman Sykes, the historian of the English 18th-Century Church, believes that the Whigs' first attempt at a Church-Whig alliance failed because they had not yet fully accepted their responsibility for insisting on non-cooperation with the queen, unless she granted them control of ecclesiastical appointments. His view, benefiting from hindsight, may fail to consider that politics in the reign of Anne were not, strictly speaking, organized by real political parties in a two-party system;[16] the queen intended to be above

---

[14] Sykes, "Queen Anne and the Episcopate", *English Historical Review*, Vol. L (July, 1935), p. 436. Harlay and St. John had been educated in the dissenting academy of Sheriffhales, and their devotion to the Church was generally regarded as more a matter of political expediency than of conviction, unlike the genuine clericalism of Queen Anne and Archbishop Sharp.

[15] Queen Anne to Marlborough, September, 1707; William Coxe, *Memoirs of the Duke of Marlborough, With His Original Correspondence* (London, George Bell, (new edition, 1876-85), Vol. II, pp. 158-159.

[16] Robert Walcott, *English Politics in the Early Eighteenth Century* (Cambridge, Harvard University Press, 1956), p. 160.

party and for some time succeeded. Until the Tory triumph of 1710
and the one-party ministry it ushered in, the personal element in English politics characterized Anne's reign: her own vigorous desire to
rule as well as reign stamped the period 1702-1710.[17] Of the eleven
clerics elevated to the episcopate by Queen Anne before 1710, six
were reputed to be Tories, and five Whigs. The abortive Church-
Whig alliance could not succeed under a monarch who exerted effectively her independence of politicians; she was the last British
monarch to reject a bill passed by Parliament. Finally, there could be
no Church-Whig alliance without a Whiggish sovereign; Anne was
heart and soul a Tory.

## III

It is to the work of Norman Sykes that we owe our understanding of
the chief characteristics of early Hanoverian Church patronage. It had
been believed that the renowned team of Queen Caroline and Sir
Robert Walpole, in ruling England from 1727-1737 by managing the
inclinations of George II, had also managed ecclesiastical patronage
in this way, Caroline's preoccupation with the Church matching that
of Queen Anne, although along more heterodox lines. Sykes has
offered a reinterpretation: the phenomenon of the Church-Whig
alliance and its "pope", Edmund Gibson, bishop of Lincoln and
London.[18] The Church-Whig alliance was motivated by both ecclesiastical and civil considerations. Its ecclesiastical progenitor, had
been Archbishop Tenison, and his motivation had been a strikingly
conservative one: the maintenance of the establishment status quo
as it emerged from the Glorious Revolution — the Church enjoying
the protection of the Test and Corporation Acts, the dissenters
enjoying the fruits of the Toleration Act, and the Protestant Succession intact. His position had been born in the days of the aggressive behavior of James II and in the high church agitation against
King William and later for the return of the Pretender. The ecclesiastical status quo required the preservation of the Protestant Succession.
Walpole, it may be said, was the lay founder of the alliance: if for

[17] William Thomas Morgan, *English Political Parties and Leaders in the Reign
of Queen Anne 1702-1710* (New Haven, Yale University Press, 1920), pp. 399-400.
[18] Sykes' reinterpretation dates from his biography of Gibson which appeared
in 1926; it took the form of an "historical revision" in "Queen Caroline and the
Church", *History*, Vol. XI (January, 1927), pp. 333-339.

Tenison the Church needed the Protestant Succession, for Walpole the preservation of the Protestant Succession — perhaps his one public passion — needed the support of the Church. Viewing the body of the clergy as deeply suspicious of the Whig Party's known anti-clericalism, low churchmanship, and alliance with non-conformity, and knowing of its active and passive labors on behalf of the Tories, Walpole feared the cry of the "Church in danger". The outburst of high church sentiment liberated by the Sacheverell Affair had defeated the Whig electoral position and very nearly had risen into a ground swell perhaps sufficient to have restored the Pretender. Walpole was resolved never again to permit the political peril to Whiggery latent in a hostile Church and clergy to materialize. He also feared that the excesses of the Whig anticlericals would give the suspicious churchmen additional ground for their fears. Thus the Whig political position and the preservation of the ecclesiastical status quo were interdependent. The Church-Whig alliance was the alliance of moderates in both groups to preserve the status quo against anti-clericalism and disestablishment on the one hand, and quasi-Jacobitism on the other. The Glorious Revolution and the Hanoverian dynasty were at stake.[19]

The clergyman expected by both lay and ecclesiastical partisans of Church-Whig moderation to develop the policy of Archbishop Tenison under the new king from Hanover, now that the Jacobites had been defeated in battle and the Tories in their failure to prevent the

---

[19] In a pamphlet which he wrote after the Tory electoral triumph in 1710 Walpole posed the question, who was the true friend of the Church? "What had become of our Nation, or Europe, of every thing that is or ought to be dear to us; if Non-Resistance had been the Doctrine in vogue, when the late King came over to our Deliverance? What had become of the Church it self, which was then in danger with a witness, if the Principles of this Doctor [Sacheverell] had been believ'd and follow'd? And is he now become her Champion, and those that impeach'd him her Enemies? . . . If her Majesty, and those that were then her Ministers, endanger'd the Church, it must have been by such Acts as these: By giving part of her own Revenue to support it, and by promoting and passing an Act in order to enrich it more: By excluding all Papists for ever, and destroying their Hereditary Right to this Crown: By filling the vacant Bishopricks with such Anti-christian Antimonarchical Bishops, as would in time have converted most of our Dissenters: By reducing the greatest Enemy of our Church, and of the whole Protestant interest, after eight successful Campaigns, to the limits of his own Dominions. These have been the terrible Designs of the Queen and those Ministers against this poor Church; and therefore it was high time for the Doctor and his Friends to redouble their Cry of its Danger . . ." *Four Letters to a Friend in North Britain, Upon the Publishing the Tryal of Dr. Sacheverell* (London, 1710), p. 19.

Hanoverian Succession, was the new Primate of England, William Wake. Wake had been elevated to the episcopate in the reign of Queen Anne at the insistence of her Whig ministers; he held to the principle of Tenison that the Protestant Succession was indispensable to the well-being of the Church. Gibson rested content in the expectation that Wake would build a Church-Whig alliance to support the establishment in Church and State against the extremists of both sides. The new government of George I, however, not only did not endeavor to quiet the fears of most churchmen that the new dynasty augured ill for their interests, but in a positive way it confirmed some of their worst apprehensions. The final elevation of Benjamin Hoadly to the episcopate — a promotion petitioned for by a pro-Hanoverian House of Commons in 1709 but blocked by the Tory victory in 1710 — touched off clerical apprehension. Raised to episcopal rank primarily for his pamphleteering on behalf of the electoral house of Hanover during the lean years of officially sanctioned Jacobite nostalgia, Hoadly lost no time in publicizing his unorthodox theological views. The ensuing Bangorian controversy was disputed over the nature of the kingship of Christ and the ecclesiastical authority of the Church. Hoadly's essentially liberal interpretation of the Protestant tradition, to the effect that the Church could legitimately exercise no ecclesiastical authority after the lifetime of its Founder, aroused the bitterness of conservatives and moderates. The only ecclesiastical authority, according to Hoadly, which could be justified was that which encouraged civil order, and that could be exercised only by the State. Thus, Hoadly combined a liberal doctrine of the nature of the Church with a thorough-going Erastianism. The government of George I led by Sunderland and Stanhope not only did not curb Hoadly's divisive speculations, but it dismissed royal chaplains who had entered the lists against him and dissolved Convocation hastily lest it demand his censure. The significance of Hoadly's theories and of the failure of the ministry to repudiate them was that they subverted one of the bases of Church-Whig cooperation: namely, no assault on the status quo of 1689. A leading Church-Whig partisan, Bishop Nicolson of Carlisle, expressed the fear that Hoadly's views implied that bishops and priests were to " '. . . derive their authority by commission out of the chancery or the war office' ".[20]

If the churchmen's dissatisfaction with Hoadly and the patronage

[20]    Nicolson to Wake, November 5, 1716; quoted in Sykes, "Archbishop Wake and the Whig Party, 1716-23", *The Cambridge Hist. Journal*, VIII (1945), p. 98.

he found in the royal closet had not been enough to estrange Wake, the policies of Sunderland designed to reward the dissenters for their staunch Hanoverianism and to preclude a resurgence of Toryism in Parliament did succeed in alienating him from both the king and from his Church-Whig brethren on the bishops' bench. Only the Tories were pleased with the turn of events. The government desired the repeal of the Occasional Conformity Act and the Schism Act which had been passed in the Tory years of Queen Anne's reign to deprive dissenters of political office and educational opportunities. Their repeal appeared reasonable to Gibson and the other Church-Whigs since it would have restored the status-quo-ante balance between Anglican monopoly and the toleration of dissenters — a balance distasteful to extremists of right and left. The Tories had upset this balance in the direction of a dry liquidation of dissent; the government of George I sought the restoration of the balance. Opposed to these Acts when they had been debated during the reign of Anne, Archbishop Wake now chose to oppose their repeal on the grounds that they had successfully encouraged more than token conformity to the Church; he feared their repeal would see the return of masses of former dissenters to their chapels. Wake desired the dissenters to rest content with toleration.

A second ministerial scheme — this time opposed with more consistency by Wake — sought to modify the Corporation Act of the Cavalier Parliament in order to permit dissenters to seek election to municipal corporations, thereby to decrease the possibility of Tory victories in the Parliamentary elections in the numerous English boroughs which returned members to Westminster. The repeal of the Corporation Act would have innovated for partisan political reasons: only out of loyalty to the overriding cause of the Protestant Succession could Gibson agree to it. Wake's opposition was undisguised, dismaying his friends in Church and ministry. His distinction between the Church interest and the State interest formed no basis for Church-Whig cooperation. Gibson predicted that if Wake would only agree to the relief of dissenters for the sake of destroying Tory electoral might, he would so please the ministry that in the future it would allow him a predominant influence over its ecclesiastical policy; whereas, his refusal endangered all the expectations of the moderates.[21] Gibson was more than Wake a follower of Tenison:

[21] Sykes, *William Wake, Archbishop of Canterbury 1657-1737* (Cambridge, University Press, 1957), Vol. II, pp. 117-118.

"... All my political reasonings proceed upon these two positions; that there is no way to preserve the Church but by preserving the present establishment in the State; and that there is far greater probability that the Tories will be able to destroy our present establishment in the State than that the Dissenter will be able to destroy our establishment in the Church." [22]

Wake sufficiently displeased the Sunderland ministry to cause himself to be ostracized and ignored in the formulation of ecclesiastical policy and preferment, succeeding to the unenviable position of Sharp under King William and Tenison in the last years of Queen Anne. The building of the Church-Whig alliance awaited an ecclesiastical champion more single-minded than Wake, and a civil champion more cognizant than Sunderland of the fears which close Whig relations with Dissent encouraged in the hearts of otherwise loyal churchmen: the alliance awaited Edmund Gibson and Robert Walpole.

Gibson's importance in 18th-Century English Church history derives from the fact that reflecting on the state of ecclesiastical politics he asked himself the right question. His query was, why so many years after the Glorious Revolution was the mass of the Anglican clergy still in varying degrees disloyal to the Protestant Succession in the House of Hanover? His response was the key to the problem of how to build an effective Church-Whig alliance: the failure lay in the fact that the ecclesiastical patronage of the Crown had been misused; promotions in the Church

have not been so ordered and disposed of in such way as to create a general dependence, and raise a general expectation among ye clergy; but have been bestowed uncertainly and as it were, by chance, and been understood to fall only to ye share of the favourites of particular Persons in power and Office; and by consequence have had no influence, nor raised any expectation, except in such favourites only.[23]

It was, thus, the rational and motivated use of the vast ecclesiastical patronage vested in the Crown which was Gibson's solution to the problem of building the indispensable Church-Whig alliance. He knew from experience during the Convocation disputes that it had been insufficient to name Whig bishops, for as latitudinarians they had estranged the lower clergy who, displeased to see mitred "Pres-

[22]  Gibson to Nicolson, December 3, 1717; quoted in *ibid.*, Vol. II, p. 119.
[23]  Bishop Gibson's Scheme of Promotions; Sykes, *Edmund Gibson, Bishop of London, 1669-1748* (Oxford, University Press, 1926), Appendix B, p. 399.

byterians" in their midst, had threatened the very episcopal order they theoretically revered. The solution was the use of patronage to encourage clerical loyalty to the dynasty: this necessitated a firm maintenance of the Toleration Act and the Test Act, and the avoidance of nominating latitudinarians and others holding theological tenets which might alienate the orthodox clergy.

Gibson's aim, in effect, was to show the Tory clerics that for the price of loyalty to the dynasty orthodoxy would be preserved from danger and even rewarded by the preferment of its adherents. Only the disloyal Tory clergy would be ostracized — along with the radical low church clergy. For, it must be emphasized, Gibson was a high churchman; he would doubtless have been a Tory had it not been for James II and the Jacobite menace. His views on Convocation and ecclesiastical courts were those of a Tory who valued a strong, Laudian Church establishment. The clerics whom Gibson would promote within the Church would not pass with mere loyalty to the royal family; they needed to be orthodox. Sykes observes quite correctly that if Gibson were guilty of "prostitution . . . to serve the ends of a single political party", his formula was not Erastian, but Laudian.[24] His aim was a reconciliation of Church and Crown — but a Church which was nothing less than that for which he and his colleagues had broken their passive obedience in 1688. His differences with Archbishop Wake would seem to have been differences of degree, not of kind. Gibson was willing to bend a little more to achieve what Wake also desired; when his job was done Gibson joined Wake in the disgrace of being vilified with the name of Tory.

The rational use of patronage as enunciated by Gibson required an inevitable attack upon royal patronage exercised by private persons. Out of some 777 benefices in the patronage of the Crown at that time, only 65 were vested personally in the sovereign; the Chancellor of the Duchy of Lancaster controlled 36, while the remaining 676 lay in the hands of the Lord Chancellor.[25] It was the incompatibility of these realities with the requirements of a rational administration of patronage which made of Gibson nothing less than a genuine reformer. He proposed that the patronage of the Crown be transferred directly into royal hands, and that vacancies be filled only with officiating clergymen of the diocese in question or with university

---

[24]  *Ibid.*, p. 119.
[25]  *Ibid.*, p. 109.

clergy who were natives of the diocese. The reasoning behind this scheme was this: if the diocesan clergy knew that benefices were exclusively designed for them, they would pay more heed to the interests of the ministry. Secondly, through the employment of bishops as the vehicles and advisers for nomination to royal benefices below the episcopal level, the lower clergy would come to cultivate the patronage of bishops, and thereby would the split be healed between upper and lower clergy.

Gibson's assault upon the Lord Chancellor's power was a complete and thorough one. Neither the policy of Anne's Lord Chancellor Cowper in laying before her for her approval all his nominations, nor the later policy of the Duke of Newcastle in bargaining with Lord Chancellor Hardwicke for his patronage were as rationalistically and thoroughly reformist as the intention of Gibson. But it was too revolutionary for the Whig politicians.[26] The Church-Whig alliance rested on compromise, and here Gibson had to yield, even though the king had approved his schemes: the great ecclesiastical offices — bishoprics and deaneries — were entrusted to Gibson for distribution, while the lesser Church plums in the royal gift were to continue to be at the disposal of politicians in exchange for public and private favors.

The unbending posture which Gibson maintained in naming bishops and his interest in reformist measures created a party of malcontents hostile to him. His indispensable stipulation that the clerics he elevated be more than merely loyal to the ministry, that they be orthodox churchmen, antagonized large segments of the low church Whigs. As Walpole's "pope", Gibson saw his opponents join Walpole's foes in the first manifestation of what was to become a Hanoverian tradition in England: the expression of opposition to the ministry by paying court to the heir apparent who had become estranged from the reigning sovereign. The political and ecclesiastical malcontents hovering about the Prince of Wales and his consort, Caroline von Ansbach, were hostile towards Gibson as well as towards Walpole. The accession of the Prince of Wales as George II did not see the end of Gibson's power only because the new monarch needed

---

[26]   It is true that Gibson's reforming spirit stopped short of attacking the citadel of private lay patronage over Church livings — a practice which bestowed about 48% of all Church livings before the reform measures of the 1830's. As we shall see below, however, Gibson's proposals for general ecclesiastical reform were far from petty; nor was his opposition. *The Clerical Guide and Ecclesiastical Directory* ..., 1836. For Gibson's other reforms see Appendix IV.

Walpole in the ministry, and Gibson was indispensable to Walpole. Nevertheless, the reign of George II saw Gibson's eventual fall from power.

In the 1730's the Church-Whig alliance as conceived by Gibson and Walpole was subjected to more storms than it could weather, and it fell apart. The issues which shook its foundation concerned questions of Anglican privilege and dissenters' rights, the latter championed by what may be designated the left wing of the ministry's Parliamentary supporters. In 1730 the ministry was forced to exert its authority to crush two bills which were strongly favored by the House of Commons. One bill sought to make illegal suits instituted for the payment of Church tithes which had not been paid for a number of years; the other struck at the system of episcopal translations which would have weakened the ministry's hold over the advancement-hungry episcopate. In 1733 a bill passed the lower house which was designed to curtail the power of ecclesiastical courts to receive certain suits and to have jurisdiction over the probate of wills; the measure also sought to discontinue the civil disabilities still remaining against those excommunicated from the Church. Again the ministry had to use its influence to kill the measure — through its supporters in the upper house. In 1732 Walpole had advised dissenters who were seeking the abolition of the sacramental test on office holders that they remain content with the wide liberties they already enjoyed. The crushing of these "anti-clerical" bills and the refusal to woo dissenters' votes by further concessions were as far as Walpole was prepared to go in upholding his cherished alliance with Gibson; the minister was torn between the need for ecclesiastical support in the coming election of 1734 and the necessity of keeping united his lay supporters, many of whom were anti-clericals. By 1736 the ministry had drawn the line on further yielding to Gibson: the Mortmain Act passed both houses, aiming at the restriction of the right to bequeath property to the Church and to charitable institutions. The Quakers' Tithe Bill initially even received ministerial approval; it sought to make it more difficult for the Anglican parsons legally to harass Quakers for payment of tithes; it was defeated in the upper house where the bishops led by Gibson were strongly hostile to it. Both these measures resulted from the anti-clerical sentiment which had crystallized around Walpole's refusal in 1732 to rock the boat for the benefit of the dissenters who supported his ministry. The ministry and Gibson were losing their common ground of cooperation as Parliamentary political requirements moved Walpole to a position less favorable to Church-Whig principles.

The immediate cause of Gibson's fall was the issue of the elevation of heterodox clerics to the episcopate. Such nominations openly violated the basis of Gibson's control of episcopal appointments. He stood inflexible, refusing to agree to a policy of political subservience advocated by those who still strove to keep together the alliance. The plea for compromise which Gibson received from Bishop Hare of Chichester was reminiscent of his own attitude toward Archbishop Wake's difficulty with the politicians twenty years before. Hare wrote:

Your lordship's rule of *Principiis obsta* is certainly a very good one. But yet I can't but think 'tis not only prudent, but absolutely necessary in public Ministers, either in Church or State, to recede on some occasions, and make some concessions in compliance with ye times and circumstances of things; . . . one must be content to choose the *minus malum*; and such it is to agree to such a promotion [of unorthodox clerics] rather than draw down upon us the resentment of those who have it so much in their power to hurt us, and at ye same time are not unfriendly disposed towards us; and such a compliance is ye more necessary as we have so many declared enemies, who can't but rejoice in all opportunities that may tend to alienate our friends from us.[27]

How similar to this advice was Gibson's, years before, that if Wake would but yield, he would retain great control of future episcopal nominations.

Some indication of the hostility which grew in opposition to the alliance of Walpole and Gibson may be found in the opinions and diatribes of the witty Lord Hervey, a close associate of both Walpole and Queen Caroline. Hostile to churchmen in general and to Gibson in particular, Hervey sought to contrast the ecclesiastical policy of Sunderland with that of Walpole; he cited two episcopal appointments at the commencement of George II's reign which he believed revealed the different principles of ecclesiastical politics pursued by the ministers.

. . . As these two men [Hare and Sherlock] were perhaps the two ablest in the whole body of the clergy, they were the last that Lord Sunderland would ever have set at the head of them. It was a maxim of his never to put

---

[27]  Hare to Gibson, August 7, 1736; included in an appendix of documents in Sykes, *Edmund Gibson* . . ., p. 405.

power into the hands of those who knew how to use it; and one which Sir Robert Walpole seemed to steer by in temporal affairs, though he deviated from it in spiritual ones. Lord Sunderland's policy was always to keep up the power of the Church in general though never to agrandize [sic!] that of particular churchmen. For which reason he took care to stock the Bench with a parcel of mean blockheads who wanted both understanding to know their strength and resolution to exert it, if they had known it — men whose ignorance was a counterpoise to their power, and who by the ridicule and contempt that attended their private characters lost all the dignity and authority that their profession would otherwise have given them — and by which means all the power they had was his proxy. It was an engine in his own hands which he could order or direct them to play whenever he stood in need of it and which he kept dormant when he did not.[28]

Discounting Hervey's wit and malice, we still have an example of the outrage of the low church and no church Whig politicians at the power of Walpole's ecclesiastical minister.

Hervey denied Gibson any particular credit for making loyal Hanoverians of the clergy through his elaborate schemes, preferring to ascribe the clergy's desertion of Jacobitism to the course of events:

... As long as translations were part of the prerogative of the Crown it was not at all surprising that every Bishop who desired to be translated should do the business of the Crown. Nor was it more to be wondered at, that the inferior clergy, whose appetites for preferment were no less keen than their cormorant superiors, should after seventeen years' Whig administration, slacken their efforts to promote a common desperate cause which jarred so strongly with their own private and particular interest.[29]

Hervey's attempt to deprive Gibson of his glory as reconciler of Church and Crown by making such a reconciliation an inevitable result of the establishment of the Hanoverian dynasty and the increasing frustration of the Jacobite cause ignored the fact that Gibson also worked to destroy the connection in the popular mind and in the ecclesiastical mind of Whiggery with anticlerical and low church sentiments. Queen Caroline's desire to elevate latitudinarians to the bench of bishops was thwarted only by the vigor of Gibson who enjoyed

[28] John, Lord Hervey, *Some Materials Towards Memoirs of the Reign of King George II*, ed. by Romney Sedgwick (London, KEP, 1931), Vol. I, p. 90. In commenting on the appointments of Hare to St. Asaph and Sherlock to Bangor, Lord Hervey did not mention that both these appointments were correctly numbered among the few which the Queen managed to intrude in spite of Gibson. Both these bishops were unquestionably orthodox in Gibson's view, but Sherlock's political associations were Tory — that is, he had associated with those in opposition to the present ministry.
[29] *Ibid.*, Vol. I, pp. 91-92.

Walpole's support. It is difficult to believe that Walpole would have supported his ecclesiastical adviser for so long — straining the allegiance of his lay followers and even his indispensable *modus operandi* with Queen Caroline — had it not been necessary. Perhaps Walpole was obsessively haunted by the Sacheverell Affair which had brought down the Whigs in 1710; nevertheless, he was politically astute enough accurately to assess the dangers which an alienated Church held in store for his ministry. What could account for his rejection of the dissenters' pleas in 1732 for an elimination of discrimination against them — pleas with which he was strongly sympathetic — other than his need of clerical support in Parliament and in the country? One suspects that Hervey was merely voicing his well-known anti-clericalism. His antipathy to the idea of a cleric wielding any political power revealed itself in his charge that Gibson's opposition to the elevation to the episcopate of Dr. Thomas Rundle was not based on the latter's alleged Arianism:

Nobody doubted but that the Bishop of London's sole reason for opposing Rundle was because my Lord Chancellor [Talbot] had made application to the Court in his favour, not through the Bishop of London, but merely upon his own weight and interest; and as the Bishop of London had always disliked what he called lay recommendations, he was determined to make a stand upon this occasion, thinking, if he could show that even so great a man as my Lord Chancellor could not get any one preferred in the Church without applying to him, for the future no other person would attempt it.[30]

It was, of course, true that Gibson sought to decrease lay interference with Crown patronage; this desire, characterized by Hervey as an attempt at personal aggrandizement, might better be seen as the emergence of the high churchman in Gibson. In defeat, Gibson came to be denounced as a Tory — in terms previously used for Wake; his *Codex Juris Ecclesiastici*, a scholarly treatise which revealed that he was no low churchman, was offered as evidence. In a sense, Gibson's eventual defeat had been inevitable; the alliance of Church and ministry rested on certain incongruities and incompatibilities. But was its defeat not a sign of its success and utility — a sign that it had so succeeded in making loyal the body of the clergy and in rendering less suspect Whig designs on the Church, that it no longer was necessary and, indeed, now worked to constrict political development? Natural or unnatural, the alliance of Walpole and Gibson had served to integrate the clergy into the loyal political life of the nation and had

[30]    *Ibid.*, Vol. II, p. 400.

helped to establish more firmly the new dynasty. The period from the death of Queen Anne until Gibson's fall was critical for the Protestant Succession: Gibson's management of English ecclesiastical preferment served to decrease the danger to it. Whig anti-clericalism brought Gibson down; but the alliance's connection of the Church with Whig politicians served to temper this anti-clericalism until it became far less virulent and dangerous. When the dynasty was no longer in as much danger as in its earliest years,[31] when the Whigs no longer truly feared the "church in danger" cry, they could afford to dispense with Gibson who had done his job so well. Because Gibson was concerned with more than political considerations, he prevented the Church-Whig alliance from degenerating into the camp-following characteristic of Church-State relations under the ecclesiastical ministry of the Duke of Newcastle. Newcastle's control of the English *feuille des bénéfices* was purely a politically motivated one; he converted the alliance of Gibson and Walpole into the subservience typical of the rest of the 18th Century. These were the dangers inherent in Gibson's policy. Nevertheless, in making the leading Whig politicians patrons of the established Church, the alliance of Walpole and Gibson did encourage them to be moderate towards the establishment.

Although involved in the trafficking in Church livings as early as 1723, the Duke of Newcastle did not become the undisputed ecclesiastical minister of the government until after the fall of Gibson in 1736, the appointment of the former's old crony, Hardwicke, as Lord Chancellor, and the death of Queen Caroline who would otherwise undoubtedly have assumed the mantle of Gibson. From 1737 until his death in 1768 — only the years 1762-65 when Lord Bute forced him from office excepted — Newcastle was the recognized ecclesiastical minister. He turned the principles of Gibson into a sham, for

[31] It is the considered view of Basil Williams that although there was never any serious danger to the dynasty, the continual plotting by Jacobites at home and abroad did give the ministry cause for sustained concern for thirty years. Had the issue of which king was to rule been decided by a Jacobite attempt to install James III as his sister's successor by proclamation of the Tory ministry of St. John, the Jacobites' weakness would have been realized and the Whig ministers acquitted of the fear of them. Because the Tory ministers of Anne had not been bold enough to attempt this, the actual strength of Jacobite sentiment and the actual danger it posed to the new ruling house remained an unknown quantity. In any case, the fear of a revival of Jacobitism was the "mainspring" of Walpole's policy. *The Whig Supremacy 1714-1760* (Oxford, Clarendon Press, 1939), pp. 144-145; 174.

after the collapse of the last Jacobite adventure in 1745-46, his rule of conduct, "'... to recommend none whom I did not think most sincerely well-affected to his majesty and his government, and to the principles upon which it is founded ...,'"[32] was no more than a fraud. Newcastle "principles" did not include the reformist and extra-political principles of Gibson, and the political future of the Protestant Succession was no longer in doubt. He used Church preferment solely for political and private ends: to support the ministry; and after the death of Frederick Louis, the Prince of Wales, to guarantee his continued office under the deceased prince's son, the future George III, by prefering some so-called former Tories in the Church. There was nothing more to fear from former Tories because of the impotence of Jacobitism — more to fear from them as the exclusive advisers of a new monarch. When one of his nominees was suspected of continuing devotion to the lost Stuart cause, Newcastle, knowing his protégés, reassured a doubtful colleague that "'... if you will only tell me what you would have him to do, and what public or private declarations he should make, I am sure of his compliance'".[33]

Newcastle's passion for ecclesiastical politics was a means of aiding the ministerial party to which he was sincerely devoted and of satisfying his vanity and his desire to be influential and to have many indebted to him. His greatest fear next to loss of office was reproach, and in the *feuille des bénéfices* reproach and ridicule were unavoidable. Nevertheless, his heart was occasionally warmed by the expressions of gratitude which he did receive — like this paean of devotion from an unnamed bishop whom he had elevated:

After passing through the largest part of my diocese finding nothing disagreeable either in my task or the people with whom I have to do, and resting two or three days in a very pleasant dwelling, I might deserve to be numbered among the unthankful, did I not with the warmest sentiments of gratitude acknowledge Your Grace's goodness in being the instrument of placing me in so happy a situation. Your Grace knows how little I am a dealer in words, 'tis generally my choice to let my actions speak for me; and I think it a very lucky circumstance in my present station that in conforming them to Your Grace's noble and generous way of thinking they will seldom fail of being conformable to the public good.[34]

[32]   Newcastle to Hoadly, May 31, 1760; quoted in Sykes, "The Duke of Newcastle as Ecclesiastical Minister", *English Historical Review*, Vol. LVII (January, 1942), p. 64.
[33]   Newcastle to Earl of Coventry, October 3, 1759; quoted in *ibid.*, p. 70.
[34]   Donald G. Barnes, "The Duke of Newcastle, Ecclesiastical Minister, 1724-54", *The Pacific Historical Review*, Vol. III (June, 1934), p. 180.

The desire which Newcastle had to be beloved by office-seekers led him to promise more than he could deliver and to raise false hopes.[35] To meet the ever mounting number of benefice-seekers whom he had vowed to satisfy he was led to seek a stranglehold on an increasing number of benefices: the patronage of no one was safe from the uncontained ambition of Newcastle and his protégés. Edmund Pyle, a royal chaplain during the Duke's heyday, wrote of the quandary in which this ecclesiastical "Fac Totum" found himself:

... He has involved himself in promises of church preferments to the greatest degree of perplexity. There are now two vacant stalls; one at Durham, & one at Canterbury; and he durst not dispose of either of them. He torments the poor Archbishop of Canterbury for everything that falls in his gift, so that if a thing drops, he is forced to give it away the moment he is informed of it, for fear of the Duke of Newcastle. He is as great a plague to the other Bishops, asking even for their small livings. . . . As to the Lord Chancellor, it is a kind of bargain made with every one that enters upon that high office, "that the Minister shall dispose of most of the church preferments in his gift." [36]

This was Newcastle's system: it owed much to Gibson's desire to centralize royal patronage and make episcopal patronage conform to royal policy, but its perversion was self-evident. One prelate rejoiced that the prebends in his cathedral were already in the gift of the Lord Chancellor, freeing him from the pestilential attentions of Newcastle.[37] Another called Newcastle's machinations by their rightful name:

My Lord, the bishops as well as the inferior clergy take the oaths against simony; and as I should think an express promise of preferment to a patron *beforehand* an express breach of that oath and would deny institution upon it, so I should think a tacit promise a tacit breach of it.[38]

Such was Newcastle's administration of ecclesiastical affairs. He turned the principled system of Gibson — with its admitted implications of Erastianism — into the use of episcopal benefices solely for Parliamentary and personal advantage. There was still the Jacobite

[35]  Newcastle's machinations were described as an "ecclesiastical lottery" by the future Bishop Warburton. Warburton to Richard Hurd, September 19, 1757; *Letters From a Late Eminent Prelate to One of His Friends* (London, T. Cadell, 2nd edition, 1809), p. 256.
[36]  Pyle to Dr. Samuel Kerrich, October 8, 1754; Edmund Pyle, *Memoirs of a Royal Chaplain, 1729-1763* (London, John Lane, 1905), p. 218; also cited in Barnes, *loc. cit.,* p. 168.
[37]  Sykes, *Church and State in England in the XVIIIth Century* (Cambridge, University Press, 1934), p. 176.
[38]  Bishop Butler of Bristol to Newcastle, August 5, 1750; quoted in *ibid.,* p. 178.

hobgoblin to exorcise and the Tories to denounce, but it all had a hollow ring. From Newcastle's day until the end of the century, the royal prerogative to name bishops for the established Church was an unabashed means of winning or rewarding political support, and it was so used by successive ministries. An interesting exchange of letters in the year 1810 revealed that the Newcastle policy had fundamentally survived at least that long and was coming to an end only over the objections of chagrined traditionalists. These concern the established Church of Ireland, but as we shall see below this Church was an integral part of the Anglican establishment even before the Union. The marquess of Ely wrote to the Prime Minister to effect the translation of his brother — Lord Robert Ponsonby Tottenham Loftus, the bishop of Killaloe — to the see of Elphin; his mood was one of annoyance:

... I have ... learned from the Duke of Richmond [Lord Lieutenant of Ireland] that the plan of his Administration is to be a total neglect of parliamentary influence in his ecclesiastical arrangements. ... I have at an expense of many thousand pounds returned two members to support you in Parliament, in the place of two decidedly hostile, and I cannot help saying it would have been but fair to have informed me at first that the only object I had in view was not to be obtained. ...[39]

The Prime Minister's reply was most revealing:

... With respect to the determination of Government not to advance to the bench, either of the law or of the church, any persons on the mere ground of parliamentary interest, I do not now perfectly recollect at what period I first heard of it. It was, however, in the first instance from Lord Liverpool [Home Secretary 1804-06, 1807-09], after my coming into my present offices; and upon Mr. Ryder succeeding to Lord Liverpool the Duke of Richmond wrote to Mr. Ryder stating to him that such had been the determination of himself and Lord Liverpool, adding that he hoped the same determination would be adhered to on our part. To Mr. Ryder and myself nothing could be more acceptable than such a determination, the propriety and merit of which at all times and under all circumstances, but most especially at the present time, considering the state of the Protestant Church in Ireland, could not fail to be felt; and we therefore did not hesitate to assure the Duke of Richmond that he might depend on our support and concurrence in carrying it into execution. I am sure I have now stated to your Lordship enough to show how entirely you have yourself put it out of my power by your letter to interfere in favour of the Bishop of Killaloe.

[39]    Marquess of Ely to Spencer Perceval, January 7, 1810; *Richmond Manuscript 66/888*, National Library of Ireland; *English Historical Documents 1783-1832*, ed. by A. Aspinall and E. Anthony Smith (New York, Oxford University Press, 1959), p. 649.

It is no longer a question upon the merits and pretensions of his Lordship as compared with those of any other competitors. . . .[40]

Thus, the use of the Church's patronage as another means of government-through-influence so characteristic of the 18th Century had a long life. We can perhaps apply Holdsworth's terminology and say that Newcastleian churchmanship had become a "convention of the Constitution".[41]

The 18th Century not only saw the elimination of the direct influence of the clergy in the nominations made to bishoprics — the change from an ecclesiastical commission to the domination of Gibson, to the domination of Newcastle and his epigones — but also the gradual elimination of the monarch himself, in whose name everything was done, from control over episcopal nominations. Anne was the last monarch to exert any independence in the dispensation of bishoprics; Georges I and II were dominated by Gibson and Newcastle; George II did make a pretense of resisting the nominations of Newcastle, but he eventually gave in, while Queen Caroline managed only a few elevations to her own liking. The needs of the ruling ministry to win support and manage the House of Commons took precedence over the personal whim of the monarch. Chaplain Pyle dismissed the possibility of George II's choice being elevated to the desirable see of Durham with finality: ". . . His Majesty has not always the best interest at Court." [42] In his autobiography, Zachery Pearce, bishop of Rochester, related an incident concerning George III's role in ecclesiastical appointments. Pearce had entreated the king for permission to resign and go into retirement and had received the royal approval. When Lord Bath who was not in the ministry heard of Pearce's intentions and the king's acquiescence, he proposed that his protégé, Bishop Newton of Bristol, be translated to the expected vacancy at Rochester. The ministry thereupon became alarmed lest someone in the opposition have any success in making and translating bishops; they tormented the king until he changed his mind, and Pearce was forbidden to resign.[43] Not even the supposedly "willful" George III was very successful in having his own way.

[40] Perceval to Lord Ely, January 11, 1810; *Richmond MSS, 66/889,* National Library of Ireland; *ibid.,* pp. 649-650.
[41] Sir William S. Holdsworth, "The Conventions of the Eighteenth Century Constitution", *Iowa Law Review,* Vol. XVII (January, 1932), pp. 161-180.
[42] Pyle to Kerrich, August 20, 1752; Pyle, *op. cit.,* p. 179.
[43] *The Lives of Dr. Edward Pocock, the Celebrated Orientalist, by Dr. Twells; of Dr. Zachary Pearce, Bishop of Rochester, and of Dr. Thomas Newton, Bishop*

## IV

Having investigated the methods of and the motivations for promoting clerics to the episcopate of the Anglican Church in the period 1660-1836, it is time to ask who the bishops were. Macaulay contended in his magnificent work on *The History of England from the Accession of James II* that since the spoliation of the Church at the Reformation, the English nobility had ceased to send its younger sons into clerical careers, leaving the Church the domain of a plebeian clergy.[44] He cited the fact that only two bishops at the close of the reign of Charles II were the sons of peers. Contemporary observers perceived something of a change in the social composition of the episcopate from the Restoration to the end of the 18th Century. Eight years before his elevation to a bishopric, William Warburton predicted that the vacant see of Durham would be awarded to a noble cleric:

> Our *Grandees* have at last found their way back into the Church. I only wonder they have been so long about it. But be assured that nothing but a new religious revolution, to sweep away the fragments that Harry the VIIIth left, after banqueting his courtiers, will drive them out again. The Church has been of old the cradle and the throne of the younger nobility. And this nursing-mother will, I hope, once more vie with imperious Berecynthia. . . .[45]

Such aristocratic notions from a cleric of no high origins were re-echoed at his own consecration, when Dr. Thomas Newton, the future bishop of Bristol and also no aristocrat by birth, offered an explanation of the Church of England's social recruitment:

> Though the apostles for wise reasons . . . were chosen from among men of low birth and parentage: yet times and circumstances are so changed that persons of noble extraction by coming into the church, may add strength and ornament to it; especially as long as we can boast of *some*, who are honourable in themselves as well as in their families; and whose personal merits and virtues; if they had not been nobly descended, would have en-

---

*of Bristol, by Themselves; and of the Rev. Philip Skelton, by Mr. Burdy* (London, Rivington, 1816), I, pp. 406-407.

[44] (London, Longman, Brown, Green, and Longmans, 1849), Vol. I, p. 327. For a discussion of the controversy touched off by Macaulay, see C. H. Mayo, "The Social Status of the Clergy in the Seventeenth and Eighteenth Centuries", *English Historical Review*, Vol. XXXVII (1922), pp. 258-266.

[45] Warburton to Hurd, July 5, 1752; William Warburton, *op. cit.*, pp. 118-119; quoted also in Sykes, *Church and State . . .*, p. 157. Berecynthia was another name for the Cybele, the Magna Mater of antiquity.

titled them justly to the rank and pre-eminence that they enjoy. God forbid that the Church of England should ever be reduced to the state and condition of the Gallican Church, incumbered with the weight of prelates of quality without learning or virtue.[46]

A trend, then, towards the greater prominence of the highly born in the ranks of the English bishops was noted by contemporaries, and the appropriate apologies were offered. The statistics provided by tables VI-X offer a means of determining what the actual trend in the period 1660-1836 was.[47]

Beause English social classes were not defined with the legal rigidity common to those on the European continent, there was no way to identify those of genteel status by means of their titles and specific legal privileges. What was called the nobility in a country like France was in England identified as the nobility and gentry. The English nobility was a very small group of titled peers whose titles devolved only upon its eldest male heirs; the gentry was a far larger group, identifiable only sometimes by knighthoods and baronetcies, but always characterized by the possession of landed property. The nobility and the gentry together comprised the *genteel* group identified in our statistical tables.

The tables provided for an analysis of the social composition of the Anglican episcopate are based on a minimum of guess work as to the social status of individuals whose backgrounds were ambiguous. It would perhaps be a temptation to classify those bishops who were the sons of brandy merchants, town clerks, bankers, and schoolmasters and parochial clergymen as plebeian on the assumption that such bourgeois occupations would have been alien to the classes legitimately identified as genteel. Indeed, certain occupations may be taken as reliable indications of membership in the lower classes: that of a jour-

---

[46]   Sermon of January 20, 1760; quoted in Sykes, *Church and State* . . ., p. 186.
[47]   Data on the family backgrounds of the English bishops have been derived from the following sources:

G. E. C[okayne], *The Complete Peerage* (London, The St. Catherine Press, Revised Edition, 1910-53), 12 volumes.

*Dictionary of National Biography.*

Joseph Foster, ed., *Alumni Oxonienses (1500-1714)* (Oxford, James Parker, 1891), 4 volumes.

Joseph Foster, ed., *Alumni Oxonienses (1715-1886)* (London-Oxford, Joseph Foster, and Parker & Co., 1888), 4 volumes.

John Venn and J. A. Venn, eds., *Alumni Cantabrigienses,* Part I, From Earliest Times to 1751 (Cambridge, University Press, 1922-27), 4 volumes.

J. A. Venn, ed., *Alumni Cantabrigienses, Part II, 1752-1900* (Cambridge, University Press, 1940-51), 4 volumes.

## TABLE VI

### English Bishops Classified According to Social Status of Their Fathers, 1660-1836

| Reign | Total | Father was a Peer or Close Kin of a Peer | | Father was a Gentleman | | Father was a Bishop | | Total of Genteel Station | | Plebeian | | Uncertain Status | |
|---|---|---|---|---|---|---|---|---|---|---|---|---|---|
| | | # | % | # | % | # | % | # | % | # | % | # | % |
| Charles II (including leftovers from Charles I) | 73 | 5 | 7 | 18 | 25 | 3 | 4 | 26 | 36 | 18 | 25 | 29 | 40 |
| James II | 8 | — | — | 3 | 38 | — | — | 3 | 38 | 2 | 25 | 3 | 38 |
| William III | 21 | 1 | 5 | 5 | 24 | 1 | 5 | 7 | 33 | 3 | 14 | 11 | 52 |
| Anne | 17 | — | — | 8 | 47 | — | — | 8 | 47 | — | — | 9 | 53 |
| George I | 24 | 2 | 9 | 6 | 25 | — | — | 8 | 33 | 5 | 21 | 11 | 46 |
| George II | 44 | 6 | 14 | 14 | 32 | (1, included under Peer) | (2) | 20 | 45 | 4 | 9 | 20 | 45 |
| George III (1760-90) | 39 | 6 | 15 | 11 | 28 | — | — | 17 | 44 | 2 | 5 | 20 | 51 |
| George III (1791-1820) | 32 | 9 | 28 | 9 | 28 | 2 | 6 | 20 | 63 | 1 | 3 | 11 | 34 |
| George IV | 14 | 3 | 21 | 4 | 29 | (1, included under Peer) | (9) | 7 | 50 | — | — | 7 | 50 |
| William IV | 5 | — | — | 3 | 60 | — | — | 3 | 60 | — | — | 2 | 40 |
| Grand Totals | 277 | 32 | 12 | 81 | 29 | 6 (2 in Peers) | 2 (3) | 119 | 43 | 35 | 13 | 123 | 44 |

TABLE VII

*English Bishops' Fathers' Social Status: Comparison of Pre-French Revolutionary Period with Post-Revolutionary Era*

| Reign | Total | Peer or rel. to Peer | | Gent. | | Bishop | | Total Genteel | | Plebeian | | Un-certain | |
|---|---|---|---|---|---|---|---|---|---|---|---|---|---|
| | | # | % | # | % | # | % | # | % | # | % | # | % |
| 1660-1790 | 226 | 20 | 9 | 65 | 29 | 4 (+1) | 2 (2) | 89 | 39 | 34 | 15 | 103 | 46 |
| 1791-1836 | 51 | 12 | 24 | 16 | 31 | 2 (+1) | 4 (6) | 30 | 59 | 1 | 2 | 20 | 39 |

TABLE VIII

*Grenville's Breakdown into Bishoprics of "Business" and Bishoprics of "Ease". Occupants of Each Type Compared*

| Type of See | Total | Peer or rel. to Peer | | Gent. | | Total Genteel (+ bishops) | | Plebeian | | Un-certain | |
|---|---|---|---|---|---|---|---|---|---|---|---|
| | | # | % | # | % | # | % | # | % | # | % |
| All sees 1660-1836 | 277 | 32 | 12 | 81 | 29 | 119 | 43 | 35 | 13 | 123 | 44 |
| Sees of "ease" Durham, Salisbury, Winchester, Worcester, 1660-1836 | 55 | 11 | 20 | 15 | 27 | 26 | 47 | 9 | 16 | 20 | 36 |
| Sees of "business" Canterbury, York, London, Ely, 1660-1836 | 56 | 6 | 11 | 20 | 36 | 26 | 46 | 6 | 11 | 24 | 43 |
| Sees of "ease" during 1760-90, Grenville's Time | 11 | 7 | 64 | 1 | 9 | 8 | 73 | 1 | 9 | 2 | 18 |
| Sees of "business" during 1760-90 Grenville's Time | 11 | 3 | 27 * | 6 | 55 | 9 | 82 | — | — | 2 | 18 |

* Grenville's distinction shows up in greater number of Peers' sons in sees of "ease".

TABLE IX

*Bishops From Ecclesiastical Families*

| Reign | Total | Father Was a Bishop | | Father Was a Clergyman | | Total Sons of Clergy | |
|---|---|---|---|---|---|---|---|
| | | # | % | # | % | # | % |
| Charles II | 73 | 3 | 4 | 14 | 19 | 17 | 23 |
| James II | 8 | — | — | 1 | 13 | 1 | 13 |
| William III | 21 | 1 | 5 | 3 | 14 | 4 | 19 |
| Anne | 17 | — | — | 7 | 41 | 7 | 41 |
| George I | 24 | — | — | 4 | 17 | 4 | 17 |
| George II | 44 | 1 | 2 | 15 | 34 | 16 | 36 |
| George III (1760-1790) | 39 | — | — | 9 | 23 | 9 | 23 |
| George III (1791-1820) | 32 | 3 | 9 | 7 | 22 | 10 | 31 |
| George IV | 14 | — | — | 6 | 43 | 6 | 43 |
| William IV | 5 | — | — | — | — | — | — |
| Grand Totals | 277 | 8 | 3 | 66 | 24 | 74 | 27 |

TABLE X

*Proportion of Uncertain Bishops who were from Ecclesiastical Families*

| | Number of Uncertain | Fathers Were Clergymen | |
|---|---|---|---|
| | | # | % |
| Charles II | 29 | 12 | 41 |
| James II | 3 | 1 | 33 |
| William III | 11 | 3 | 27 |
| Anne | 9 | 7 | 78 |
| George I | 11 | 4 | 36 |
| George II | 20 | 12 | 60 |
| George III (1760-1790) | 20 | 6 | 30 |
| George III (1791-1820) | 11 | 6 | 55 |
| George IV | 7 | 5 | 71 |
| William IV | 2 | — | — |
| | 123 | 56 | 46 |

neyman tanner, a menial servant, a wood-turner, or a drayman in a brewery. However, the younger sons of both titled nobility and untitled landed gentry went into professions and business ventures; attention only to their occupations may obscure connections with kinsmen of high social standing and influence. Consequently, in the tables of statistics I have labeled as plebeian only those bishops whose fathers were specifically so designated — on class lists in the universities or by common repute. Only those have been considered of the gentry whose fathers clearly were considered gentlemen — on class records or by repute in their local communities; there is of course no problem with those whose fathers possessed knighthoods and baronetcies. All those from neither the titled nobility, the spiritual nobility (that is, the sons of bishops), or the recognized gentry, nor specifically designated as plebeian, have all been placed in an unknown category: regardless of various claims by contemporaries and modern writers that some of these were from "old families" or "humble circumstances". Such terms conceal varying degrees of social rank, not to mention deliberate attempts to assume undeservedly a higher rank for personal motives or to ascribe to some a lower rank to prove greater social mobility. Consequently, for the sake of accuracy, only those have been categorized as peers, gentry, and plebeians who were specifically so recognized at the time; a minimum of guessing has been employed. The result is a large category of bishops whose status is *uncertain*, the largest single subdivision of whom were sons of clergymen.

Our uncertain category remains reasonably constant throughout the period 1660-1836, averaging 44% of the total: the range goes from 53% in the reign of Queen Anne to 34% in the second half of that of George III; thus, of those whom we can classify with a high degree of accuracy, we are dealing with between one-half and two-thirds of the total number of 277 bishops in this period. The reign of George III has been divided into two because of its length, and particularly because it was divided historically by the French Revolution which, it can be shown, had some effect on the makeup of the Anglican episcopate. In all of the social categories used on the tables, the social position of the fathers and paternal ancestors of the bishops has been utilized; information on maternal and marital relationships was not complete enough to be used.

Having noted these limitations, we can see from the tables that there was a real decline in the percentage of bishops in our 176-year-long period who were of plebeian origins. The proportion of bishops who came from plebeian families dropped from 25% of those named to the episcopate before 1688 and 21% during the reign of George I, to a mere 9% in George II's reign, 4% in the entire reign of George III, and to nothing in the remaining years of the pre-reform period. The reign of George I was the only exception in an otherwise generally downward trend, with Anne's reign seeing the elevation of no plebeians to the episcopate.

Except for the reigns of William IV and James II when episcopal nominations were too few to yield meaningful statistical data, and the reign of Anne which appeared generally exceptional, the 29% of bishops who came from the untitled gentry remained reasonably constant throughout the different reigns, deviating only from a low point of 25% in the reigns of Charles II and George I to a high point of 32% in the reign of George II. If the percentage of gentry did not rise meaningfully, nor the percentage of unknowns change greatly, the fall in plebeian representation was counterbalanced only by the notable rise in the proportion of bishops who were the sons or close relatives of peers: from 7%, 5%, and 9% in the reigns of Charles II, William III, and George I, respectively; to the levels of 14% in the reign of George II, 15% in the first half of George III's reign, 28% in the second half of his reign, and 21% in that of George IV. The decline in the plebeian representation, then, was matched by an increase in the representation of the sons of the titled nobility. This can be taken as an unequivocal sign of an aristocratic resurgence in the procurement of bishoprics in the Anglican Church.

In both the plebeian and the aristocratic trends, the one downward, the other upward, the period from the French Revolution until the reforms of the 1830's appeared as the time of greatest aristocratic predominance in the Church. It is helpful to split the entire period into two, 1660-1790 and 1791-1836. Comparing figures for the two periods, we find that gentry representation in the episcopate rose only from 29% to 31% and the *uncertain* proportion dropped only from 46% to 39%; however, the proportion of peers' sons and close relatives rose from 9% to 24%, while that of plebeians fell from 15% to 2%. Between our two periods, the total percentage of what we can call the genteel classes — the titled nobility, the landed untitled gentry, and the clerical nobility — increased from 39% to 59% of the total. If merely the proportion of bishops who were themselves the *sons of peers* are considered, we find that this proportion rose from 3% in the reign of Charles II and from nothing in those of

James II, William III, and Anne, to the hights of 15% and 22% in the two halves of George III's reign and 14% in that of George IV. Making the French Revolution again the watershed, we find that the bishops who were sons of peers in the first period made up only 5% of the total, while those in the later period comprised 18% of the total — certainly a significant difference.

When Warburton in 1752 hailed the reappearance of the nobility in the ranks of the clergy he was describing a perceptible trend. The difference in the nominations made between even the reigns of the first two Georges was significant: with the unknown quantity remaining stable around a 45%-46% level, the proportion of plebeians dropped from 21% to 9% while that of the genteel classes rose from 33% to 45%; the proportion of sons and close relatives of peers from 9% to 14%. However, what Warburton saw in 1752 was only the beginning of a trend whose most striking development was revealed in the reign of George III.[48]

The danger which the French Revolution augured for the established social order in unreformed England was met by a tightening up of the unreformed and abusive institutions and practices rather than by their reformation. The British ministry responded not by concessions but by repression and postponement of reform. The French reform of their established Church, the emigration of substantial numbers of the French clergy to England, and the joining of the cause of the French Church with that of the Old Régime — an identification proclaimed both by revolutionaries in France in the grips of revolutionary fervor, suspicion, and insecurity, and by conservatives in France and out — all these worked for the identification of the unreformed clergy, English or French, with the general defense of order and morality against regicide and atheism. The genteel classes in England sent their sons into the Church in greater numbers than before, and in greater numbers they were elevated to episcopal rank to assist in reversing the tide towards revolution and its vanguard, irreligion. The abuses in the established Church, once the objects of reformist endeavors, were now often elevated to the rank of sacred symbols of tradition, indispensable for preventing the French fever from spreading to England.[49] Our statistics indeed show that the

---

[48]  George III had the reputation for viewing low birth an offense to his sensibilities. He judged fitness for high office, lay and ecclesiastical, by rank rather than by talent. Henry Richard Vassall Fox, Third Lord Holland, *Further Memoirs of the Whig Party 1807-1821* (New York, E. P. Dutton, 1905), p. 64.

period between the French Revolution and the reformist decade forty years later was one of reaction and retrenchment in the Church.

The identification of the old abuses with the defense against the revolutionary movement was made no more forcefully than by Edmund Burke. His was a defense of privilege and aristocratic ascendancy in the Church:

The people of England know how little influence the teachers of religion are likely to have with the wealthy and powerful of long standing, and how much less with the newly fortunate, if they appear in a manner no way assorted to those with whom they must even exercise, in some cases, something like an authority. What must they think of that body of teachers, if they see it in no part above the establishment of their domestic servants? . . . Our provident constitution has therefore taken care that those who are to instruct presumptuous ignorance, those who are to be censors over insolent vice, should neither incur their contempt, nor live upon their alms; . . . For these reasons, whilst we provide first for the poor, and with a parental solicitude, we have not relegated religion (like something we were ashamed to show) to obscure municipalities, or rustic villages. No! we will have her to exalt her mitred front in courts and parliaments. We will have her mixed throughout the whole mass of life, and blended with all the classes of society. The people of England will show to the haughty potentates of the world, and to their talking sophisters, that a free, a generous, an informed nation honours the high magistrates of its church; that it will not suffer the insolence of wealth and titles, or any other species of proud pretension, to look down with scorn upon what they look up to with reverence; not presume to trample on that acquired personal nobility, which they intend always to be, and which often is, the fruit, not the reward . . . of learning, piety, and virtue.[50]

Burke's prejudices were those of the greater part of the ruling oligarchy of England; the period from 1790 until the reform era saw the implementation of much of the above outlined program. Whatever its liberalizing effects in France and in the western world, the immediate effects of the French Revolution in a nation such as Britain which was able to resist French military incursion were reactionary. The trends in the Anglican Church bore this out.

In idealizing the abuses and inequalities of the Church of England into the sacred ramparts of justice, piety, and morality — whose overthrow would reproduce in England the bestial horrors of the French Revolution — Edmund Burke led his readers to believe that

[49]   Sykes, *Church and State* . . ., p. 407.
[50]   Edmund Burke, *Reflections on the Revolution in France* (London, Everyman's Library, 1910), pp. 99-100; also quoted by Sykes, *Church and State* . . ., p. 408.

the natural state of the Anglican Church and its hierarchy was one of liberty and independence. It is well worth quoting Burke at length to expose the flight of fancy to which his counter-revolutionary ardor carried his perception of reality. He bitterly condemned the Civil Constitution of the Clergy which marked the reformation of the Gallican Church and demonstrated the superiority of English institutions. He wrote:

The people of England think that they have constitutional motives, as well as religious, against any project of turning their independent clergy into ecclesiastical pensioners of the state. They tremble for their liberty, from the influence of a clergy dependent on the crown; they tremble for the public tranquillity from the disorders of a factious clergy, if it were made to depend upon any other than the crown. They therefore made their church, like their king and their nobility, independent. . . . [The National Assembly] . . . has made a degrading pensionary establishment, to which no man of liberal ideas or liberal condition will destine his children. It must settle into the lowest classes of the people. . . . The Assembly has provided in future an elective clergy; an arrangement which will drive out of the clerical profession all men of sobriety; all who can pretend to independence in their function or their conduct; and which will throw the whole direction of the mind into the hands of a set of licentious, bold, crafty, factious, flattering wretches, of such condition and such habits of life as will make their contemptible pensions . . . an object of low and liberal intrigue. . . . I hope their partisans in England . . . will succeed neither in the pillage of the ecclesiastics, nor in the introduction of a principle of popular election to our bishoprics and parochial cures. . . . I know well enough that the bishoprics and cures, under kingly and seignoral [sic!] patronage, as now they are in England, and as they have been lately in France, are sometimes acquired by unworthy methods; but the other mode of ecclesiastical canvass subjects them infinitely more surely and more generally to all the evil arts of low ambition, which, operating on and through greater numbers, will produce mischief in proportion.[51]

It was only by the grossest kind of self-deception that Burke could have pretended that the existing system of naming bishops in England avoided the mean subservience inherent in an elected episcopate. It was common knowledge that bishops were made as rewards for past political favors or inducements for future ones: certainly since the fall of Gibson any vestige of disinterested religious sentiment had ceased to carry any weight with those in high position, and even Edmund Gibson's principles of orthodoxy were never proclaimed without those of political reliability. Whether any bishops could have

[51]   Burke, op. cit., pp. 97; 144-145.

been elected by the people who would have been more subservient than those obliged to the Duke of Newcastle is highly improbable; where the glorious independence of the episcopate was remains a mystery. Indeed, even the highly born did not deceive themselves so egregiously as Burke. Spencer Cowper, the younger son of William, Earl Cowper, Lord Chancellor of England, was contemplating entering holy orders; however, he shunned preferment to the episcopate with an explanation which was more forthright than any which Burke would have deemed proper to express:

... If I put on the Gown, very probably I might get a considerable addition to my present Fortune, but there, if I expect to rise to any height of Preferment in the Church, Self-Interest must be my guide, and entire submission to command, especialy [sic!] if I hope for a Seat in the Bench in your House [of Lords], nay after I have it, if I intend to make it worth my while the sitting there; but in that way I had no such views; I had rather content myself with a moderate Preferment in the Church, and be my own Master, than do any thing disagreeable, or be the Humble Slave of any one for the best Mitre on the Bench.[52]

This young aristocrat's confession of what being a bishop involved was common knowledge; it could not have escaped Edmund Burke.

Nor could Burke have ignored the existence of incidents like that related in the autobiography of Bishop Pearce of Rochester — revealing the kind of political loyalty expected as a matter of course from a cleric by his ministerial or parliamentary makers. Pearce wrote of the advice he received from his friend and patron, William Pulteney, the political foe of Walpole, better known as the Earl of Bath:

As soon as it was known that Dr. Pearce was to be the Dean of Winchester, his friend Mr. Pulteney came to congratulate him on that occasion; and among other things which he then said, one was, "Doctor Pearce, though you may think that others besides Sir Robert have contributed to get you this dignity, yet you may depend upon it, that he is all in all, and that you owe it entirely to his good will towards you. And therefore as I am now so engaged in opposition to him; it may happen that some who are of our party, may, if there should be any opposition for Members of Parliament at Winchester, prevail upon me to desire you to act there in assistance of some friends of our; and Sir Robert, at the same time, may ask your assistance in the election for a friend of his own against one whom we recommend. I tell you, therefore, before-hand, that if you comply with my re-

[52]    Spencer Cowper to his brother, the 2nd Earl Cowper, May 23, 1736; *Letters of Spencer Cowper, Dean of Durham 1746-74*, ed. by Edward Hughes (=*The Publications of the Surtees Society*, Vol. CLXV) (1950), published in 1956, p. 6.

quest rather than with Sir Robert's, to whom you are so very much obliged, I shall have the worse opinion of you." [53]

Finally, the observations of a bishop who suffered ecclesiastical ostracism because he refused to play the game the way the ministry desired are enlightening. Bishop Watson of Llandaff was undeniably an example of the wrong approach to the ministry. For all Watson's elaborate talk about the reform of ecclesiastical abuses and his various schemes which were submitted for the consideration of the ministry, it must be recalled that he was a notorious non-resident and was far more interested in politics than in religion; his writings were larded with rampant self-righteousness. But perhaps from such a man — typical of the secular clerics of the 18th Century in his attitude though not in his fate — we can learn much. Writing of the time before he had become bishop of Llandaff, he explained:

My temper could never brook submission to the ordinary means of ingratiating myself with great men; . . . I was determined to be advanced in my profession by force of desert, or not at all. It has been said, (I believe by D'Alembert,) that the highest offices in church and state resemble a pyramid whose top is accessible to only two sorts of animals, eagles and reptiles! My pinions were not strong enough to pounce upon its top, and I scorned by creeping to ascend its summit. Not that a bishoprick was then or ever an object of my ambition; for I considered the acquisition of it as no proof of personal merit, inasmuch as bishopricks are as often given to the flattering dependants or to the unlearned younger branches of noble families, as to men of the greatest erudition; and I considered the profession of it as a frequent occasion of personal demerit; for I saw the generality of the Bishops bartering their independence and the dignity of their order for the chance of a translation. . . .[54]

He went on to claim that his eventual promotion to a bishopric was based on the erroneous notion of some in the ministry that he would use his literary talents on its behalf; when it was fully realized that he would be the political hack of no political faction ". . . it is probable that I may continue to be Bishop of Landaff [sic!] as long as I live".[55] He did; he was never translated to a better see.

Hidden away in the middle of Burke's dubious discussion of English practices in the dispensation of benefices there was at least one grain of truth. Concerning the ecclesiastical establishment he

---

[53]   *The Lives of Dr. Edward Pocock, . . .*, Vol. I, p. 392.
[54]   *Anecdotes of the Life of Richard Watson, Bishop of Llandaff* (written by himself) (Philadelphia, Abraham Small, 1818), p. 62.
[55]   *Ibid.*, p. 81.

did express this desire: "We will have her mixed throughout the whole mass of life, and blended with all the classes of society." [56] While the aristocratic entry into the Church during the French Revolution and in the years before the reformist decade meant that the Church as represented by its prelates was becoming less and less blended with all the classes of society, Burke's desideratum — incompatible with his general thesis — was reasonably characteristic of the Anglican establishment. Our statictics show an average *uncertain* group of 44% for the entire 176-year period under consideration: 46% of the uncertain group were the sons of clergymen below the rank of bishops, mostly rectors, parsons, and curates. While a parson could originate from any kind of social background, he had many blood and social ties, not to mention occupational ties, with various classes of his local society. Many of the *uncertain* group of bishops were the sons of men with occupations which, if they did not indicate low birth necessarily, must have often done so; furthermore, those younger sons of genteel families who were engaged in commerce often had close business and other relations with widely diversified social groups. All this is by way of saying that the English episcopate was socially fairly well integrated into the social fabric of the nation.

The trend towards the greater reservation of high positions for the well-born came relatively late in the 18th Century. There was always room in the Anglican episcopate for those whose lack of birth was compensated by literary merit, political service to some influential patron, or personal service in the household of a peer or landed gentleman. While the aristocracy did through its control of the ministry dominate the appointment of bishops, it never attempted in this period to monopolize these offices for its own kin; at least, it often used its influence for the preferment of low-born clerics who had been chaplains, secretaries, or other retainers. When Thomas Newton, bishop of Bristol and no well-born person, was in 1764 offered the archbishopric of Armagh, the Primacy of the Irish Church, he informed George Grenville that he preferred a translation within the English bench of bishops. Grenville replied

... that he considered bishoprics as of two kinds, bishoprics of business for men of abilities and learning, and bishoprics of ease for men of family and fashion. Of the former sort he reckoned Canterbury, and York, and London, and Ely ...; of the latter sort Durham, and Winchester, and Salibury, and Worcester. He mentioned the Bishops Egerton and Lyttelton [the first, the

56    Burke, *op. cit.*, p. 100.

son of the bishop of Hereford and grandson of the Earl of Bridgwater; the second, the son of a baronet] as likely to succeed to some of the latter sort, and informed the Bishop of Bristol that he was designed for one of the former. . . .[57]

As unfair as such a scheme would have been to the lowly born, it would not have reserved all the high offices of the Church for the nobility: Grenville did not flinch at seeing ordinary commoners in the archiepiscopal sees of Canterbury and York. The fact that for the ruling classes bishoprics had not only social uses but also political uses opened them to men whose political talents compensated for deficiencies of blood.

The English aristocracy's policy on the nomination of bishops was perhaps best expressed by the Earl of Liverpool, the Prime Minister from 1812-27. It was partly to him that the policy of ceasing to name bishops for Parliamentary favors was attributed. He expressed himself in these terms, typical of the belief in a mean between an episcopate of merit and an episcopate of birth:

I believe that as to the Church patronage in England no Minister has ever paid more attention to merit or so little to political objects, as myself. But it is impossible where pretensions are nearly equal, wholly to set aside all other considerations. The aristocracy of the country will naturally expect to have some share in the patronage of the Church, and it is desirable even for the sake of the Church itself that this should be the case. The man of learning and talents who is made a bishop is of more consequence as such when he finds at his side a man of rank and family holding perhaps a bishopric inferior in rank and importance to his own. It is of great consequence, however, that the proportion of men of rank raised to the bench should not be too large. In England there is no ground for complaint on this head. I cannot quite say as much of the distribution of patronage heretofore in Ireland. If, however, individuals of rank and connection are to be promoted, it cannot be expected that friends should not be preferred to foes. . . .[58]

Even the violent attack on the political and ecclesiastical status quo which has come down to us as the *Black Book* had to admit that the English aristocracy did not acquire all the lucrative places solely for the members of their own families. Alongside the bitter contention that "to England . . . the spirit of ecclesiastical improvement has not

[57] *The Lives of Dr. Edward Pocock, . . .*, Vol. II, p. 154; partly quoted in Sykes, *Church and State . . .*, p. 157; concerning Grenville's distinction, see Table VIII.
[58] Lord Liverpool to Earl Talbot, Lord Lieutenant of Ireland, September 19, 1819; British Museum Additional MSS. 38279, f. 323; in *English Historical Documents 1783-1832*, p. 650.

yet extended; though usually foremost in reform we are now behind all nations in our ecclesiastical establishment; though the Church of England is ostentatiously styled the *reformed* Church, it is, in truth, the most *unreformed* of all the churches. Popery, in temporal matters at least, is a more reformed religion than Church of Englandism" — alongside this, the critics of the establishment had to concede that the retainers and servants of the well-born were preferred to the episcopate in spite of their low birth: "... They have mostly been indebted for promotion to marriage, or to their connexions with the aristocracy, either by relationship, or from having filled the office of tutor or secretary in their families." [59]

[59]  John Wade, ed., *The Extraordinary Black Book: An Exposition of Abuses in Church and State* ... (London, Effingham Wilson, new edition, 1832), pp. 5; 24.

# THE IRISH FIEF: THE RECRUITMENT OF ITS BISHOPS

In every meaningful sense the episcopal Church of Ireland was a part of the Church of England. From the period of the Restoration until the Act of Union in 1800 which joined the two established Churches together, the only separation between them was the provision that clerics could not at the same time hold English and Irish benefices.[1] The head of the Irish Church was also the head of the Church of England, and the primatial see of Canterbury enjoyed ecclesiastical jurisdiction over the four ecclesiastical provinces of Ireland, even over the Primate of *All* Ireland at Armagh and the Primate of Ireland at Dublin. Since the Irish Parliament in the period 1660-1836 only had independence from Great Britain for a short time (1782-1800), the British ministers of the king were able to control Irish ecclesiastical patronage in much the same way as English patronage. Temporal affairs in Ireland were administered by the Lord Lieutenant and his deputies, appointed by the king on the advice of his British ministry. The gentry and nobility of the Irish Parliament were managed through the dispensation of governmental patronage. Although only six men in our period were bishops of both Irish and English dioceses, the proportion of Irish bishops who were English by birth was always considerable, at one point attaining a level of 50%.[2] Consequently, with the sole proviso that clerics resign their English livings before accepting Irish benefices, there were never any legal obstacles in the way of men being translated from ecclesiastical livings in the one Church

---

[1]  17 & 18 Charles II, chapter 10.
[2]  The phrase *by birth* denotes born in England rather than of English ethnic origin. If figures on the bishops in Ireland who were English by birth included those who came from families relatively new to Ireland, the non-Irish proportion would be much larger. However, in view of the frequent difficulty of determining whether an inhabitant of Ireland with English relations was truly Irish or English (or Scottish), I have chosen only to distinguish according to place of birth.

to those in the other. For all practical purposes, the Churches were one.

The men named to the twenty-two bishoprics of the Church of Ireland received their appointment directly from the king, no pretense of *congés d'eslire* having been made since the Reformation. The Irish bishoprics did not vary as much as the English in terms of annual revenue. The estimates of Arthur Young for the years 1776-78 showed a variation from £ 2,000 for the sees of Dromore and Ossory to £5,000 for Dublin, £ 7,000 for Derry, and £ 8,000 for Armagh. In 1833 the Ecclesiastical Commissioners gave the following spread for the Irish sees based on net annual revenue and including benefices annexed to the bishoprics: Armagh, Derry, Clogher, and Dublin led with £ 14,494, £ 12,159, £ 8,669 and £ 7,787, respectively; while the least of the bishoprics, Clonfert, Ossory, and Killala, enjoyed revenues of £ 2,971, £ 3,323, and £ 3,411, respectively.[3] The average Irish episcopal income in the 1833 report was £ 5,864, differing little from the average English episcopal income in the 1835 report on England which reached £ 5,937. The Irish sees involved far less administration, however, for there were more bishoprics in proportion to the population in Ireland than in England. The Irish population in 1800 was about 5 million leaving about one diocese every 230.000 persons; in England the population in 1800 was about 9 million, or one diocese for every 330,000 people. However, where in England the established Church represented the large majority of the people, in Ireland it comprised no more than one-tenth. The Irish sees, thus, were high paying sinecures for the most part — especially in the West and the South of the kingdom where conformists to the established Church were scarce indeed.[4]

The Irish bishops' ecclesiastical duties were small; often their political responsibilities were greater. They sat in the Irish House of Lords where, save when some of them ventured to oppose specific ministerial measures, they were important as the government's trusty

[3]    Arthur Young, A *Tour in Ireland*, Part II (1780), pp. 56-57; 166; given in English Historical Documents 1714-1783, ed. by D. B. Horn and Mary Ransome, p. 703. "Summary of Digest of Inquiry into Revenues and Patronage in Ireland", *Sessional Papers, House of Commons*, 1833, Vol. XXVII, microprint, pp. 449 ff.
[4]    Irish population figures are derived from the revised estimates given in K. H. Cornell, *The Population of Ireland 1750-1845* (Oxford, Clarendon Press, 1950), p. 25. The religious subdivisions in the Irish population derive from Wolfe Tone's estimates, given in E. H. Stuart Jones, An *Invasion That Failed, the French Expedition to Ireland, 1796* (Oxford, Basil Blackwell, 1950), p. 33.

faction; lay members of the House of Lords outnumbered them, but these either had no estates in Ireland and remained in England or else resided in England as absentee landlords. The twenty-two bishops, consequently, usually comprised a majority of the normally attending Irish peers.[5] The Lords Lieutenant of Ireland, the real rulers of the kingdom, were usually non-residents also, and their authority was wielded by the several Lords Justices named: these almost always included the archbishop of Armagh and frequently the archbishop of Dublin. Jonathan Swift's mordant description of the heavy labors of the Irish prelates deserves to be remembered:

The Maintenance of the *Clergy*, throughout the Kingdom, is precarious and uncertain, collected from a most miserable Race of beggarly Farmers; at whose Mercy every *Minister* lies to be defrauded: His office, as *Rector*, or *Vicar*, if it be duly executed, is very laborious: As soon as he is promoted to a *Bishoprick*, the Scene is entirely and happily changed: his Revenues are large, and as surely paid as those of the *King*; his whole Business is once a Year to receive the Attendance, the Submission, and Proxy-Money of all his Clergy, in whatever Part of the Diocese he shall please to think most convenient for himself. Neither is his personal Presence necessary, for the Business may be done by a *Vicar-General*. The Fatigue of Ordination, is just what the Bishops please to make it, and as Matters have been for some Time, and may probably remain, the fewer Ordinations the better. The rest of their visible Office, consists in the Honour of attending Parliaments and Councils, and bestowing Preferments in their own Gift; in which last Employment, and in their Spiritual and Temporal Courts, the Labour falls to their *Vicars-General, Secretaries, Proctors, Apparitors, Seneschals,* and the like.[6]

As in England, in Ireland the welfare of the established Church was seen as intimately tied to the preservation of the political and social order. The Irish bishops realised that only a small segment of the Irish population adhered to the Church of Ireland, while the remaining population was not only non-conforming, but hostile to the point of violence; this had been the experience of Irish episcopalians at the hands of Catholics and dissenters alike in the period from the fall of Strafford to the victory of William III. Only upon the Irish gentry and officialdom could the Irish bishops rely for support

[5]  Archbishop King of Dublin to Archbishop Tenison of Canterbury, September 30, 1714; William King, *Correspondence*, National Library of Ireland, microfilm.
[6]  Jonathan Swift, "Considerations upon Two Bills, etc.", *The Prose Works of Jonathan Swift*, Vol. XII, *Irish Tracts, 1728-1733* (Oxford, Shakespeare Head Press, 1955), pp. 191-192.

and defense.[7] As a minority of the population, the conforming gentry learned from the experiences of the 17th Century that the only sanction for their minority rule short of the permanent presence of British troops in the kingdom was the statutory monopoly of office enjoyed by conformists to the established Church.[8] In its exclusive right to sit in the Irish Parliament and its monopolistic holding of Crown offices, the Irish gentry found a guarantee of minority rule. No Catholic could vote for members of Parliament until the reforms of 1792-93; no Catholic could hold Crown offices until the repeal of the Test Act in 1828; and no Catholic could be seated in Parliament until the Catholic Emancipation of 1829. However, the Irish Church was dependent on the king and on his British ministers for its bishops. Just as the Ascendancy in Ireland did not always agree with the Irish policy of the British ministry and House of Commons, so also did segments of the Irish episcopate find themselves in opposition. Those bishops whose birth and connections were in Ireland found themselves in positions of increasing hostility to the British government and to the bishops who came over from Great Britain. They opposed the attempt of the British Whigs to modify legislation against dissenters: the toleration of 1719 was passed only over the strong opposition of the greater part of the Irish bishops, while subsequent attempts to repeal the Test Act failed.

Because the bishops necessarily relied so heavily on the Irish gentry, their own interest in the reform of abuses in the Church establishment was frustrated. The gentry suported the Church *as it was*; any reform of abuses could dislodge it from its advantageous position and was opposed. Bishops and gentry clashed on such issues as the payment of tithes which the latter often managed to avoid in part, and the question of lay patronage and impropriations; the problem of episcopal land leases was also a cause of conflict. In Ireland, lay patronage accounted for approximately 21% of the total Church patronage. Irish and English patronage compared as follows: [9]

---

[7]    Archbishop King to Bishop Stearne of Dromore, September 25, 1714; King, *Correspondence.*

[8]    J. C. Beckett, "The Government and the Church of Ireland Under William III and Anne", *Irish Historical Studies*, Vol. II (March, 1941), p. 282.

[9]    "Third and Fourth Reports of Commissioners of Ecclesiastical Inquiry, Ireland", *Sessional Papers, House of Commons*, 1837, Vol. XXI, p. 672; 1836, Vol. XXV, p. 616; microprints. *The Clerical Guide and Ecclesiastical Directory . . .,* 1836.

|                             | Irish | English |
|-----------------------------|:-----:|:-------:|
|                             |   %   |    %    |
| Crown:                      |  10   |    9    |
| Deans and Chapters          |   —   |    7    |
| Bishops                     |  61   |   12    |
| Individual Clarics          |   8   |   17    |
| Total eccl.                 |  69   |   36    |
| Universities and Hospitals  |   —   |    7    |
| Private Lay and Corporations|  21   |   48    |
| Total Lay                   |  21   |   55    |

Although episcopal and ecclesiastical patronage was far larger in the Irish than in the English Church, the best benefices in the Irish Church were either in the patronage of the Crown and its viceroys or in that of laymen. Archbishop King lamented that he had very few good livings to bestow.[10]

Archbishop King sincerely desired a reform of the various abuses of the Irish Church. He did not, however, delude himself about the obstacles to reform in Ireland and in London. Early in his career, when he was bishop of Derry, King had lamented that the Church's petition to be granted the impropriations [ownership of part or all of the tithes of a parish] owned by Catholics whose estates had been forfeited following their rebellion on behalf of King James II was ignored in London; instead of dispensing these revenues for the maintenance of the poorer clergy the government granted much of it to laymen, and King expected that they would all be given to laymen.[11] The archbishop's remarks upon his translation to Dublin revealed his assessment of the hopelessness of inducing the government and the gentry to support reform. He wrote of his new see:

It is cramped with peculiars [that is, exemptions from episcopal jurisdiction], oppressed with lay patronages, appr[opr]iations and impropriations, and the jurisdictions and discipline so sunk and lost and personages so powerfull that need reforma[t]ion. . . . It is like an old cross body that will

[10]  Archbishop King to Bishop Browne of Cork, May, 1725; the same to the same, December 12, 1724; quoted in Richard Mant, Bishop of Down, *History of the Church of Ireland from the Revolution to the Union of the Churches of England and Ireland* (London, John W. Parker, 1840), pp. 426-427.
[11]  Bishop King of Derry to Bishop Burnet of Salisbury, October 5, 1696; quoted in Mant, *op. cit.*, p. 66.

not endure physick, and therefore must be suffered to lye in quiet for fear of irritating diseases that will admit of no cure.[12]

The disposition of Irish bishoprics by the British ministry generally followed political necessity. As members of the Irish House of Lords and sometimes Lords Justices, the bishops were important politically, and the ministry sought to have their support for the maintenance of the Irish status quo. The Irish Parliament was managed by patronage, and the appointment of bishops from prominent parliamentary families who controlled borough elections was desirable. Some bishops also held pocket boroughs, while in some more open boroughs ecclesiastical influence in elections was strong.[13] Before 1768 the Irish Parliament had been subject to general elections only at the accession of a new sovereign; there had, consequently, been few general elections. Once the government had gotten the support of a majority of the Parliament through a judicious use of patronage, it had to concentrate on keeping it intact.

Another motive for promoting men to the Irish episcopate was the need to be rid of them in England. It was the common opinion that those in England whose orthodoxy was suspect to such watchmen of orthodoxy as Gibson but who needed for one or another reason to be satisfied with Church preferment, would be given Irish benefices. When Dr. Rundle was refused an English see because of his alleged Arianism, he received an Irish one: "Last Saturday Dr. Rundle kissed his Majesty's hand for the Bishopric of Ireland [Derry]. ... The town saith thereon that my Lord Chancellor has interest to make an Irish Bishop, but not an English one, and that a person unfit to be a small Bishop in England is good enough for Ireland." [14] Warburton also held the Irish bishops in poor esteem: "The Bishop of Clogher, or some such heathenish name, in Ireland, has just published a book. It is made up out of the rubbish of old Heresies; of a much ranker cast than common Arianism. ... This might be Heresy in an English Bishop; but in an Irish, 'tis only a blunder." [15] Because Gibson did not

---

[12]   Archbishop King to Bishop Compton of London, February 12, 1703; King, *Correspondence*.
[13]   J. L. McCracken, "Irish Parliamentary Elections 1727-68", *Irish Historical Studies*, Vol. V (March, 1947), p. 210.
[14]   Historical Manuscripts Commission, *Diary of the First Earl of Egmont (Viscount Percival)* (1920-23), Vol. II, February 19, 1735, p. 151; also quoted in Appendix F of Sykes, *Edmund Gibson . . .*, p. 419, with incorrect page references.
[15]   Warburton to Hurd, November 18, 1751; *Letters From a Late Eminent Prelate to One of His Friends*, p. 92.

have much to do with Irish preferment,[16] the British ministry was free to prefer men whose Hanoverian loyalty was certain without needing to trouble unduly about their theological position. Newcastle had a decisive voice in granting Irish bishoprics before he acquired such a position in English ecclesiastical patronage. He usually intruded upon the former privilege of Irish Lords Lieutenant in the nomination of men to fill the Irish sees. Three successive Primates of *All* Ireland — Hugh Boulter, John Hoadly, and George Stone — were obliged to the patronage of the Duke for their high station; the last of these, Stone, was the brother of the Duke's own private secretary.[17] It is accurate to say that the Irish bishoprics in large measure served as a safety valve for clerics whose Whiggery was too severe for the Church-Whig alliance in England, but whose political connections and services made their preferment desirable to the ministry. Heterodox clerics in Ireland were not expected to alienate the orthodox clergy as in England because the Irish clergy was anyway so firmly dependent upon the British ministry. It was the besieged predicament of the minority Church of Ireland which permitted the British ministry to treat it far less gingerly than the Anglican Church.

The chief representative of the British ministry's ecclesiastical policy in Ireland for many years was Hugh Boulter, the archbishop of Armagh. He was an Englishman, formerly the bishop of Bristol, and a loyal Hanoverian Whig. Eighteen years at Armagh saw no diminution of his English reactions to Ireland and its problems. Boulter viewed his task as simply that of securing the Hanoverian succession in Ireland: all else was subordinated to this end. It was largely on the advice of Boulter that Newcastle named bishops to the Irish sees. He had been sent to Ireland probably to restrain the liberalizing tendencies of the new Lord Lieutenant, Carteret, who had been given the vice-royalty as a means of precluding anti-ministerial activities by him in England; Boulter sought to win full control of Irish episcopal recommendations, thereby removing the Lord Lieutenant from his traditional influence in such matters.[18] Boulter's own words offer the best description of his self-concept. Writing to the Duke of Newcastle

---

[16]  Bishop Gibson told Egmont that he corresponded little with Primate Boulter because of the latter's policy of preferring heterodox clerics; he corresponded not at all with the heretical John Hoadly, archbishop of Dublin. *Diary of the First Earl of Egmont*, Vol. I, Macrh 15, 1732, pp. 238-239.

[17]  Basil Williams, *Carteret and Newcastle* (Cambridge, University Press, 1943), p. 41.

[18]  *Ibid.*, pp. 74-75.

shortly after his arrival in Ireland, Boulter expressed himself in this way:

Your Grace knows very well that I was very content with what I had in *England,* and my just expectations there; and that it was purely in obedience to his Majesty's pleasure, that I came hither: and now I am here, the only thing that can make me uneasy, is, if I should not be enabled to carry on his Majesty's service here; the prospect of doing which is the greatest confort I have in my present station. But if the Bishopricks here, are to be disposed of elsewhere, without leaving me room for any thing more, than (as it may happen) objecting against a person, who may be sent over to the best promotions here, when I have done so; and if I be not allowed to form proper dependencies here, to break the present *Dublin* faction on the bench, it will impossible for me to serve his Masjesty further than in my single capacity. I do not speak this, as if I did not think there are some on the *English* bench, that would do very well in *Dublin,* and would heartily join with me in promoting his Majesty's measures; or that I do not esteem it wise gradually to get as many *English* on the bench here as can be decently sent hither; but that I think being on the *English* bench alone, is not a sufficient qualification for coming to the best promotions here; and that an imprudent person may easily be temped by *Irish* flattery, to set himself at the head of the Archbishop of *Dublin's* [King's] party, in opposition to me. And besides, as there is a majority of Bishops here that are natives, they are not to be disobliged at once.[19]

Boulter received virtually sole permission to recommend men to the British ministry for preferment to Irish sees. His policy of gradually reducing the native Irish representation on the bishops' bench grew out of not only his conviction that English bishops in Ireland would be more trustworthy and loyal to the dynasty, but also out of the fact that the "Dublin faction" of Archbishop King participated in Irish resistance to British ministerial policy — particularly on relief for dissenters and the coinage scheme of William Wood, both of which aroused vigorous opposition within the Ascendancy. The well-being of Ireland and its connection with Great Britain were endangered in Boulter's eyes by the presence of an Irish interest apart from a British interest; his task was to reduce the Irish interest on the bench of bishops.

Boulter was not pleased with a policy which sent to Ireland clerics whose only merit was failure to qualify for English benefices. A requirement of his was that bishops-elect not only be English but also sufficiently depend upon him so as to accept unquestioningly his

---

[19]    Boulter to Newcastle, March 4, 1725; *Letters Written by His Excellency Hugh Boulter, D. D., Lord Primate of All Ireland to Several Ministers of State in England* (Dublin, Geo. Faulkner, 1770), Vol. I, pp. 12-13.

tutelage.[20] But true to his political subservience to the British ministry, Boulter accepted those English clerics who failed to qualify in the Anglican Church. His reaction to the nomination of Rundle to Derry was indicative: "I confess I am very sorry to hear that the publick service has made it necessary to give the bishoprick of Derry to Dr. Rundle, because your Grace cannot but be sensible it will give a handle to some clamour here. But to be sure our affairs must give way to the more weighty concerns in England." [21] One concern, however, remained constant — that if he was to do the ministry's work in Ireland, no other person in Ireland should interfere with him. The threat of other Irish interests being able to influence episcopal nominations drew his angry response. Replying to rumors that an Irishman would be named to the archiepiscopal see of Cashel at the insistence of the Speaker of the Irish Commons, Boulter announced: "I shall ... write a letter to the Duke of Newcastle, to desire the ministry to consider who is the proper person to recommend to bishopricks here, an *Irish* Speaker, or an *English* Primate." [22] The preferment of Englishmen, then, was Boulter's policy for the Irish episcopate — the only guarantee of the political loyalty of the kingdom. The thought that at one point in his Irish career there were only nine Englishmen on the Irish bench of bishops drove him to warn London that many more were required.[23]

The policy of preferring Englishmen to Irish sees was very evident to the Irish. From 1660 to 1790 between 45% and 50% of all the clerics named to Irish bishoprics were born in England (including seven from Scotland) and had emigrated to Ireland at the time of their first Irish preferment or shortly before. Both episcopal and lesser benefices were filled with imported Englishmen. Archbishop King was known to deplore this policy publically. He not only denounced the preferment of "strangers", but also criticized the disposal of benefices from London, causing Irish clerics who could afford the expenses and the absence from parochial cares to flock to London to court members of the ministry.[24] King tried to inform the English prelates of the disastrous effects of such a policy. To the bishop of Carlisle he lamented:

[20]  Boulter to Newcastle, January 1, 1727; *ibid.*, Vol. I, p. 94.
[21]  Boulter to the Duke of Dorset, February 20, 1735; *ibid.*, Vol. II, pp. 105-106.
[22]  Boulter to Gibson, April 25, 1727; *ibid.*, Vol. I, p. 127.
[23]  Boulter to Newcastle, February 18, 1727; *ibid.*, Vol. I, p. 111.
[24]  King to Tenison, August 19, 1714; King, *Correspondence*; King to Dr. Goodwyn, September 21, 1714, *ibid.*

... The best of ours [benefices] are taken away by strangers that come from time to time out of Engl[an]d with our Chief Governours, that commonly are changed every three years. ... I have very deserving and learned men that have served as assistant curates for 13 and 14 y[ea]rs for £ 30 per annum, and if it had not been by great indulgence of my L[or]d L[ieuten-an]t the Earl of Sunderland, I shou'd not have been able to help one of them on this occasion. I wish the people with you that have the disposal of our best benefices understood a little the miserable estate of our Ch[urc]h. If they did, I persuade myself they wou'd see the hardship of providing for their cast clergymen here.[25]

Archbishop King found that the English-born bishops in Ireland disposed of their own patronage in the same way as the ministry — preferring friends from England or of English birth.[26] However he was not incapable of a bit of humorous comment on the state of the Irish patronage; from his sickbed he wrote to the Lord Lieutenant:

'Tis confidently reported here, that 10 English B[isho]ps were striving for this void Archb[isho]prick, if this be so I conclude when it pleaseth God to remove me, 20 will contend for mine; but I am no ways inclined to throw a bone of contention amongst my Brethren and therefore am Resolved to take all possible care of my health, and do all that I can to prolong my Life as long as God and nature will allow me.[27]

It was natural that in a country ruled from London the bishoprics would be opened to those of English birth. The Lord Lieutenant of Ireland had the customary right to make his first chaplain a bishop,[28] and as he was always an Englishman, so also was his protégé. However, the ministry in pursuing such a policy did rupture its connections with the dominant gentry and anger the native Irish clergy who seemed to find favor neither with the vast majority or Irishmen nor with the British government and its agents. One disappointed Irish cleric was Jonathan Swift. It had been only with difficulty that he had ever acquired a deanery, and once the Whigs had gained the upper hand he could expect little in the way of preferment. Dean Swift's description of the Irish prelates was mordant indeed:

Those Gentlemen who have been promoted to Bishopricks in this Kingdom for several years past, are of two sorts; First, certain private Clergymen

[25]   King to Bishop Nicolson of Carlisle, December 14, 1714; *ibid.*
[26]   King to Edward Southwell, December 29, 1725; *ibid.*
[27]   King to Carteret, March 18, 1727; *ibid.*
[28]   Lord Chesterfield to Newcastle, January 11, 1746; Sir Richard Lodge, ed., *Private Correspondence of Chesterfield and Newcastle, 1744-46* (= *Camden Society Publications,* Series 3, Vol. XLIV) (1930), p. 103.

from England, who by the force of friends, industry, sollicitation, or other means and merits to me unknown, have been raised to that character by the *mero motu* of the Crown. Of the other sort, are some Clergymen born in this Kingdom, who have most distinguished themselves by their warmth against Popery, their great indulgence to Dissenters, and an implicit readyness to fall into any measures that will make the Government easy to those who represent his Majesty's person.[29]

In writing to the Lord Lieutenant, the sympathetic Carteret, Swift championed the cause of the neglected Irish clergy:

Since your Excellency has had an opportunity so early in your government of gratifying your English dependents by a bishopric, and the best deanery in the kingdom, I cannot but hope that the clergy of Ireland will have their share in your patronage. There is hardly a gentleman in the nation, who has not a near alliance with some of that body; and most of them who have sons, usually breed one of them to the Church, although they have been of late years much discouraged, and discontented, by seeing strangers to the country almost perpetually taken into the greatest ecclesiastical preferments. . . . The misfortune of having bishops perpetually from England, as it must needs quench the spirit of emulation among us to excel in learning and the study of divinity, so it produces another great discouragement, that those prelates usually draw after them colonies of sons, nephews, cousins, or old college companions, to whom they bestow the best preferments in their gift, and thus the young men sent into the Church from the University here, have no better prospect than to be curates or small country vicars, for life. . . . There is not another kingdom in Europe, where the natives, even those descended from the conquerors, have been treated, as if they were almost unqualified for any employment either in Church or State.[30]

During controversies between the Irish gentry and the bishops over the non-payment of tithes and the question of leases on Church lands,[31] a spokesman of the gentry accused the Church of failing to encourage the gentry to send its sons into the Church by its preference for

[29]  Jonathan Swift, "On the Bill for the Clergy's Residing on Their Livings", *The Prose Works of Jonathan Swift*, Vol. XII, p. 181.
[30]  Swift to Carteret, July 3, 1725; *The Correspondence of Jonathan Swift, D.D.*, ed. by F. Elrington Ball (London, G. Bell, 1912), Vol. III, pp. 247-248.
[31]  The gentry sought the repeal of a statute of Charles I which set the maximum number of years for which bishops and ecclesiastical corporations could lease their land at twenty-one years; the statute also imposed a minimum on the amount of rent to be charged. Both these provisions prevented the alienation of Church lands by prohibiting bishops from granting long leases of their lands to laymen at low rents in return for large fines (or bribes, to be more correct); bishops could no longer mortgage Church lands for their own immediate aggrandizement at the expense of future incumbents of their sees. The gentry in the long run profited from such virtual alienation of Church lands. Louis A. Landa, *Swift and the Church of Ireland* (Oxford, Clarendon Press, 1954), pp. 97-111.

strangers; as a result the gentry had to send younger sons into commerce. The gentry's spokesman advocated a closer union between Church and gentry:

If our Gentry were to partake according to their Proportion of the Profits of the Church . . . either in Leases from the Bishops as formerly, whereby many good Families were maintained in Gentility and Hospitality under their Wings, and consequently were always their Humbler Servants in Causes, wherein the Church was any way interested, both in Country and Parliament, and also in a proper and fair Distribution of Promotions and Dignities Ecclesiastical amongst their Sons, answerable to the Number of Graduates of Birth and Distinction bred in our own University, then they wou'd see their Interest in supporting the Church and Clergy. . . .[32]

## II

Contemporary observations on the social composition of the Irish episcopate matched those on the English episcopate: the earlier part of our period of interest, 1660-1836, was seen as one in which the well-born played a minor role in the episcopate of the national Church. The bishop of Killala wrote to the favorite of Queen Caroline, Mrs. Clayton (a relation of his and the future Viscountess Sundon), concerning promotions in the Irish Church:

It has not been customary for persons either of birth or fortune, to breed up their children to the church, by which means, when preferment in the church is given by their Majesties, there is seldom any one obliged but the very person to whom it is given, having no near relations either in the House of Lords or Commons that are gratified or kept in dependence thereby. The only way to remedy which is, by giving extraordinary encouragements to persons of birth and interest whenever they seek for ecclesiastical preferment, which will encourage others of the same quality to come into the church, and may thereby render ecclesiastical preferments of the same use to their Majesties with civil employments.[33]

---

[32]   "Reasons for the Present Clamours against the Clergy of Ireland", (Dublin, 1736); quoted in *ibid.*, p. 170.
[33]   Robert Clayton, bishop of Killala, to Mrs. Clayton, March 19, 1730; *Memoirs of Viscountess Sundon*, ed. by Mrs. Thompson (London, Henry Colburn, 1847), Vol. II, pp. 9-10. According to J. H. Plumb, Bishop Clayton was the brother of the future Viscountess Sundon; this relationship, however, is not supported by the *Dictionary of National Biography*. See Plumb's *Sir Robert Walpole* (London, The Cresset Press, 1956-60), Vol. II, p. 97.

Statistics for the two hundred men who sat on the Irish bench
of bishops from 1660-1836 reveal trends similar to those found in
England.[34] The total figures for the two episcopates may be compared
as follows: 47% of the Irish prelates were classifiable as of *uncertain*
origin compared with 44% of the English; 48% of the Irish were from
genteel families as compared with 43% of the English; 5% of the Irish
were surely plebeian, 13% of the English. Within the genteel class,
the following comparisons obtained: 9% of the Irish were sons and close
kin of peers, 12% of the English; 31% of the Irish were from the untitled
gentry and 9% from the clerical nobility, while of the English bishops
the corresponding percentages were 29% and 2%. Thus, the social
origins of the Irish bishops in this period were not very different from
the English — except for a slightly higher Irish representation from
the genteel classes.

The real difference between the Irish and the English figures lay
not in their respective totals, but in the strength of their trends.
Among the English bishops, the 50% mark for those of genteel origins
was not reached until the second half of the reign of George III
(1791-1820); in Ireland the 50% mark, except for the reign of Anne
which saw relatively few Irish nominations, was reached in the reign
of George II (1727-1760). Furthermore, in the second half of George
III's reign, the proportion of Irish bishops who were the sons or close
relatives of peers rose to 42% while in England the figure was only
28% — both high-points in the respective kingdoms. The following
comparison between the 1660-1790 and 1791-1836 periods reveals
that the difference between them was more marked among the Irish
bishops:

|  | 1660-1790 | | 1791-1836 | |
|---|---|---|---|---|
|  | England | Ireland | England | Ireland |
|  | % | % | % | % |
| Sons and Kin of Peers | 9 | 4 | 24 | 32 |
| Gentry | 29 | 30 | 31 | 32 |
| Total Genteel | 39 | 44 | 59 | 68 |
| Plebeian | 15 | 5 | 2 | 5 |
| Uncertain | 46 | 51 | 39 | 30 |

[34] The sources for the family backgrounds of the Irish bishops are the same as
those for the English, with the addition of: George Dames Burtchaell and Thomas
Ulick Sadleir, eds., *Alumni Dublinenses* (London, Williams and Norgate, 1924).

TABLE XI

Irish Bishops According to Social Status of Their Fathers
1660-1836

| Reign | Total | Father was a Peer or Close Kin of a Peer | | Father was a Gentleman | | Father was a Bishop | | Total Genteel Status | | Plebeian | | Uncertain Status | |
|---|---|---|---|---|---|---|---|---|---|---|---|---|---|
| | | # | % | # | % | # | % | # | % | # | % | # | % |
| Charles II (plus hangovers) | 54 | 1 | 2 | 9 | 17 | 7 | 13 | 17 | 31 | 6 | 11 | 31 | 57 |
| James II (None) | | | | | | | | | | | | | |
| William III | 20 | — | — | 7 | 35 | — | — | 7 | 35 | 2 | 10 | 11 | 55 |
| Anne | 8 | — | — | 3 | 38 | 1 | 13 | 4 | 50 | — | — | 4 | 50 |
| George I | 13 | — | — | 4 | 31 | 1 | 8 | 5 | 38 | — | — | 8 | 62 |
| George II | 37 | 2 | 5 | 13 | 35 | 5 | 14 | 20 | 54 | — | — | 17 | 46 |
| George III (1760-90) | 31 | 3 | 10 | 13 | 42 | 2 | 6 | 18 | 58 | 1 | 3 | 12 | 39 |
| George III (1791-1820) | 26 | 11 | 42 | 5 | 19 | 1 (+ 1 peer) | 4 (8) | 17 | 65 | — | — | 9 | 35 |
| George IV | 8 | — | — | 5 | 63 | — | — | 5 | 63 | 1 | 13 | 2 | 25 |
| William IV | 3 | 1 | 33 | 2 | 67 | — | — | 3 | 100 | — | — | — | — |
| Grand Totals | 200 | 18 | 9 | 61 | 31 | 17 (18) | 9 (9) | 96 | 48 | 10 | 5 | 94 | 47 |

TABLE XII

*Irish Bishops from Ecclesiastical Families*

| Reign | Total | Father Was a Bishop | | Father Was Other Clergy | | Total: Sons of Clergy | |
|---|---|---|---|---|---|---|---|
| | | # | % | # | % | # | % |
| Charles II | 54 | 7 | 13 | 8 | 15 | 15 | 28 |
| William III | 20 | — | — | 5 | 25 | 5 | 25 |
| Anne | 8 | 1 | 13 | 2 | 25 | 3 | 38 |
| George I | 13 | 1 | 8 | 3 | 23 | 4 | 31 |
| George II | 37 | 5 | 14 | 6 | 16 | 11 | 30 |
| George III (1760-90) | 31 | 2 | 6 | 7 | 23 | 9 | 29 |
| George III (1791-1820) | 26 | 2 | 8 | 2 | 8 | 4 | 15 |
| George IV | 8 | — | — | 2 | 25 | 2 | 25 |
| William IV | 3 | — | — | 1 | 33 | 1 | 33 |
| Totals | 200 | 18 | 9 | 36 | 18 | 54 | 27 |

TABLE XIII

*Proportion of Uncertain Bishops who were from*

*Ecclesiastical Families*

| | Number of Uncertain | Fathers Were Clergymen | |
|---|---|---|---|
| | | # | % |
| Charles II | 31 | 6 | 19 |
| William III | 11 | 3 | 27 |
| Anne | 4 | 2 | 50 |
| George I | 8 | 3 | 38 |
| George II | 17 | 6 | 35 |
| George III (1760-1790) | 12 | 3 | 25 |
| George III (1791-1820) | 9 | 2 | 22 |
| George IV | 2 | 2 | 100 |
| William IV | — | — | — |
| Totals | 94 | 27 | 29 |

The significant difference between English and Irish trends in these two-period comparisons lay in the category of sons and kin of peers: in sons and kin of peers, the Irish showed an increase of 8 times, the English under 3 times. The Irish bishoprics, then, more than the

English became in the course of the 18th Century the possession of a large number of noble families. The dangers posed by the French Revolution were greater in Ireland than in England, and the consequent rallying to the Old Régime by the nobility that much greater. Although as in England, in Ireland the high places in the Church were never closed to men of low birth provided they had influential patrons or political merit, by the end of the 18th Century it became more common to witness the return of the great ecclesiastical magnates of noble blood to the hierarchy of the Church. A contemporary's description of the bishop of Derry's progress to Dublin to take his seat as a delegate to the National Convention of 1783 was the description of a decidedly untypical Irish bishop; nevertheless, Frederick Augustus Hervey, Earl of Bristol and bishop of Derry, was more typical of the latter 18th Century than of any other period since the Restoration:

Through every town on the road, he seemed to court, and was received with, all warlike honours; and I remember seeing him pass by the parliament-house in Dublin — lords and commons were then both sitting — escorted by a body of dragoons, full of spirits and talk, apparently enjoying the eager gaze of the surrounding multitude, and displaying altogether the self-complacency of a favourite marshal of France, on his way to Versailles, rather than the grave deportment of a prelate of the Church of England. [*sic!*] [35]

### III. A SUMMARY OF RECRUITMENT

The significant differences which have emerged between the nomination of bishops to the established Churches of France on the one hand and of England-Ireland on the other, lay in the source of episcopal personnel and in the motivation for its preferment. The following comparison between the social composition of the Gallican and the English-Irish episcopates shows that the former more than the latter was recruited from a single source. The French bishops, narrowly recruited, were socially isolated from the generality of the French population; the English prelates did, however, represent something of a cross-section of the population. Owing to the nature of the Irish "colonial" problem, this cannot be said of the Irish prelates.

[35] From Francis Hardy's *Life of the Earl of Charlemont*, quoted in Mant, p. 689.

|  | England 1660-1790 | Ireland 1660-1790 | England-Ireland 1660-1790 | France 1682-1790 | England-Ireland 1791-1836 |
|---|---|---|---|---|---|
|  | % | % | % | % | % |
| Genteel | 39 | 44 | 41 | 87 | 63 |
| Plebeian | 15 | 5 | 11 | 4 | 2 |
| Uncertain | 46 | 51 | 48 | 9 | 35 |

A cross-section of pre-democratic 18th-Century society may be defined only with caution. An 18th-Century cross-section may not numerically present a microcosm of the entire population of a nation. People were worthy of attention only as they had education and political, social, and economic power, rights, and privileges. Edmund Burke identified the "public" in this manner:

In England and Scotland I compute that those of adult age, not declining in life, of tolerable leasure for such discussions, and of some means of information, more or less, and who are above menial dependence, . . . may amount to about four hundred thousand. . . . This is the British public. . . .[36]

For Tocqueville, the public included "ceux qui y occupent les régions moyennes et hautes de la société, les seuls qui se fassent voir. . . ."[37] A cross-section, then, would include the nobility and gentry, and that part of the bourgeoisie which had economic and professional power and reputation, either nationally or locally. The mass of the peasantry and the wage-earning classes would be eliminated from consideration. Any wider view of a cross-section would do violence to the character of the 18th Century.

Recalling that among the English and Irish bishops the *uncertain* group included both those who might have been genteel and many who were probably plebeian, we can see that in the period before the French Revolution the contrast between French and English-Irish bishops was striking: the English and Irish far more represented the generality of the important and educated population than did the French, whose origins were in a social caste and whose episcopal rank also constituted a caste. It was only after 1790 that the English-

[36] "First Letter Addressed to a Member of the Present Parliament on the Proposals of Peace with the Regicide Directory of France", 1796; *The Works of Edmund Burke* (London, Bell and Daldy, 1872), V, p. 190.
[37] Tocqueville, *op. cit.*, I, p. 143.

Irish establishment came close to resembling the French — and, even then, only incompletely. In spite of statistical errors and uncertainties, the care taken in assigning individuals to these social categories leads me to believe that the above picture is reasonably accurate and significantly striking.

That the English-Irish bishops were selected largely for political reasons has been made abundantly clear. The political nature of their appointment is borne out by their average age of elevation and length of tenure. In France, the average age of elevation to the Gallican episcopate in our period was 40 years; in England it was 53, in Ireland 48, and in England-Ireland as a whole 51. Naturally then, the average length of tenure of each bishop was shorter in England-Ireland than in France, where bishops began their episcopal careers earlier: the average length of incumbency in England-Ireland was 11 years; in France it was 19 years. What is remarkable, however, is that given the later start of English-Irish prelates, they, nevertheless, held a greater number of sees and enjoyed more translations than their French counterparts: the average number of sees held by each English bishop was 1.65, by each Irish bishop 1.84, and by each English-Irish bishop 1.73; the average number of sees held by each French prelate, however, was 1.22. Thus, although the French became bishops approximately 11 years before their English-Irish counterparts, they occupied fewer sees and were translated less frequently. Given the briefer time in which English and Irish bishops could be translated and retranslated, and given the smaller number of English and Irish dioceses to begin with — 49 English-Irish against 130 French — the English-Irish bishops still obtained more translations than the French. Political needs in England and Ireland required a greater shifting around of bishops to keep patrons with parliamentary influence happy; in France, the more exclusively social motives behind the nomination of bishops, and the lack of any dependency on an elected Parliament, resulted in far fewer translations.[38]

---

[38]   The failure of Watson to be translated from the poor see of Llandaff was a topic of conversation only because of its rarity. In Ireland, it appears that frequent translations were a matter of course. Bishop Clayton of Killala expressed his pique at not having been translated with the following resume: "... Give me leave to inform you, that my predecessor, Dr. Howard, was but just three years Bishop of Killala, when he was translated ... The Bishop of Killala before him ... was, indeed, near six years Bishop of Killala, and I should not wonder if he had been Bishop of Killala to this day. The next before him ... was not quite three years Bishop of Killala when he was also removed to Elphin. I have now

Norman Sykes has observed that contentions like those of Thomas Newton that the social composition of the Anglican Church placed it in a golden mean between apostolic simplicity and Gallican aristo-cracy were exaggerations — that the Anglican Church actually re-sembled the Gallican Church socially, the latter more than the former appearing to be the refuge of useless nobles only because its greater number of bishoprics left many prelates without any real spiritual functions.[39] It is true that a French population in 1790 of $26\frac{1}{2}$ million meant that there was one French diocese for approximately every 203,000 persons, while in the England of 1790, with a population of perhaps $8\frac{1}{2}$ million, there was one diocese for every 311,000 persons. However, since the Irish Church was an integral part of the Anglican establishment, its relationship to the population must be included. The population of Ireland at the time of the French Revolution was 4,750,000, or one diocese for every 216,000 persons: England and Ireland together had 1 see for every 268,000 compared to France with 1 see for every 203,000.

To draw an accurate picture, however, one must consider the large non-conformist population of Ireland. If we subtract from the total population of Ireland the number of Catholics and dissenters, 450,000 people remain as conformists — or one see for every 20,000; when the dissenting and Catholic populations of England are deducted, the total population of conformists yields 1 see per 302,000 persons: the total for England and Ireland, then, was 1 see for every 175,000 conformists. Similarly, in France a deduction of 600,000 Protestants brought the total to 1 see per 198,000 conformists. On this basis, there were more superfluous Anglo-Irish sees than Gallican sees.[40] It becomes important, consequently, to recognize that the Church of Ireland with a number of dioceses and a revenue almost totally super-fluous for the genuine needs of the Irish episcopalians provided for

been four years Bishop of Killala, during which time the Bishop of Cloyne has already been once removed." Bishop Clayton to Mrs. Clayton, January 3, 1733; *Memoirs of Viscountess Sundon*, Vol. II, pp. 197-198.
[39]   Sykes, *Church and State . . .*, pp. 186-187.
[40]   Estimates of the non-conformist Protestant population of England in the late 18th Century may be found in C. E. Fryer, "The Numerical Decline of Dissent in England Previous to the Industrial Revolution", *The American Journal of Theology*, Vol. XVII (1913), p. 239. An estimate placing the Catholic popula-tion of England in the 1780's at 48,000 is cited by Basil Williams, *The Whig Supremacy*, p. 67. Estimates of the Protestant population of France is given in Burdette C. Poland, *French Protestantism and the French Revolution* (Princeton, University Press, 1957), p. 8.

the episcopal clergy of Great Britain and Ireland what some of the superfluous sees of France provided for the Gallican clergy. When viewed in this light — the Church of Ireland serving as a safety valve for the patronage of the Church of England — the differences between the utility of the Gallican and Anglican bishoprics are revealed to have been less remarkable than has often been alleged.

Sykes, however, is correct in emphasizing that the Gallican Church did not share the flexible social policy of the Anglican, such that although the aristocracy monopolized ecclesiastical appointments, its retainers shared with its offspring access to high ecclesiastical office; the French nobility monopolized these places for itself alone. Both French and English society in the 18th Century were aristocratic: but where English society was led by its responsible aristocracy, French society was divided by an aristocracy which, having been deprived of a significant political role, took refuge in its legal privileges. Through its control of the king's ministry, the English aristocracy controlled episcopal appointments; it rewarded the political and literary talent of its retainers; the French nobility succeeded in making the Gallican episcopate into its exclusive domain. The consequence was that the Anglican episcopate represented a type of cross-section of the entire literate, educated, and significant population, while the Gallican episcopate was a closed caste recruited from an increasingly closed caste. The English episcopate consequently blended with the whole of society; the French was conspicuous as a subdivision of the nobility; the one was integrated into the political life of the nation by the very nature of its recruitment; the other was but another reflection of the gulf between the different classes and corporate bodies in a France increasingly lacking any principle of national unity or common interest.[41]

Finally, it must be emphasized that the French prelates came to be recruited more and more from one part of the nobility — from the non-magisterial nobility — furthering the development of a split within

[41]    A French pamphleteer of 1789 wrote that as a result of the aristocratic bias reflected in the use of the *feuille des bénéfices*, "instead of bringing together the subjects like the members of the same family, they are disunited and separated; it seems that one fears that the noble would be soiled by contact with a plebeian. Thus it is that in the shadow of Gothic prejudices, each day a formidable aristocracy is fortified which, placing itself at the entrance to rewards, honors, and all the paths of fortune, allows entry only to those whom it finds branded with its sign." Thomas-Guillaume Bér[anger], *Haro sur la F[euille] des B[énéfices]* (Grenoble, 1789), pp. 21-22.

the nobility on questions concerning the role of the Church and its bishops in society. The Jansenist controversy estranged the Parlements from the episcopate, and the recruitment policy of the government sought bishops from the section of the nobility not as obviously tainted with Jansenist sympathies. The Parlements were able to utilize their popularity to attack the bishops; they had at hand institutional means of attacking governmental policies in Church and State. There was a *noblesse mitrée* and a *noblesse de robe* whose differences accentuated the lack of common purpose between groups and classes and within them. In contrast to the contribution of the Gallican episcopate to the division of the French nation into inimical bodies, the English episcopate was recruited from a broader social base, and no particular group of its nobility and gentry were excluded; the excluded Jacobites and non-jurors had no institutional means of opposition like those available to the French *robins* because in England the Parliament was the only political body in the nation. The British Parliament was not alienated from the Anglican bishops as occurred in France's Parlement-Episcopate relations because the Church-Whig alliance tempered the anti-clericalism of the ministry's supporters, and the episcopate was composed of men acceptable to, and obliged to, the ministerial leaders of the Parliament. Thus in a country whose social cleavages were strictly defined and jealously guarded, the episcopate was narrowly recruited and mirrored the fragmentation of society; in a country whose social stratification was more customary and flexible and not legally defined, the episcopate was drawn from a broader social base and did not develop into an exclusive social caste. Both the Gallican and Anglican episcopates closely resembled their nation's social order, the one tending towards exclusionism, the other towards assimilationism.

# V

# FRANCE: THE EPISCOPATE AS AN ESTATE: GENERAL ASSEMBLIES AND TAXATION

Of the three estates of the French nation only the clergy enjoyed a corporate status which expressed itself in regular, national deliberative and legislative assemblies. Convened every five years and whenever otherwise required, the General Assemblies of the Clergy constituted the supreme governing body of the Gallican Church — of all French dioceses except those in the territories united to the Crown since the 17th Century, 116 dioceses in all. Although as originally constituted these assemblies had been designed primarily for the discussion of the temporal affairs of the Church, with the decay of national and provincial councils which had exercised authority in spiritual and disciplinary affairs, the only surviving ecclesiastical convocation in 18th-Century France was the General Assembly. The last provincial council had been held in 1727 at Embrun, and its sole purpose had been an inordinate one: the condemnation of the patriarchal leader of Jansenism, Bishop Soanen of Senez. The General Assemblies were convened solely at the pleasure of the king and predominantly for the furthering of royal policy: above all financial, except in 1682 when the king desired support for his claim to the *droit de régale*, and in 1713 when the Bull *Unigenitus* was officially received.

Three types of assemblies were distinguishable by their membership and their intent. The regular quinquennial convocations alternated between a *greater* assembly and a *lesser* assembly whose distinctiveness rested upon the number of delegates attending and their nominal business. The greater assemblies comprised four deputies from each of the sixteen provinces of the clergy *dit de France* — half from the episcopate and half from the lower ranks of the clergy — while the lesser assemblies contained exactly one-half of that number of deputies, both from the episcopate and the lower clergy. The former were termed *greater* not only because of their larger membership, but also because their nominal task was the renewal of the ten-year contract between the clergy and the Hôtel de Ville of Paris by means of which the clergy, through helping to retire the public debt of the city of Paris, contributed to the public revenue. The lesser assemblies' nominal business was the examination of the general accounts of the clerical estate. However, since both the greater and lesser assemblies enjoyed equally the competence to grant *dons gratuits*, or free offerings, to the royal treasury and the right to petition the king for a redress of grievances, they were identical in all but size of membership. A third kind of convocation, the *particular* assembly, was attended by whatever prelates and other ecclesiastics found themselves in Paris at the time that it pleased the king to require their deliberation. These irregular assemblies were generally designed to meet emergencies, whether the problem of the *droit de régale* in 1682 or the insufficiency of the treasury for the successful conduct of war. Where the quinquennial assemblies were composed of a fixed number of elected deputies, the particular assemblies were the accidental assemblying of Church dignitaries residing in the capital who had not been "elected" for that purpose by their clergy.[1]

All assemblies of the clergy, whether greater, lesser, or particular, were convened only with the express consent of the king. The process of convening one of the regular quinquennial convocations began with a royal order for the convocation of ecclesiastical assemblies in the sixteen Church provinces which were to elect deputies to the General Assembly in Paris. Thereupon, in each diocese there assembled a meeting of all the beneficed clergy to select a delegate from among its own ranks to accompany its bishop to the provincial assembly where delegates would be selected for the national assembly. The sharing of diocesan representation by the bishop with a lower cleric was purely formal, since at the provincial conclave each diocese had a single vote — for all practical purposes, the vote of the bishop and the acquiescence of his colleague. These elaborately prepared elections in the archiepiscopal towns were never free, for the king's government both directly and indirectly made known through the controller-general and other high officials to local functionaries, lay and ecclesiastical, its choice of deputies to be sent to Paris. The government desired that clerics attending the General Assemblies be well known to the ministry, the intendants, the provincial and Parisian

---

[1] Albert Cans, *L'Organisation financière du clergé de France à l'époch de Louis XIV* (Paris, Librairie A. Picard, 1909), pp. 39-40.

magistrates, and the court bishops — men who could be relied upon to accede to every temporal and disciplinary request of the government on the one hand and to abstain from raising the divisive issues of Jansenism, ultramontanism, or clerical independence on the other. Certain troublesome and dissenting prelates were excluded from attendance, while others, like Bossuet in 1682, were dragged from a preferred anonymity to attend against their will.[2] A typical example of royal interference was the letter of the comte de Pontchartrain to the archbishop of Arles:

The king has several particular reasons for desiring that M. the bishop of Saint-Paul-Trois-Chasteaux not be sent to the assembly of the clergy, and His Majesty has commanded me to write to you to prevent, through the most gentle means, the choice from falling on him — without anyone knowing that His Majesty has excluded him; unless you are compelled, in which case you can simply declare to those who will form the assembly that it is His Majesty's intention that M. de Saint-Paul-Trois-Chasteaux not be delegated.[3]

While the non-episcopal delegates to the General Assembles were according to a reiterative regulation of 1715 required to be clergy beneficed and resident in the province electing them, these provisions were only applied when particular deputies were challenged. In practice, only holy orders was a requirement of delegates and it was legitimately met by reception of minor orders below that of the priesthood. The contingent of delegates rarely included ordinary *curés*: from 1715 to 1774 the non-epiescopal delegates were virtually always men without cure of souls but with high ecclesiastical rank. The year 1680 had seen the last of the simple *curé*-delegates.[4]

Decisions of the General Assemblies according to regulation were taken by a majority vote by province, except that a two-thirds vote was required for the granting of pensions and gratuities and for the naming and dismissal of the Receiver-General, who was the lay financial officer of the clergy. In spite of this regulation, however, except in the most important matters voting was generally by head. The Assembly of 1700 succeeded in depriving the non-episcopal delegates of any but a consultative voice in deliberations when non-temporal

[2]   *Ibid.*, pp. 57-58.
[3]   Comte de Pontchartrain to the archbishop of Arles, Jan. 20, 1700; *Correspondance administrative sous le règne de Louis XIV*, ed. by G. B. Depping (Paris, Imprimerie Nationale, 1850-55), Vol. IV, p. 192.
[4]   Gabriel Lepointe, *L'Organisation et la politique financières du clergé de France sous le règne de Louis XV* (Paris, Recueil Sirey, 1923), pp. 28-29.

questions of faith and morals were treated.[5] Actually, in its public image the assemblies usually appeared to be united on all questions before them. The official *procès-verbaux* sacrificed individual opinion and dissent to the needs of corporate unity; it characteristically presented merely a summary of various proposals and votes by provinces. Opposition views within the body of delegates were either suppressed or abridged sufficiently to vitiate any meaningful divergence.[6] To the public the *procès-verbaux* presented a picture of unanimity and cohesion. Only notably in 1755 when the question of refusing the sacraments to "notorious" Jansenists arose did the bishops parade their disagreement publicly; it was noteworthy for its rarity.

As the only surviving form of national ecclesiastical convocation, the General Assemblies of the Clergy persuaded themselves that they retained the independent power and spiritual authority of the defunct national councils of the Gallican Church It was the fact that no general assembly could be convened save by royal order and that the granting of ecclesiastical funds to the royal treasury was the general purpose of the assemblies which led the Parlements, apart from their fear of clerical pretensions, to claim that the assemblies were "purely economic" bodies. Characteristic of the Parliaments' position on the nature of these assemblies was the following manifesto of the Paris magistrates:

It is known that they meet every five years for the temporal affairs of the clergy, or more often when circumstances demand that the clergy more frequently contribute to the needs of the State. It is also known that if the deputies have sometimes disputed matters relating to religion, it was to defer to the express demands of the Sovereign or to present to the king in their *cahiers* what in the Assembly they had believed necessary or useful for the good of religion.[7]

The Paris Parlement's feeling here was one of intense opposition to the ecclesiastical drive for independence; its argument that the assemblies were "purely economic" had been previously used by the appellant party in opposing the assemblies' propagation of *Unigenitus*.[8]

---

[5] *Collection des procès-verbaux des assemblées générales du clergé de France* (Paris, Imprimerie de Guillaume Desprez, 1774), Vol. VI, column 347.

[6] Cans, *op. cit.*, p. 89.

[7] *Arrest de la cour de parlement, July 8, 1766* (Paris, G. Simon, 1766), p. 14; found in the Speer Library of the Princeton Theological Seminary collection, "Jansénisme: pamphlets", Vol. XXI, number 37.

[8] M. Picot, *Mémoires pour servir à l'histoire ecclésiastique pendant le dix-huitième siècle* (Paris, Librairie Adrien Le Clere, 3rd edition, 1853-57), Vol. IV, pp. 185-186.

The bishops realised that the magistrates' attack upon their general assemblies was but a part of the latter's general assault upon ecclesiastical jurisdiction, and they replied accordingly. The Assembly of 1765 insisted that its predecessors had always been competent to deal with non-temporal affairs, even when the immediate cause of their convocation had been fiscal. It was the voice of Loménie de Brienne, archbishop of Toulouse, which enunciated the episcopal position at that time:

It is in vain that, to camouflage its enterprises, your Parlement of Paris pretends to reduce the General Assemblies of the Clergy to the status of *purely economic assemblies*. How could the bishops united together not do what each of them could do in his diocese? The right to teach and to instruct is inseparable from their person, and their reunion gives only a new force to their teaching. Thus, the General Assemblies of the Clergy have always been regarded *in a certain way* as the council of the nation.[9]

From the position that the assemblies were a type of national council the bishops went on to assert that the work of the assemblies was only in a secondary sense temporal. Far higher were its aims and its achievements:

Of all the duties which the Assemblies of the Clergy have to fulfill, ... there is none more sacred, and none of which they have at all times more faithfully acquitted themselves, than that of defending religion against the attacks of all kinds to which Divine Providence has permitted it to be exposed. It is by the labors of these Assemblies that the errors of the Pretended Reform have been entirely proscribed; the maxims of the kingdom solidly established; the true doctrine of Grace faithfully preserved; the obedience to the judgments of the Church maintained; the illusions of false mystics dispelled; the excesses of a relaxed morality arrested and confounded; and in the more than two hundred years since their present form has been fixed, error has been able to attempt no enterprise which they have not vigorously repressed, both by censures, declarations, and expositions which regulate and assure the faith, and by instructions, admonitions, and notifications which develope its principles and motives.[10]

Despite these high pretensions, however, the bishops knew that if their assemblies were not solely economic bodies, they were, indeed, primarily assembled for the support of the royal treasury and only secondarily for religious affairs. In their regular *cahiers* of grievances

---

[9]   September 8, 1765; *Procès-Verbaux*, Vol. VIII, Part II, cols. 1379-1380.
[10]   "Avertissement du clergé de France, aux fidèles du royaume, sur les dangers de l'incrédulité", 1770; *ibid.*, Vol. VIII, Part II, pièces justificatives, col. 574.

the assemblies rarely failed to petition for the convocation of provincial councils which would deal solely with spiritual affairs. They never received any but evasive replies. Indeed, Cardinal Fleury had shunned the demands of the fanatical opponents of the Jansenists, the Cardinals de Bissy and de Rohan, that a national council be convened to stamp out dissent, preferring the milder policy of enforced silence on questions of *Unigenitus*. Fleury realized fully the polarizing consequences which would have followed a national council's collision with a hostile Paris Parlement, and he avoided them.[11] The Assemblies as organized and utilized were neither the purely economic bodies of the Parlements' imagination nor the national councils of the bishops' desire. The Assemblies were, however, pre-eminently the instrument of the fiscal autonomy of the Gallican clergy and merit being treated as such.

A striking characteristic of the resurgence of the episcopate as an aristocratic body in 18th-Century France was the increasing difficulty of the royal government in controlling membership in the General Assemblies. The letter of the comte de Pontchartrain to the archbishop of Arles cited above was characteristic of that period. Documents from the Regency also reveal that the government successfully controlled the membership of the Assemblies and needed to fear nothing unexpected from them.[12] After surveying all the possible permutations and combinations of vacant benefices, the writer of a "Projet sur la disposition des bénéfices vacants" went on to observe that "it is not at all necessary to await the Assembly of the Clergy and even less the day of its adjournment in order to nominate to benefices, on the pretext that the hope of obtaining some will make its members do more easily what is desired of them, because the clergy is so habituated and inclined to grant whatever the Court asks of it that one is not to fear anything but its powerlessness." [13] However, as the century progressed the government chose to interfere less in the composition of the ecclesiastical assemblies and the clergy more openly and successfully resisted such interference. In a provincial assembly of 1740 the archbishop of Sens refused to choose a deputy to the

---

[11] Georges Hardy, *Le Cardinal Fleury et le mouvement janséniste* (Paris, Librairie Ancienne Honoré Champion, 1925), p. 297.
[12] Copy of a form letter from the king to a bishop ordering him to absent himself from a provincial assembly of the clergy; Jan. 15, 1725, *AN*, 01° 276, folio 22.
[13] *AAE*, Mémoires et Documents, Fonds France, Vol. 1253, folios 139-141 (December 8, 1722).

General Assembly because five years before his province's nominee had been barred from participation by the Court. In 1750 several provinces with impunity selected deputies who were famed for their opposition to the bruited reforms of Machault; these same deputies in 1755 were permitted to be sent to the new Assembly.[14] A letter of the *agents généraux* of the clergy, the representatives of the Assembly between its sessions, to the minister of the *feuille* revealed that the government was becoming loath to use direct secular pressure to control Assembly membership and that the officers of the clergy were becoming less inclined to obey:

Before executing the orders which you have done us the honor of giving respecting the deputation of M. the bishop of Rodez to the next General Assembly of the clergy, permit us to offer you our very humble remonstrances on this subject. As it is without example that our predecessors have acted to bar prelates from attending the Assemblies when they were preparing to arrive there, we would have cause to fear that the next Assembly would disapprove the steps which we would have taken against the deputation of M. the bishop of Vabres. [The change from Rodez to Vabres is unexplained; it may have been an error.] If it has sometimes happened that our predecessors have used their ministry to this end, these examples are very rare; they were authorized by the order of the minister and it was a question of prelates whose doctrine was suspect; but it does not seem that M. the bishop of Vabres is in that group. Moreover, Monseigneur, as we know that your views tend in all things only to the greatest good, we are ever ready to do all which you direct us to do; we beg you only to have us given an order of M. the comte de Maurepas which could guard us from the reproach of the clergy in this matter.[15]

It is doubtful whether such a letter could have been written under Louis XIV or even under the Regent; at that time, the government directly made known its will and its wishes were respected. Like the Parlements which opposed them, the General Assemblies in the course of the 18th Century enjoyed a resurgence of independence and manifested a desire for greater power.

The immunity of the Gallican clergy from direct taxation by the royal government basically meant exemption from payment of the ignoble *taille*. The medieval principle which held the property of the Church so sacred a trust that it was totally inadmissible for it to be used for secular purposes had been modified drastically: first, ecclesiastical contributions for the waging of religious wars had been

---

[14]    Lepointe, *op. cit.*, pp. 29-30.
[15]    The *agents généraux* to Boyer, August 14, 1744, AN, G8* 2568, no pages.

deemed a not improper use of Church wealth; then, the prosecution
of national wars to preserve the Capetian monarchy had been included in the area of permissible clerical taxation; finally, by the
epoch of Louis XIV, any governmental fiscal need was considered a
legitimate reason for clerical contributions to the royal treasury. The
medieval position that the pope and clergy had to consent to taxation
was reduced in practice to the single point that the clergy maintained
an autonomous administration of its revenues and tax contributions,
employing its own tax officials and making its own apportionment.
While theoretically the clergy could refuse to grant the king the sum
he desired, such behavior in the 18th Century was rare and revolutionary; in practice, the king determined what the contribution of the
clergy was to be; the clergy apportioned it according to its own
lights and collected it through its own officials. It was, thus, the
separate taxation of the clergy arranged by a type of treaty between
sovereign bodies which characterized ecclesiastical fiscal immunity.
The clergy paid taxes in much the same form as the *pays d'états* of
Languedoc, where the estates enjoyed self-apportionment and self-
collection of direct taxes for the royal treasury.

This system of financial autonomy coupled with fairly regularized
ecclesiastical contributions to the public revenues stemmed from the
16th Century. Much of the French public debt had existed in the
form of redeemable bonds [*rentes*] which had been issued, not directly
by the royal government, but indirectly through the large cities of
the realm: Toulouse, Lyon, and especially Paris. According to the
contract of Poissy in 1561 [16] the clergy undertook to redeem a portion
of this municipally incurred public debt: it agreed to pay during the
years 1562-67 an annual sum towards the retirement of the debt of
the cities other than Paris, and to pay for a ten-year period another
sum towards the redemption of the debt of the Hôtel de Ville of
Paris. The contract of Poissy also sanctioned the self-assessment of the
clergy. It was significant that the obligations agreed to by the clergy
provided ecclesiastical support only for the liquidation of the public
debt — not for the current expenses of the government.[17] The contract
of Melun in 1580 bound the clergy to an annual payment for a sixteen-
year period of 1,300,000 livres, most of which was earmarked for

[16]   The term *contract* best describes the financial relationship of Church to
Crown under the Old Régime.
[17]   A. Esmein, *Cour élémentaire d'histoire du droit français* (Paris, Librairie du
Recueil Sirey, 15th edition, 1925), pp. 605-606.

Paris and the remainder for Toulouse. The renewal of this arrangement in 1586 for a ten-year period commenced a practice which became traditional: the signing of a ten-year contract between king and clergy for the payment of an annual sum to the Hôtel de Ville of Paris; this renewal by every greater General Assembly provided for the normal and regular contribution of the clergy to the royal treasury.[18] The annual payment was successively reduced until it amounted to only about 660,000 livres annually under Louis XIV and 440,000 livres in the 18th Century. Since the expenses of government and the unpaid public debt mounted, the diminishing return from the clergy's contract with the king for the debt of the Hôtel de Ville indicated that the ten-year contract had become an outmoded means of financial assistance and had been replaced by the clergy's grant to the king of *dons gratuits*.[19]

Under Louis XIV the *don gratuit* as a means of ecclesiastical contribution to the treasury overshadowed the payment of *décimes ordinaires* because the two great dynastic struggles found peacetime taxation everywhere insufficient. The *don gratuit* was the means of increasing the voluntary taxation of the clergy without its loss of fiscal autonomy. The requirements of the War of the League of Augsburg led Louis XIV's government to levy a *capitation* on laity and clergy alike. The opposition of the clergy to this infringement of its immunity, based as usual on the sacred character of its wealth, was strenuous, and the king yielded on the principle of equal subjection to taxation in favor of a *don gratuit* of 4 million livres anually for the duration of the war. The clergy willingly voted this sum in order to maintain the contractual nature of its fiscal contributions to the State and to keep its own assessments and tax officers. The *capitation* survived the war by a year and, in all, the clergy supplied about 9 million out of the 80 million livres collected [20] — a sum not inconsonant with the relative wealth of the clergy. However, the clergy's success in buying its way out of the national *capitation* aggravated an already inequitable assessment of clerical taxes. According to the Edict of January 18, 1695 establishing the new levy, the poor were to be exempt.

[18]  *Ibid.*, p. 609.
[19]  Marcel Marion, *Histoire financière de la France depuis 1715* (Paris, Arthur Rousseau, 1914-31), Vol. I, pp. 38-39.
[20]  Albert Cans, *La Contribution du clergé de France à l'impôt pendant la seconde moitié du règne de Louis XIV (1689-1715)* (Paris, Librairie A. Picard, 1910), pp. 29-30.

Through its separate arrangement with the government the clergy levied its 9-million-livres contribution on all of the clergy: a lighter burden for the wealthy ecclesiastics and a correspondingly heavier one for the *curés*.

The War of the Spanish Succession necessitated the imposition of a second *capitation*, the clergy's exemption from which the king was willing to acknowledge in exchange for as favorable a free gift as he had received in 1695-96. The clergy freely voted a sum of 1,500,000 livres for 1701 and 4 million livres annually thereafter. The king's desire was primarily to raise money, a consideration which overrode the principle of equality of taxation. The royal declaration announced:

[We] desire that none of our subjects ... be exempt from this *capitation*, with the exception of the clergy and the secular and regular ecclesiastics whom we have excepted, not doubting that this body which composes the first Order of our kingdom, will itself demonstrate its zeal at this juncture by granting us voluntary help proportionate to its abilities and to the needs of the State, as it did during the last war.[21]

From this viewpoint, the king could have rested content, for the clergy paid almost 12% of the annual levy of the *capitation* during the period of the War of the Spanish Succession.[22] However, even the king's emphasis on revenue rather than on fiscal principle was myopic, for in 1710 the clergy was permitted to pay to the treasury a lump sum of 24 million livres in exchange for exemption from further subjection to the *capitation*. The *capitation* levied on the laity, however, survived the Peace of Utrecht; through its lump payment in exchange for freedom from the *capitation* the clergy had won exemption from a possible figure of over 300 million livres during the remainder of the 18th Century. The government had lost a source of permanent ecclesiastical revenue.[23]

In the early years of Louis XV the same pattern of official surrender to the fiscal autonomy of the clergy obtained. In seeking to include the clergy among those subject to the new *cinquantième* in 1725 the government quite deliberately endeavored to appease clerical sensibilities: the clergy's contribution to the new levy was to be labelled a *don gratuit*; a five-year limit was promised on its assessment; and

---

[21] Declaration of March 12, 1701, article iii; *Correspondance des contrôleurs-généraux des finances avec les intendants des provinces*, ed. by A. M. de Boislisle (Paris, Imprimerie Nationale, 1874-97), Vol. II, p. 505.
[22] Cans, *La Contribution du clergé ...*, p. 57.
[23] *Ibid.*, pp. 75-77.

bishops and their diocesan fiscal bureaux were to be given extensive, even final, power to decide disputes between tax collectors and tax-payers. None of these preliminary concessions, however, satisfied the more extreme ecclesiastical pretensions; the clergy reiterated its fiscal immunity, compelling the government to yield by allowing the clergy to purchase its exemption with a *don gratuit*. Adding to the semblance of defeat for the government was its declaration of October 8, 1726 in which it proclaimed the principles of ecclesiastical independence so baldly that it surely violated the fundamental laws of the realm. The edict was never sent to the Parlement of Paris where vigorous opposition was certain to arise.[24]

The climax of these continuing impasses between the fiscal needs of the government and the fiscal immunities of the clergy was reached in 1749-51 under the Controller-Generalship of Machault. Machault's view of the needs of the treasury led him to seek to besiege the battlements of ecclesiastical privilege. His program was, first, to restrict the further acquisition of property by the Church, and second-ly, to create a permanent national tax to which clergy as well as laity would be subject without exception. The first measure, an attack on mortmain, was designed to arrest the continuing degeneration of taxable property and revenue into a non-taxable status; the second sought to restrict a large degree of clerical fiscal autonomy. The Edict of August, 1749 concerning mortmain, more the work of d'Agues-seau than of Machault, was partly a reiteration of the already estab-lished necessity for royal approval of all new religious foundations. New foundations were only to be authorized by letters patent, re-gistered in Parlement, and only after extensive investigations by lay and Church officials in the localities concerned; all legacies for the founding of such establishments were declared null and void. A second part of the edict was substantially new — a prohibition against the acquisition by ecclesiastics of immovable property without specific letters patent. With slight alterations the edict on mortmain was en-forced for the duration of the Old Régime.[25]

Machault's scheme for the creation of a permanent *vingtième*, in the place of the *dixième*, to be levied on all revenues without excep-tion and to be channelled exclusively towards the retirement of the national debt was a more direct challenge to the clergy's position. The subjection of the clergy to a permanent exaction violated its im-

[24] Marion, *Machault d'Arnouville* (Paris, Librairie Hachette, 1891), pp. 202-203.
[25] *Ibid.*, pp. 407-408.

munities and the feeling that clerical contributions to the State should only be given in time of acute distress; here was a permanent levy — promulgated not in wartime but after a general European peace treaty. Furthermore, coupled with the new levy was an order that the clergy re-evaluate the worth of its benefices for the inspection of royal officials — a forthright attack upon the last stronghold of the clergy's privilege, the right to self-assessment. Even admitting that the *dons gratuits* were virtually permanent taxes, which the clergy was loath to admit, self-assessment in practice remained the heart of the Church's independent fiscal position. Machault's program threatened both without dissimulation.

The General Assembly of 1750 concluded that the privileges of the First Estate were in danger because the government intentionally had avoided regarding the new demands made upon the clergy as free gifts and had implied that all the estates of the realm were equally obligated to redeem the public debt.

It has seemed that one wished to reduce Ecclesiastical Immunities to the sole practice of apportioning the aid offered to the king, something which one pretends even to regard as a concession of the Sovereigns and an emanation of their authority. This directly attacks the liberty of our gifts, the essential point of our Immunities.[26]

Characteristically, the Assembly's stand was made to rest not merely on its immunities *per se*, but on its whole function in society. It lectured the king: "Sire, today you owe to religion a protection more striking than ever, *because it has never been as sharply attacked....*"[27] Against the royal directive for a new evaluation of benefices the Assembly reacted by claiming no substantial inequalities existed in the old evaluations. The remonstrance of the Assembly on August 17, 1750 admitted that some inequalities existed between different dioceses and were legitimately remediable, but it conceded no need for reform within dioceses between the different sorts of benefices — an idealization of an apportionment system which based itself on ecclesiastical function as well as income. The Assembly, finally, expressed the fear that the directive for a re-evaluation of benefices was an evident calumny of the bishops' diocesan administration.[28]

The clergy was eventually victorious in its battle with Machault

---

[26]   *Procès-Verbaux*, Vol. VIII, Part I, col. 259.
[27]   *Ibid.*, Vol. VIII, Part I, pièces justificatives, col. 68. Italics added.
[28]   *Ibid.*, Vol. VIII, Part I, pièces justificatives, cols. 84-89.

not only because the anti-Pompadour party at Court, its protagonist, was able to exploit the weaknesses of Louis XV, but more important-ly because Machault challenged not just ecclesiastical privileges but all privileges. The Parlement of Paris and the provincial Parlements did not take a leading role in resisting reform at this time. Having been opposed to Machault's reforms, the Parlements acceded and registered the new edicts — perhaps because their traditional hos-tility to ecclesiastical independence was partly incorporated into them.[29] Indeed, whatever opposition to Machault's schemes the Paris magistrates did offer was far removed from concern for ecclesias-tical privileges; without protest, they had registered the declaration directing a new evaluation of benefices and publication of ecclesias-tical revenues.[30] The important manifestation of lay opposition to Machault came from the *pays d'états* where the estates correctly saw their own fiscal autonomy and its corresponding monetary benefits threatened. The clergy's immunities were very similar to those of the *pays d'états*: separate taxes separately negotiated and self-assessed.[31] The *pays d'états* opposed Machault on the grounds made respectable by Montesquieu: the necessity of a variety of intermediate bodies to restrain royal despotism and maintain the privileged liberties of cor-porate bodies, without which there could be no Liberty.[32] The *Esprit des lois* was freely circulated in 1750,[33] and while it was no comfort to either king or clergy in its philosophical basis, its conservative defense of corporate privileges and liberties was of use to the *pays d'états*, which, in defending themselves, were also defending the immunities and the autonomy of the clergy. Thus was lost the most serious 18th-Century effort to establish equality of taxation between the three estates of France. Faced with vigorous, institutionalized opposition and a weak vacillating king, a forward-looking reformer like Machault was brought down to defeat. The next attempt to achieve equal submission to taxation succeeded. But it needed the Revolution.

[29] Alfred Maury, "Les Assemblées du Clergé en France sous l'ancienne mo-narchie; Part IV: Les Assemblées du Clergé à la fin du XVII$^e$ et au XVIII$^e$ siècle", *Revue des deux mondes*, Vol. XL (July-August, 1880), p. 645.
[30] E. Glasson, *Le Parlement de Paris. Son Rôle politique depuis le règne de Charles VII jusqu'à la Révolution* (Paris, Librairie Hachette, 1910), Vol. II, p. 158.
[31] Barbier, *op. cit.*, Vol. VI, p. 332.
[32] Marion, *Machault d'Arnouville*, pp. 289-291.
[33] Peter Gay, *Voltaire's Politics: The Poet as Realist* (Princeton, University Press, 1959), p. 137.

The actual amount contributed by the clergy *dit français*, the clergy represented in the General Assemblies, to the royal treasury in the period 1700-88 was 358,050,000 livres. Annually, this sum averaged 4,023,034 livres; the annual payment of 440,000 livres for the retirement of the debt of the Hôtel de Ville was offset by an annual rebate to the clergy to help meet the burden of interest which was accumulating owing to the clergy's increasing preference for borrowing to pay its *dons gratuits*. Thus the 4 million annual sum was about the average actually received by the treasury. The clergy not represented in the General Assemblies contributed to the royal treasury separately. Necker estimated that the "foreign" clergy taxed itself annually at a sum equal to about one-eleventh of the self-taxation of the "French" clergy, whereas they probably enjoyed one-eighth of the revenue of the latter. Necker circumspectly noted that the lighter load of the "foreign" clergy was simply a characteristic of the new provinces whose overall tax burden was less than that of regions integrated into France earlier.[34]

The clergy's real share of public taxation seemed larger to it than it actually was because the amount which it levied upon its own members was higher than its contribution to the king. This difference — in the reign of Louis XV the difference between 213.5 million livres paid to the king and 288 million collected [35] — was accounted for by the internal expenses of the clerical estate and the payment of interest on the mounting ecclesiastical debt. The discrepancy between what the clergy annually paid in *décimes* and the sum remitted to the king in the form of *dons gratuits* increased throughout the 18th Century as the burden of ecclesiastical debt weighed down more heavily upon the clergy. In the decade 1726-35 the clergy taxed itself 2,686,620 livres annually and paid to the king 2,542,650 livres; in the decade 1763-72 the annual discrepancy was between 7,352,108 collected and 4,272,650 paid out.[36] This burden of debt permitted the clergy to plead its mounting obligations when confronted with demands for increased free gifts.

How much of its annual revenue did the clergy actually pay in contributions to the royal treasury? In the eleven-year period 1723-1733 the clergy's contributions reached the sum of 28,250,000 livres

[34] Necker, *De l'Administration des finances de la France* (Paris, 1784), Vol. II, pp. 332-333.
[35] Lepointe, *op. cit.,* pp. 314-315.
[36] *Ibid.*

or 2,568,182 annually. A 1725 estimate of revenue made by the clergy's own *agents généraux* was 61,600,000 livres. This would have constituted an annual contribution in this decade of 4.17% of the clergy's income. If the 1725 estimate of revenue was too low, as may be expected from such an official declaration, the clergy in this period undoubtedly paid less than 4% anually. For a mid-century estimate, we may indirectly estimate the annual revenue of the clergy in the year 1760. Official figures for the archdiocese of Lyon in 1760 listed its revenue as 1,574,168 livres. Now, in 1760 Lyon was expected to raise 21,373 livres for each 1 million levied upon the entire clergy in *décimes*, or 2.14%. Thus, if Lyon's share of *décimes* corresponded roughly to its share of the total ecclesiastical income, the total ecclesiastical income in 1760 would have been about 74,600,000 livres. Lyon's share of *décimes* in 1765 was the same 2.14% and its income was about the same as in 1760. The *dons gratuits* in the decade 1760-69 reached 35,500,000 or 3,550,000 livres annually; accordingly, the clergy in this period contributed 4.76% of its revenue to the public treasury. Finally, in the reign of Louis XVI the clergy paid in *dons gratuits* an annual sum of 5,782,857 livres. Using Necker's 1784 estimate of the total income of the "French" clergy as 110 million, we find that its contribution to the public treasury was 5.24%. Using, on the other hand, Talleyrand's higher figure of 150 million, the clergy's contribution would have been 3.92%. Higher estimates of ecclesiastical revenues just before the Revolution would have brought the clergy's contribution down to at least as low as 3.21%.[37]

Clearly a public contribution of 3%, 4%, or even 5% throughout the 18th Century could hardly have been burdensome in itself. What did burden the clergy was its debt. The clergy's resort to borrowing for the payment of its public obligations began in 1686 to cover the costs of the *nouveaux convertis* forced into conformity by the Revocation of the Edict of Nantes. Actually, the first example of its borrowing to furnish the king with a free gift occurred in 1690 when, under heavy royal pressure to provide 12 million livres for the war effort, the clergy borrowed 5.5 million of that sum. The tax needs of Louis

[37] Marion, *Machault d'Arnouville*, p. 211; 205-208. *Archives du Rhône*, nouvelle côte, 6G 65*, "Rôles des revenus et impositions des bénéfices, 1760"; nouvelle côte, 6G 70*, "Extrait du rolle des décimes du clergé du diocèse, 1744-69"; nouvelle côte, 7G 56, "Pièces générales", folios 122-127. Necker, *op. cit.*, Vol. II, p. 317. *Réimpression de l'ancien Moniteur* (Paris, Plon Frères, 1847), Vol. II, Session of October 10, 1789, p. 37. Pierre de la Gorce, *Histoire religieuse de la Révolution française* (Paris, Librairie Plon, 1912-24), Vol. I, pp. 10-12.

XIV evoked this expedient whereby the clergy could avoid the alienation of its property or the immediate increase of its internal taxation
to meet the increased costs of its fiscal autonomy. In 1710, for the first
time the whole sum of a free gift was borrowed — the 24 million livres
required to redeem the clergy's *capitation* — a practice repeated in
1711 and 1715, so that in the period 1710-15 alone, 44 million livres
of free gifts were borrowed.[38] Because the clergy paid the interest on
its debt but rarely redeemed any of the principal — in order not to
alienate property — its debt grew more burdensome and required
increasingly higher *décimes*. At the Assembly of 1788 the archbishop
of Reims, Talleyrand-Périgord, noted:

In adopting this means [of borrowing] provoked by the government, your
taxes and your debts have increased to such a point that they make it almost impossible for you to offer new sacrifices to the state, and they at
least deprive you of the sweet satisfaction of making your sacrifices as effi-
cacious and as useful as they could be.[39]

The clergy's debt, which already by 1715 had reached about 50
million livres, by 1784 had attained the level of approximately 134
million, at a cost of 5.86 million livres for interest annually.[40] On
behalf of the Constituent Assembly the marquis de Montesquiou
estimated this debt at 130 million, of which 85 million was held by
private, lay creditors and the remainder by ecclesiastical foundations
and individuals.[41]

The growing size of the clergy's debt, the result of its unwilling-
ness to raise its free gifts through either more equitable self-taxation
or through the alienation of some of its property, was of concern to

[38] Cans, *L'Organisation financière du clergé* ..., pp. 174-177.
[39] Procès-verbaux of 1788, AN, G8* 706, p. 2. The discrepancy between *décimes*
and *dons gratuits* showed itself clearly in the see of Lyon: the archdiocese paid
12.66% of its 1769 income in *décimes*; only 9.48% went to the Receiver-General;
finally, the probable rate of the *dons gratuits* in this period was under 5%. Thus
the expenses of fiscal management in Lyon itself consumed over 3% of the
*décimes*, and another 4%-5% were consumed by the expenses of the Receiver-
General. *Archives du Rhône*, nouv. côte, 7G 62*, "Registres de 1762-1769".
[40] Necker, *op. cit.*, Vol. II, p. 309. Calonne's estimate of the annual sum paid in
interest was 7 million livres; "Mémoire sur le remboursement des dettes du
clergé", *Assemblée de Notables*, 1787, Bibliothèque nationale, Le 21 .7, Box I,
p. 4.
[41] Denys-Buirette, *op. cit.*, p. 111. The accounts of the "Nouvelles Rentes"
(AN, G8* 1033) show that the clergy's creditors were magistrates, advocates,
financiers, and a certain number of bishops, dioceses, and religious corporations.
For the 18th-Century investor, the ecclesiastical debt was one of the best and
safest investments.

the government. In 1750, having seen his original scheme for subjecting the clergy to the new *vingtième* failing because of strong opposition and governmental weakness, Machault had substituted a plan whereby the clergy would pay an annual subsidy of 1,500,000 livres, not to the government, but for the compulsory retirement of its own debt. The episcopal leadership opposed this measure too, on the same grounds of fiscal autonomy. Its policy was to pay the interest on its debt and leave the principal outstanding — a policy which led the Third Estate to claim in its *cahiers* of 1789 that if, in exchange for the clergy's approval of equality of taxation, its debt were assumed by the government — exactly what the clergy hoped would be done — the clergy would have, in effect, paid nothing at all in free gifts or in any other contribution to the public revenue. The Assembly of 1788 was called not merely to have the clergy provide funds for the bankrupt royal treasury, but also to effect a reform of the unmanageable debt it had contracted. Calonne proposed that the clergy like all other Frenchmen be subject to the envisaged *subvention territoriale*, while to wipe out part of its debt the clergy was to sell various of its seignorial and honorific rights and to redeem that portion of its debt held by ecclesiastical corporations and persons. According to the minister:

In order to contribute to the public revenues under the name *dons gratuits* it has contracted debts which have successively risen to an enormous sum; and, however, it has never paid under this heading what it should have furnished of the general contribution in proportion to the value of its goods. The nature of its administration is the principle of the indefinite increase of its debt, in that it does not establish its *décimes* in such a manner as to provide for the repayment of the capital at the same time as the payment of arrears.[42]

In 1789 the clergy was finally willing to concede the principle of the equal submission of all estates to taxation, but it assumed that the government would make its own a debt which the clergy had contracted while trying to ease the financial want of the State.[43]

It become clear that the fiscal autonomy of the clergy was advantageous to the First Estate. An annual burden of 3%-5% of its income as a contribution to the royal treasury was small indeed. Whatever great burden the clergy labored under was caused by its refusal to tax

[42]  Calonne, *loc. cit.*, pp. 2-3.
[43]  Denys-Buirette, *op. cit.*, p. 120. The Constituent Assembly finally did assume the part of the clergy's debt held privately — about 85 million livres — but the property of the clergy was nationalized along with its debt.

itself equitably, a matter to be discussed below, and by its resort to extensive borrowing. The clergy's small contribution was far less than that of the vast majority of the population which paid the *taille* and the other direct taxes. Necker demonstrated that the clergy enjoyed a lighter tax burden than even the nobility which was also the beneficiary of a privileged status. Since both nobility and clergy paid no *taille*, their direct contribution to the State was in the form of *capitations* and *vingtièmes* for the former and substitutes for the latter. Necker found that the clergy anually paid from 700,000 to 800,000 livres less than the nobility through its separate arrangements for the *capitations* and *vingtièmes*. Corporately, the clergy thus emerged as the most privileged of the privileged.

It is difficult with any certainty to assess the extent to which the educational and charitable institutions operated by the clergy and its relief to the poor increased the hidden contribution of the ecclesiastical estate to the common weal. Claims were made that the archbishops of Paris for over a century had distributed three-quarters of their episcopal revenues in alms; others, like some of the *cahiers* of 1789, especially singled out monastic houses as sorely delinquent in their charitable undertakings.[44] However, the increasing 18th-Century participation of the royal government in charitable and educational undertakings leads one to conclude cautiously that the churchmen's labors in this field were inadequate and were becoming increasingly less important.

The majority of primary schools in France were staffed by lay schoolmasters and mistresses who were maintained by salaries from municipal and rural communities, by additional work in their communities, and by various military and fiscal exemptions. Secondary education was also heavily supported by public authorities: the 124 Jesuit *collèges* and many of the other religiously operated secondary schools received large governmental grants; often, property confiscated from Protestants and decadent schools and monasteries were turned over by the government to the teaching orders. Bishops had visitation and licensing rights over these schools, but ecclesiastical revenues did not provide most of the support required for education. Condorcet's report to the National Convention revealed that the royal treasury had spent about four million livres annually for education

[44] Camille Bloch, *L'Assistance et l'état en France à la veille de la Révolution* (Paris, Librairie Alphonse Picard, 1908), pp. 329; 409-410.

— about one-fifth of the yearly cost of education in the 1780's.[45]

In providing charity in the form of hospitals and work houses there was an 18th-Century trend away from private, municipal, and Church charities to state charities — a movement resulting from the failure of the former to provide adequate aid. The "secularization of charity" had in the 16th Century taken the form of laicization of the administration of charitable institutions, leaving the bishops as merely presidents of hospital administrative assemblies. While the personnel of hospitals remained predominantly ecclesiastical, funds came increasingly from governmental sources. The clerical tithes contributed very little to the support of charitable establishments; the owners of tithes, the *gros décimateurs*, were very unwilling to contribute significantly to charitable assistance. The deficits of charitable institutions were made up largely by grants from the royal treasury. In addition, institutions for the care of children, the *ateliers de charité*, and the relief of mendicity were publicly supported. In general, great ecclesiastical charity obtained in periods of unusual hardship and catastrophe rather than as a regular outlay of funds. In 1790 the committee of mendicity of the Constituent Assembly estimated the needs of State public assistance at 51,000,000 livres annually. Since in his *compte rendu* of 1781 Necker had estimated such government aid at that time at 19-22 million livres annually, the government was apparently providing about 40% of the minimum charitable needs of the nation. The final nationalization of public assistance announced by the Constituent Assembly and enacted by the National Convention was the culmination of a centuries-long trend under the Old Régime.[46] In summary, then, the annual contribution of the clergy to the public treasury was undoubtedly increased indirectly through its still important educational and charitable undertakings. However, the inadequacy of these endeavors and the steadily increasing governmental participation in these areas — a participation involving great sums of direct and indirect aid — leads one to believe, albeit cautiously, that the clergy's vast fiscal privileges and caste-like independence were not seriously modified by its charitable and educational efforts. The

[45] Shelby T. McCloy, *Government Assistance in Eighteenth-Century France* (Durham, Duke University Press, 1946), pp. 411; 433. Abbé Allain, *L'Instruction primaire en France avant la Révolution* (Paris, Librairie de la Société Bibliographique, 1881), pp. 130-142.

[46] Bloch, *op. cit.*, pp. 274-276; 300; 305; 315; 327-328; 450. McCloy, *op. cit.*, pp. 460-46].

lack of episcopal accounts of expenditures — unheard of among the *grands seigneurs ecclésiastiques* — makes it extremely difficult to estimate the level of Church expenditure in charitable works.


II


The first Estate taxed its own members according to its own assessment of the value of the different benefices in the Church and its own insight into what constituted an equitable distribution of the internal tax burden. The *décime* was the clergy's internal tax. The *agents généraux* of the clergy determined the sum which the clergy would require for each year by combining the *décimes ordinaires* which were the contribution for the retirement of the debt of the Hôtel de Ville, the sums needed for the payment of the interest on and the redemption of the bonds issued to raise the *don gratuit*, and other necessary expenses, including salaries, pensions, and gratuities. This total sum was apportioned among the clergy according to its own peculiar system. It was here that innumerable inequalities and outrageous abuses were believed to have been perpetrated, and here that reformers sought to supply the light of reason. Traditionally, the individual dioceses through their financial bureaux had been virtually sovereign in raising the amount of taxes which the General Assemblies assigned to each diocese. The provincial financial bureaux (or superior chambers) had a supervisory control over the diocesan bureaux, but commonly the former deferred to the latter, and even the General Assemblies were loath to overrule the diocesan bureaux; indeed, the quotas themselves had originally been set on the basis of statements of annual revenue drawn up by the not disinterested diocesan bureaux. The General Assemblies had recommended in the 17th Century that the apportionment of taxes within each diocese consider the differences in function between benefices and had suggested that abbeys, priories, chapters, and simple benefices be taxed at a rate of $1/3$, *curés* at a rate of $1/6$, and religious and secular communities at a rate of $1/10$. In practice, however, the system of apportionment varied with each diocese, depending upon the composition of the diocesan bureaux.

There were two sorts of abuse, basically. First, the quotas assigned to each diocese, a fixed proportion of whatever sum the General Assemblies upon the advice of their *agents généraux* had decided upon for the year, had long failed to correspond to the changing fortunes of the different dioceses; the relative impoverishment of the numerous southern dioceses and the corresponding enrichment of those of the north of France were not reflected in the assigned quotas; consequently, the increasing revenue of northern sees went untaxed. Secondly, the control of diocesan bureaux, with few exceptions, by the wealthiest ecclesiastics and tithe-owners worked for the undervaluation of rich benefices and the corresponding increase in the burden borne by the poorer ecclesiastics, principally by the *curés à portion congrue* whose incomes were a matter of public knowledge. Tax rates in some dioceses might even have adhered to the principles suggested by the General Assemblies — that is, the taxation of a *curé* at a lower rate than an *abbé in commendam*; but the latter's declared income was rarely as high as his real income, and the tax rates were consequently regressive.

Throughout the first half of the 18th Century the need for a new and accurate evaluation of the worth of ecclesiastical benefices was periodically pressed for in the sessions of the General Assemblies. Adjustments in the quotas of individual dioceses were made, and in 1729-30 an eleven-class tax system which was to discriminate in favor of benefices with cure of souls was formulated as part of a general reform of the clergy's taxing procedures; however, the general investigation of the worth of benefices which had to precede such a scheme was never undertaken, and only in eight overtaxed dioceses in 1735 was the eleven-class system implemented. Thus, immediate relief was offered in certain severe cases of inequality, but a general reform was aborted. The episcopal leadership feared that lay intervention would follow any real attempt at reform, although it was the failure to implement reform which in fact led to the initiative of Machault in seeking a reevaluation of ecclesiastical property. Furthermore, there was in high Church circles always a certain reticence about publicizing ecclesiastical revenues or indeed anything at all about the mysteries of independent Church finance. In any case, the great tithe-owners — those who stood to lose most from any reform of entrenched abuse — were able to win delay. It was a depressing tale, this attempt to create a just financial order out of the chaos and abuses of traditional practices, and it may be read in detail in Lepointe's fine study without needing to have it retold at length here. Perhaps the great difficulties in cleaning a veritable Augean stable and in overcoming the systematic sabotage of effective reform were too discouraging for the well-meaning reformers within the Church. But it is sufficient to note that the clergy itself confessed its abuses and its inability to end them. In the midst of a partial reforming effort in 1755 activated by Machault's recent frontal attack upon the Church, the archbishop of Albi, La Rochefoucauld Saint-Elpis, admitted that the official declarations of wealth from individual clerics and from diocesan bureaus were worthless and that a true reformation would entail the sending of agents by the General Assembly into every diocese of the realm to determine the real state of fiscal affairs.[47]

Once the Machault affair had demonstrated to the episcopal leadership that the dangers of lay intervention would be increasingly prevalent if the Church failed to reform its own fiscal organization, the General Assembly acted with greater enthusiasm. In 1755 a commission of the Assembly recommended that a multi-class progressive tax system like that unsuccessfully proposed in 1729-30 be applied to all the dioceses of the Gallican Church represented in the Assemblies. However, the general investigation of the annual value of benefices, the previous stumbling block, was to be forgotten in favor of a highly progressive class system. Actually this was a cowardly compromise: the data provided by the diocesan bureaus, long held in contempt by reformers, were to be accepted as true. It was hoped that those benefices whose revenues were most probably under-declared would be compelled to pay a given tax rate on a higher proportion of their declared income than those benefices which, like cures à portion congrue, could not as easily conceal the truth. Taxable income was to be determined by the following eight-class system and a tax of 25% was to be levied on all taxable income; the quota for each diocese was based on its estimated taxable income:

I.    A-Simple benefices: abbeys, secular priories, and
         regular priories without residency.
      B-Chapels with residency.
      C-Monastic offices
      Taxed 1/4 of all declared income.
II.   A-Bishoprics above 36,000 livres.
      B-Cures above 1800 livres.
      C-Cathedral dignities above 1500 livres.
      D-Abbeys, Men, above 10,800 livres.
      E-Abbeys, Women, above 28,800 livres.
      Taxed 1/4 of 2/3 of all declared income, or 1/6.

[47] *Procès-Verbaux*, 1755, Vol. VIII, Part I, cols. 527-529.

III.   A-Bishoprics 30,000-36,000.
       B-Cures 1500-1800 livres.
       C-Dignities 1250-1500 livres.
       D-Abbeys, Men, 9000-10,800.
       E-Abbeys, Women, 24,000-28,800.
       Taxed 1/4 of 3/5 of all declared income, or 3/20.
IV.    A-Bishoprics 24,000-30,000
       B-Cures 1200-1500
       C-Dignities 1000-1250.
       D-Abbeys, Men, 7200-9000.
       E-Abbeys, Women, 19,200-24,000.
       Taxed 1/4 of 1/2 of all declared income, or 1/8.
V.     A-Bishoprics 18,000-24,000.
       B-Cures 900-1200.
       C-Dignities 750-1000.
       D-Abbeys, Men, 5400-7200.
       E-Abbeys, Women, 14,400-19,200.
       Taxed 1/4 of 2/5 of all declared income, or 1/10.
VI.    A-Bishoprics 12,000-18,000.
       B-Cures 600-900.
       C-Dignities 500-750.
       D. Abbeys, Men, 3600-5400.
       E-Abbeys, Women, 9600-14,400.
       F-Seminaries 12,000-18,000.
       G-Church plants 200-300.
       Taxed 1/4 of 1/3 of all declared income, or 1/12.
VII.   A-Bishoprics 6000-12,000.
       B-Cures 300-600.
       C-Dignities 250-500.
       D-Abbeys, Men, 1800-3600.
       E-Abbeys, Women, 4800-9600.
       F-Seminaries 6000-12,000.
       G-Church plants 100-200.
       Taxed 1/4 of 1/4 of all declared income, or 1/16.
VIII.  A-Bishoprics 6000 and below.
       B-Cures 300 and below.
       C-Dignities 250 and below.
       D-Abbeys, Men, 1800 and below.
       E-Abbeys, Women, 4800 and below.
       F-Seminaries 6000 and below.
       G-Church plants 100 and below.
       H-Hospitals.
       Taxed 1/4 of 1/6 of all declared income, or 1/24.

According to this scheme Class I paid one-fourth of its declared income in taxes, Class II one-sixth, until Class VIII which paid one-twenty-fourth. To understand how such a system was intended to effect an improvement in the fiscal system without the painful necessity of investigating the real state of individual revenues and without challenging the veracity of the diocesan bureaux, it will be helpful to use an altogether hypothetical example. Suppose that before the reform of 1755-60 a *curé* with an annual income of 500 livres had been taxed at the rate of 10%; his income would have been relatively impossible to conceal and he would have paid a true 10%. Suppose that an *abbé in commendam* at an annual declared revenue of 500 livres had been taxed at 15%; if his real revenue had been 750 livres, he would actually have paid a tax of only 10% on his real income when he paid 15% of his declared income. Thus both ecclesiastics, the one in charge of souls, the other in possession of a sinecure, would have paid an actual tax of 10% — an abusive arrangement. Under the new eight-class system, the *abbé's* declared income of 500 livres would have been assumed accurate; however, he would have fallen into Class I which was taxed one-fourth of all declared income: thus 25% of 500 livres or 16.67% of his real 750-livre income. The *curé* at 500 livres would have fallen into Class VII where he would have been subject to a tax of one-sixteenth or 6.24%. Thus, the old abuse would have in some measure been modified, and without a fearful overhaul of the whole financial edifice. This was the reasoning of ecclesiastical reformers like the archbishop of Albi. Quite evidently, many abuses survived. The classes were arranged in such a manner that bishops enjoying declared annual revenues of 300,000 livres paid the same tax rate as *curés* enjoying revenues one-half of 1% as large; and if a bishop with a declared revenue of 300,000 livres were actually concealing perhaps another 70,000 livres, while the *curé* was concealing an additional income of 300 livres, the abuse would have been even more scandalous. Nevertheless, the episcopal leadership idealized its partial reform in glowing terms:

The division of all ecclesiastical tax-payers, like members of one great family, into many classes seems to offer a complicated plan only in order to render the tax more consonant with the first and simple ideas of distributive justice. Needs, like services, are counted as nothing in all fiscal administrations which recognize only the rigidity of their arithmetic rules. Among the clergy, the needs and the services of different classes are united and combined with an estimate of real revenue in order to form a gauge for apportioning taxes.[48]

[48] *Remontrances du clergé, présentées au roi le dimanche 15 juin 1788, sur ses droits, franchises et immunités*, AN, "Rondonneau Collection", AD XVII, 10A, p. 11.

The traditional arguments of the clergy were employed by the First Estate to block all the various secular attempts upon clerical fiscal autonomy and privilege. For the clergy it was simply a question of the divine character of its property and the reiteration of its privileges by Carolingians and Capetians, not to ignore the immunities of the priesthood under the Pharoahs of Egypt. Just before the great Revolution, however, the argument of the clergy changed from this passive defense of immemorial privilege to an active propagation of the liberal aristocratic ideas of the 18th Century.[49] By 1788 the clergy was defending itself along the lines of the laymen of 1750 — with the arguments of Montesquieu against despotism. Of course, the clergy still confessed no shift in its general opposition to royal policy. Yet, its Remonstrance of 1788 asserted that if the clergy had insisted on the *free* character of its fiscal arrangements,

it has always claimed them, not only as particular exemptions, but as the remains of the ancient national liberties. If these liberties are suspended, they are not destroyed.

The approval by the Parlements of the *capitations* and *vingtièmes* had been legitimate, but it was now time for them to declare their incompetence to approve further tax schemes and to demand an Estates-General.[50] The clergy joined the other aristocratic groups resisting despotism in the great revolutionary upsurge of 1787-88:

The natural immunity of property was not limited solely to goods consacrated to God in the hands of the ministers of religion. Other citizens, after having paid their fixed obligations and the services of their personal condition, were submitted to no extraordinary tax without their free consent.[51]

Thus did the clergy claim to see its fiscal privileges not as an abuse but rather as a right originally possessed by many corporate bodies, among which only the clergy had successfully preserved its original rights.[52] The clergy, in this light, were not medieval reactionaries whose unreasonable privileges offended Reason and Justice, but the only free body left in a despotic State and the leader of the movement to

---

[49]   Marion, *Machault d'Arnouville*, pp. 284-285; 289.
[50]   *Remontrances du clergé présentées au roi le 15 juin 1788*, p. 19. Bibliothèque nationale, Ld 5-6 .599.
[51]   *Remontrances ... sus ses droits ...*, p. 5.
[52]   Marion, *Machault d'Arnouville*, p. 289.

regain the liberties of all. The clergy, in its self-esteem, had come a long way.

If the vast majority of the bishops stubbornly had defended their fiscal privileges and had participated in the 1788 celebration of these "liberties", there were a few dissenters. The bishop of Orange, a see not included in the Gallican Church, was still a Frenchman: Mgr. du Tillet; during the period before the summoning of the Estates-General he had held that the national debt could be retired in five years by applying for this purpose two-thirds of the revenues of bishoprics and abbeys and by levying a land tax on the nobility — all without increasing the tax burden of the people. At the Estates-General he offered to give up two-thirds of his own income for the common-weal and encouraged the privileged orders to self-sacrifice:

". . . We cannot count on the resources of the people in this regard; it is already burdened with taxes; its misery is terrible. In my view, it is the higher clergy and the nobility which alone should assume the burden of the debts of France and cover the deficit of the treasury." [53]

Du Tillet was not to accept the Civil Constitution of the Clergy. One of the few prelates who did accept this reform of the ecclesiastical establishment, Lafont de Savine, bishop of Viviers, defended the new order with an honest assessment of the *ancien* clergy's fiscal privileges and autonomy:

One will always remember that there was a time when the clergy refused every kind of contribution. Its immunities, although the course of the centuries had reduced them to privileges more apparent than real, exposed it incessantly to the public hatred, and to the most grievous wranglings with the general administration of the State. The fathers of the people, the ministers of the God of justice and charity were accused of not even being citizens; and their most generous sacrifices were tarnished by the forms under which they presented themselves. One always believed, and one would have always believed, that the liberty of their gifts was made more in order to limit them than to honor them; the people subject to necessary contributions always would have viewed with a jealous eye its pastors enjoying a privilege which was refused to it; one would have believed that the tricks of selfishness were always to be seen in the guise of honoring religion. . . .[54]

[53] From Bonnel, *Notice biographique sur du Tillet, évêque d'Orange* (1880); quoted in Sicard, *op. cit.*, p. 131.
[54] Charles Lafont de Savine, évêque de Viviers, *Examen des principes de la Constitution civile du clergé* (Lyon, J. B. Delamolliere, 1792), pp. 4-5.

## III

What with the financial organization of the Gallican clergy mysterious to the uninitiated, the abuses in the levying of taxes undeniable
and undenied, and all reform measures abortive or halfhearted, there
was necessarily great distress in the ranks of the poorer clergy, particularly among the *curés*. The problem of ecclesiastical taxation was
a very central one in what came to be known as the late 18th-Century
"revolt of the *curés*", culminating in the fraternization of the lower
clergy with the Third Estate in 1789. Debatable as may be its Jansenist and Richerist foundations, this movement within the Gallican
Church was in large part nothing more than the attempt of the *curés*
to improve their meager living standards through an increase in their
*portions congrues* and to democratize by means of *curé* participation
in Church deliberations a corporate body completely dominated by
great Church *seigneurs*, the bishops. The amount of *décimes* levied
on the *curés* naturally affected their economic position, and the fiscal
abuses under which they labored merely bore witness to their collec-
tive impotence. It was the diocesan bureaux from which the *curés*
were effectively barred which symbolized for them the abuse and the
tyranny within the Church. It must be noted that no taxing system,
however just towards the mass of the *curés*, could overcome the
most unjust disadvantage of the *curés* within the French clergy:
around the year 1750 the average annual income of the bishops was
approximately 37,500 livres, compared to a *portion congrue* of 300
livres; thus each *congruiste* received less than 1% of the average annual incomes of the bishops; *vicaires*, the poorest class of all, received
about .4% of the episcopal income.

It was through the illegal voluntary association of the *curés*, their
publication and dissemination of numerous plamphlets, and their
petitioning of the *agents généraux*, over the heads of their bishops,
that the *curés* made known their demands; the Parlements often lent
a sympathetic ear to a movement hostile to the bishops and the great
tithe-owners. The large pamphlet literature of this revolt is a testimony to the naive but sincere expectations of the neglected backbone
of the clergy.[55] A typical pamphlet on behalf of the *curés'* cause was

---

[55] For an analysis of this literature see: E. Préclin, *Les Jansénistes du XVIIIe
siècle et la Constitution civile du clergé. Le Développement du richerisme, sa
propagation dans le bas clergé* (Paris, Librairie Universitaire J. Gamber, 1928),
pp. 390 ff. M. C. Hutt, "The Curés and the Third Estate: the Ideas of Reform

one attributed to the abbé Reymond. He complained that although in principle the episcopal leadership had conceded that the working lower clergy should be less severely taxed than the other strata of the clergy, in practice the omnipotent diocesan bureaux ignored all principles of justice; they were controlled by the great tithe-owners, and the *curés'* representatives, as mere appointees of the bishops, were subservient to them. Reymond claimed that from the mid 17th Century until the reforms of 1755-60 the *curés* had been taxed one-sixth of their meager 300-livre incomes. He contended, furthermore, that the eight-class system of 1760 still dealt unjustly with the *curés* since they were assigned to the same classes as ecclesiastics who held virtual sinecures. In any event, Reymond condemned a fiscal regime which accepted without question the declarations of the corrupt diocesan bureaux and which gave no voice to the mass of the clergy.[56]

As early as 1735, in seeking an improvement in their temporal status, the *curés* had complained of being excessively taxed.[57] More than the bishops, whom the largely obedient *curés* usually revered, the target of the *curés* in revolt was the great tithe-owners who controlled the diocesan bureaux and blocked reform. A *curé* in the archdiocese of Auch lamented:

... that one does not cease complaining that the [just] ratios are not followed in the assessment made in the said diocesan bureau [of Auch]; that the other taxpayers are overcharged, whereas the chapters do not contribute the share which justice and the rules of the General Assemblies of the clergy require; that in vain has the supplicant made his complaints to the bureau in this regard; that fruitlessly the lord archbishop of Auch, who desires nothing but the establishment of order and perfect equity in the assessment of ecclesiastical taxes, has insisted many times on the same principles; the abuses still remain; that not being able to conceal these abuses the diocesan bureau has decided to remedy them by reforming the tax roll: but that these decisions remain without effect, and that it is to be feared either that they will remain so for a long time or that the reform of the assessment will be inimical to the *curés*, because out of the five votes which there are in the bureau, the canons have three, so that they often have a common interest in the deliberations; that this interest can only produce

---

in the Pamphlets of the French Lower Clergy in the Period 1787-1789", *The Journal of Ecclesiastical History*, Vol. VIII (1957), pp. 74-92.

[56] Abbé Henri Reymond (authorship attributed to him by Barbier), *Droits des curés et des paroisses, considérés sous leur rapport, spirituel & temporel* (Paris, 1776, Bibliothèque nationale), E. 7316, pp. 121-148.

[57] "Réponse des curés congruistes du diocèse de Comminges, aux mémoires présentés par les décimateurs dudit diocèse, devant Nosseigneurs des Assemblées générales du clergé de France", *Rapport de l'Agence*, 1735-40, pp. 264-268.

among them a unanimity of votes, and that this unanimity must always triumph over the two other votes, namely those of the lord archbishop and of the deputy of the *curés*.[58]

The mysterious and pernicious workings of the diocesan bureaux so exasperated the *curés* that they choose to believe that as much as 100 or even 160 livres were taken in taxation on their *portions congrues*.[59] Had these sums actually been taken in taxes, they would have been illegally collected; royal edicts prohited the taxes on *portions congrues* from exceeding 60 livres annually. Some modern historians, among them Marion, have concluded that as much as one-fifth of *portions congrues* were taken in taxes.[60] However, Marion had no evidence of *curé* taxes such as will be presented below; he took at face value the *curés'* own claims of exorbitant taxes, although their "evidence" was more useful in revealing their exasperation and disappointment under a system removed from their control than in offering real tax figures.[61]

What drove the *curés* to the desperate action of illegal assemblies was the consistent refusal of the government to interfere with the workings of the diocesan bureaux. Little could be hoped for from within the Church: when in 1735 the *curés* of Comminges sought to have a representative voice in diocesan affairs, an increase in the *portion congrue*, and a more equitable assessment of *décimes*, the *agents généraux* reported to the General Assembly that these demands "... would not lead to less than the complete overthrow of order".[62] When the Parlements sought to assist the *curés* in their campaign to reform the diocesan bureaux the government repeatedly annulled the Parlements' decisions and forbade the magistrates from meddling in the internal affairs of the clergy.[63] Finally, even where the

---

[58] Included in an arrêt du conseil d'état, June 30, 1772, *Rapport de l'Agence*, 1770-75, pp. DCCXLVII-DCCLVIII. The reform of the diocesan bureau of Auch gave the *curés* two votes so that with the support of the archbishop the three votes of the canons could be equalled and thereby overridden.

[59] "Mémoire présenté au ministre et secrétaire d'état ayant le département du clergé (Laurent de Villedeuil), par les curés à portions congrues, 1788", AN, Ba 1, folio 7, no. 2, pp. 8-9.

[60] Marion, *Machault d'Arnouville*, pp. 224-225.

[61] See "Lettre du curé de M ... diocèse de T ... à un de ses amis à Paris, à l'occasion de l'Assemblée du clergé", May 23, 1755, S. 1., Bibliothèque nationale, Ld4 .2695, p. 2.

[62] *Rapport de l'Agence*, 1735-40, pp. 264-268.

[63] "Arrêt du conseil d'état du roi, 2 juin 1773", *ibid.*, 1770-75, pp. 202-204; pièces justificatives, pp. DCCXXXIII-DCCXXXVI. *Ibid.*, 1775-80, pp. 141-144.

*agents généraux* were compelled to admit the justice of the *curés'* contentions — as in 1728 when the deduction of fifty livres in advance by the great tithe-owners from the *portions congrues* of their *curés* was declared clearly illegal — the *curés* were nevertheless admonished to remember that the diocesan bureaux and the provincial superior chambers alone could be petitioned for redress.[64] The *agents généraux* were just as inflexible a half-century later when they again advised the *curés* that the diocesan bureaux alone could correct the abuses for which they alone were responsible.[65] It became impossible for the obedient *curés* to obey any longer.

In their struggle to win some representation on the all-important diocesan bureaux and thereby to reform fiscal abuses the *curés* had a notable success in the diocese of Troyes. In 1767-68 the *curés* successfully appealed to the Parlement of Paris, causing their bishop to seek aid from the conseil du roi. By chance, it was a good time for presenting *curé* demands — 1768 had seen the long-awaited increase in the *portion congrue* from 300 to 500 livres — and the government intervened on behalf of the *curés* of Troyes, ordering that they be permitted to assemble in their rural deaneries to elect two deputies to the diocesan bureau. The government persuaded the General Assembly of 1770 to approve a reform of the diocesan bureau. The episcopal leadership, notably the archbishop of Narbonne, Mgr. Dillon, believed that the clergy should reform itself in order to win royal support against the continuing hostility of the Parlements. At first the Assembly had decided upon a general reform of all diocesan bureaux, but the fear that such general reform would create *curé* unrest in dioceses still peaceful led it to reform only Troyes and to draw up a statement of principles to guide future reform of diocesan bureaux. Both clergy and government stopped at this point, refusing to extend reform to the other dioceses; the given excuse was of a piece with the particularism of the Old Régime — the "temporizing spirit": [66]

This administration [of décimes] is essentially tied to so many special circumstances that before proceeding with the said ruling [for general reform] as his Majesty has proposed, it is indispensable to obtain the most ample information about the different diocesan bureaux of the kingdom,

[64] Letter of the *agents généraux* to the syndic of the *curés* of the see of Gap, June 23, 1728, AN, G8* 2558, no. 315.
[65] Letter of the *agents généraux* to a *curé* of Lonlay, May 31, 1781, AN, G8* 2617, no. 331.
[66] Lepointe, *op. cit.*, pp. 105-106.

the acts which have established them, their composition, the rights of different bodies or individuals which customarily have a deliberative voice, by themselves or by their representatives; finally, about the different taxes other than those destined for the general treasury of the clergy or those which spring either from exceptional needs or from particular debts of the dioceses.[67]

Thus the government preferred cautious piece-meal measures to any general reformation. After the conseil d'état at the request of the archbishop of Auch in 1772 had reformed his bureau according to the principles of 1770, the *agents généraux* noted that it was to be hoped that such reform would be effected individually in the different dioceses, according to the needs of each diocese, "to avoid the commotions and the agitations which appear inseparable from a general revolution made at the same time in the universality of the dioceses".[68] The archbishop of Vienne, Le Franc de Pompignan, likewise accepted the plan of 1770 in principle but refused to implement it on the grounds that Vienne was not Troyes and that there was a danger of violent disturbance resulting.[69] It was basically the episcopal supremacy in executing reform which the *agents généraux* sought to protect.[70] The best summary of moderate enlightened opinion, lay and ecclesiastic, presented on the subject of the diocesan bureaux was that of Talleyrand. As one of the *agents généraux* of the clergy from 1780-85 the abbé de Périgord believed in the necessity of reform; however, to the revolutionary ferment of the *curés* he was unalterably opposed:

The clergy, Monseigneur, for a long time have desired to bring all the diocesan bureaux to a uniform constitution; the Assemblies of 1760 and 1765 have concerned themselves with it; that of 1770 drew up and recorded in its official proceedings the project of a general ruling on the subject. But when one has wished to execute it, one has encountered great difficulties in adopting it to the situation of a great number of dioceses, and according to all appearances it will be necessary to prefer a special settlement for each diocese, but one resembling as much as possible the general plan.

This operation, moreover, can only be the work of time [even] if it is important to accelerate it in some dioceses. It is a point whose examination could be sent to the Assembly of the clergy; but I believe, Monseigneur,

---

[67] "Arrêt du conseil d'état du roi, 5 mai 1771", *Rapport de l'Agence*, 1770-75, pièces justificatives, pp. DCCXXXVI-DCCXLIV.
[68] *Ibid.*, 1770-75, p. 206.
[69] *Ibid.*, 1780-85, p. 296.
[70] *Ibid.*, p. 303.

that it does not concern less the interest of the finances of the king than the peace of the dioceses not to defer on this point to the demands of the tax-payers whatever they may be; and it appears to me essential still to main-tain provisionally the composition of the bureau of *décimes* [of Bazas] until it pleases his Majesty to give a new form to this bureau or to authorize that one which will be proposed to him. Without this, the operation of the bureau being contested, sometimes compromised, and often even halted, the receipt of *décimes* and other taxes of the clergy would necessarily suf-fer.... The change is never [to be] the fruit of a reprehensible ferment; nothing would be more encouraging to ... turbulent spirits.

The ferment which is breaking out in the diocese of Bazas is similar in everything to the former ones. Several *curés* protest against the nomination of deputies to the diocesan bureau. I do not mean to blame their demand basically: there can be reasons to seek a change.[71]

However, the revolutionary organization of *curés* was not to be tole-rated. In this attitude, the episcopal leadership had the support of the government. In the face of the *curés'* revolt, when on the eve of the Revolution the government supported the subjection of all three estates to taxation, the bishops had little choice but to agree; sup-port for the fiscal autonomy of the clergy was growing increasingly feeble among the mass of the clergy.

Inevitably the question arises: how much did the *curés* actually pay in *décimes*? The autonomy of each individual diocesan bureau meant that tax rates varied from see to see, and short of an impossible dio-cese-by-diocese survey, any tax figures must be selective. In his study of the rural *curés* under the Old Régime, Pierre de Vaissière offers random examples of taxation: the *curé* of Acqueville in the see in Coutances in 1783 paid a tax of 200 l. on an income of 500 l., or 40%; the *curé* of Bussière-Dunoise in Tulle in 1769 57 l. on 500 l., or 11.4%; the *curé* of Lonlai l'Abbaye in Le Mans in 1767 48 l. on 500 l., or 9.6%; the *curé* of Vergy in Dijon in 1767 72 l. on 500 l., or 14.4%; and a *curé* in Nîmes in 1754 16.7% of an undisclosed income.[72] In his excel-lent study of the Church's financial organization Lepointe provides some fiscal data based on archival sources for the city and environs of Le Mans; his figures are admittedly risky because contemporary re-venue estimates were unreliable. However, for what they are worth by way of example, we find the following data:

[71]  Talleyrand to M. de Miromesnil, garde de sceaux, September 14, 1782; *AN*, G8* 2618, no. 224.
[72]  Pierre de Vaissière, *Curés de campagne de l'ancienne France* (Paris, Editions Spes, 1932), p. 204.

| Year | Curés' Tax (ten curés of whom no more than four could have been congruistes) | Abbés' Tax | Religious Communities |
|---|---|---|---|
| | % | % | % |
| 1710 | 7.38 | 7.4 | 7.44 |
| 1736-37 average | 7.27 | 12.2 | 6.09 |
| after 1755 reforms | 6.73 | 10.8 | 7.35 |

Lapointe does note that Le Mans was a rich and well-administered diocese whose taxes were unusually light.[73]

According to the diocesan bureau of Reims, to raise a *don gratuit* in 1732 in lieu of a *capitation,* taxes were levied in the following manner in Clermontois: 13 *curés* paid an average tax of 18.85 livres, 5 *vicaires* 3.35 livres, and 12 holders of simple benefices 15.71 livres. Thus, even the diocesan bureau admitted that *curés* paid an average tax higher by some 3 livres than those possessing simple benefices.[74] The diocesan bureau of Tours in 1751 provided the following official statement: *curés* were taxed at 48 livres for 500 livres of income, or 9.6%; every increase or decrease of 50 livres of income meant an 8 livres change in the tax levied; thus, *curés à portion congrue,* receiving 300 livres, paid a tax of 5.33%. Other groups in Tours paid the following rates: [75]

| | % |
|---|---|
| Archbishop | 14.29 |
| Simple benefices | 33.33 |
| Communities and Chapters | 10 |
| Dignities with residency | 16.67 |

In his study of the *département* of Ille-et-Vilaine Rebillon found that *curés à portion congrue* paid a tax of 12 livres or 1.71% and *vicaires* a tax of 5.2 livres or 1.57%è. Other groups paid as follows:

| | % |
|---|---|
| Bishop of Rennes and capitular dignities | 5.66 |
| One Abbey | 13.72 |
| Two Abbeys | 4.41 |
| Ten Priories | 17.92 |
| Endowed *curés* | 5.73 |

These figures are based merely on the 1789-90 declarations made by the clergy to the comité ecclésiastique of the Constituent Assembly

[73]   Lepointe, *op. cit.,* Appendix VIII, pp. 333-339.
[74]   *AN,* G8 43, #7.
[75]   *AN,* G8* 2479, folios 172-173.

and include only half of the revenues of the *département* in question. Rebillon concludes: "In spite of inequalities which were often considerable and inexplicable, it does seem that a certain concern for equity in the assessment of *décimes* was manifested. The upper clergy was not systematically spared; the *congruistes* and most recently founded convents which sometimes performed some useful work were kindly treated...." [76] Finally, in the diocese of Bordeaux, after the 1755-60 reforms, the eight classes of tax-payers paid the following tax rates according to the diocesan archives:

| Class | 1771 | 1781 | Theoretical Rate |
|---|---|---|---|
| | % | % | % |
| I | 21.28 | 25.0 | 25 |
| II | 13.88 | 16.5 | 16.67 |
| Archbishop (II) | 16.22 | 16.67 | 16.67 |
| III | 14.0 | 14.29 | 15 |
| IV | 10.38 | 12.5 | 12.5 |
| V | 8.24 | 10.0 | 10.0 |
| VI | 6.90 | 8.33 | 8.33 |
| VII (*congruistes*) | 5.16 | 6.25 | 6.25 |
| VIII | 3.13 | 4.17 | 4.17 |

Evidently, in Bordeaux the theoretical rates of 1760 were not applied sufficiently as late as 1771; in 1781 they were virtually what they should have been — based on official evaluations of ecclesiastical revenue.[77]

These scattered data are too spotty to reveal very much about the overall 18th-Century trends in ecclesiastical taxation and in the proportions contributed by the poorest strata of the clergy. Excellent data, however, are available for the important archdiocese of Lyon which do reveal such trends. Since the independence of the various dioceses in fiscal arrangements prevents any absolute generalization based on one diocese, except for researching in every diocese of the Gallican Church, it seems reasonable to take one important diocese and to follow through its trends; with caution a generalized view can be hazarded. As just one of 116 dioceses with representation in

[76] Armand Rebillon, ed., *Département d'Ille-et-Vilaine. La Situation économique du clergé à veille de la Révolution* (Rennes, Imprimerie Oberthur, 1913), pp. LXXVII-LXXIX.
[77] Ernest Allain, "Un grand diocèse d'autrefois. Organisation administrative et financière", *Revue des questions historiques*, Vol. LVI (October, 1894), pp. 493-534.

the General Assembly of the clergy Lyon may seem less important than it actually was. A better way of viewing its relative importance is to note its share of the taxes raised by the clergy. According to the fiscal assessment of 1755, for every one million livres levied on the clergy the see of Lyon was to provide 19,605 livres, or just under 2%. In 1760 and 1765 Lyon was responsible for 2.14% of the clergy's *décimes*. Thus, fiscally Lyon comprised about 2% of the Church as represented in the fiscal organization of the Gallican clergy — a proportion more than twice its share as just one see in over a hundred.[78]

The eight-class system of 1760 was unquestionably a reform favorable to the *curés à portion congrue* of the archdiocese of Lyon. Figures for 1720, based on the records of the diocesan bureau for 1718, reveal that the average amount in *décimes* paid by *congruistes* was 51 livres annually. The *portion congrue* in 1720 was 300 livres; consequently, the *curés à portion congrue* was taxed at 17% — just over the one-sixth recommended by the General Assemblies. *Vicaires* paid an annual tax of 8 livres and occasionally 12 livres; at a contemporary income of 150 livres, the *vicaires* were taxed 5.3% and occasionally as high as 8%.[79] These figures are to be compared with those available after the 1755-60 reformation had been initiated, in this case of Lyon, the years 1760 and 1769. In 1760 we find that the average amount of *décimes* paid by the whole *curé* body was 8.20% and in 1769 8.25%; the breakdown of the *curés* into the different classes was as follows: [80]

| Class | Cures' Income | 1760 | 1769 | Theoretical Tax |
|---|---|---|---|---|
|  |  | % | % | % |
| II | over 1800 livres | 16.67 | 16.67 | 16.67 |
| III | 1501-1800 | 16.69 | 16.22 | 15 |
| IV | 1201-1500 | 12.52 | 12.26 | 12.5 |
| V | 901-1200 | 8.53 | 8.72 | 10.0 |
| VI | 601-900 | 7.09 | 7.01 | 8.33 |
| VII | 301-600 | 6.01 | 5.90 | 6.25 |
| VIII | 300 and below | 5.33 | 5.25 | 4.17 |
| Total |  | 8.20 | 8.25 |  |

[78]  *Archives de Rhône*, nouvelle côte, 7G 56, "Pièces générales", folios 122-127.
[79]  Calculated from *Archives du Rhône*, nouvelle côte, 7G 38°, "Etat des impositions des bénéfices du diocèse dressés par les commissaires nommés par l'Assemblée du clergé du diocèse pour 1720".
[80]  Calculated from *Archives du Rhône*, nouvelle côte, 6G 65°, "Rôles des revenus et impositions des bénéfices, 1760"; nouvelle côte, 6G 70°, "Extrait du rolle des décimes du clergé du diocèse 1744-69".

Since for 1720 our archival document gives us merely the amount of
*décimes* paid by all *curés* without indicating their incomes, we have
been able to derive the tax rates of only the *congruistes*, because
their incomes are known and they were identified on the tax roles as
*congruistes*. We may compare the 17% paid in 1720 by *congruistes* to
the rate they paid in 1760 and 1769. In 1760, when the *portion
congrue* was still 300 livres, the *congruistes* paid a *décime* rate of
5.33% — less than one-third of what they had paid in 1720. In 1765 it was
decreed that *congruistes* were to be taxed as belonging to Class VIII
only it they received no *novales* (tithes on newly cultivated land) and
little *casuels* in addition to their *portion congrue*; otherwise, diocesan
bureaux could increase the tax rate on income above 300 livres according to the rate for Class VII. In 1768 the *portion congrue was*
raised to 500 livres — placing the *congruistes* in Class VII: those of
Lyon in 1769 paid a tax of 5.90%. Furthermore, in 1769 — within
Class VII — the *curés* were permitted to earn up to 600 livres without
paying at a higher rate and could thus pay the same 5.90% on their
extra incomes, excluding the *novales* which were taken away from
them in exchange for the increase of their ordinary revenue to 500
livres.[81] Thus, the position of the *curés à portion congrue* in the archdiocese of Lyon improved as a result of the 1755-60 reforms. The
*vicaires* in 1760 were still earning 150 livres annually as in 1720, but
they paid a tax of only 4 livres or 3.7%; in 1769 after a raise in income
to 200 livres they retrained the tax of 4 livres which became a rate of
but 2%.

It is clear, then, that in the archdiocese of Lyon the *décime* rate
for *curés à portion congrue* diminished considerably as a result of the
1755-60 reforms. It becomes clear also that the more highly placed
ecclesiastics were constrained to pay a higher tax rate on their incomes. The question of accuracy of revenue declarations aside — a
question to be treated below with regard to a large number of bishoprics — the following partial figures are available for Lyon:

| Benefice | 1744 | 1755 | 1760 | 1769 |
|---|---|---|---|---|
| | % | % | % | % |
| Archbishop | 7.69 | 11.36 | 6.56 | 10.0 |
| Cathedral Chapter | 7.69 | 10.28 | 14.17 | 10.77 |
| Other Chapters | 7.69 | 6.58 | 7.92 | 7.54 |
| Group of Male Communities | 7.69 | 10.74 | 13.17 | 12.39 |

[81] Vaissière, *op. cit.*, pp. 167-168; 202.

In 1769 the revenues of the archdiocese of Lyon were officially listed as 1,580,020 livres, of which 200,013 or 12.66% were taken in *décimes*. The different groups of clerics paid the following rates:

|                                                      | %     |
|------------------------------------------------------|-------|
| Archbishop                                           | 10.0  |
| *Curés*                                              | 8.25  |
| *Vicaires*                                           | 2.0   |
| Chapters, Claustral Offices, Sacristies, Chapels     | 10.23 |
| Abbeys, Priories, Communities                        | 15.03 |
| Prebends                                             | 20.99 |
| Societies                                            | 11.19 |

It is evident that the archbishop did not really pay according to the eight-class system, for with a declared income of 60,000 livres in 1769 he paid but 10% in *décimes*; however, he belonged to Class II and properly should have paid 16.67%. If his declared income of 60,000 livres concealed still more revenues, he, in effect, paid less than 10%. We may conclude from this that while the archbishop in the course of the century was constrained to be taxed at a higher rate and the *curés* at a lower rate, he unlike them was not really closely subjected to the 1760 reform. Furthermore, while the *curés à portion congrue* benefited from the 1760 reform substantially, the increase of their *portion congrue* to 500 livres in 1768 and to 700 livres in 1786 placed them each time in a higher tax class. They graduated from a theoretical tax of 4.17% at the inauguration of the system, to 6.25% in 1768, and to 8.33% in 1786. The *curés à portion congrue* in the see of Lyon paid 5.33% in 1760, 5.90% in 1769, and in 1786 in Class VI they probably paid something between 7.01% and 8.33%. The *congruistes* all over France felt that their income rise had been wiped out by increased taxes, and the government was forced to explain that a higher income necessarily demanded a higher tax rate.[82] Furthermore, some *curés* who were *congruistes* received large additional revenues, and the government had already held that the 60-livre limit on *décimes* applied only to the *portion congrue* and not to additional income. For this reason some *congruistes* did pay *décimes* exceeding the limit of 60 livres.[83] Finally, although the *curés* were being treated with in-

---

[82]   *AN*, G8* 2455, p. 543. From the "Recueil des conférences du conseil du clergé pour l'année 1770", concerning a letter sent by the *agents généraux* to an official of Chenerailles, December 28, 1770.

[83]   From the deliberations of the conseil du clergé concerning the payment of décimes to the bureau of Avranches, August 28, 1747, *AN*, G8* 2785, folio 191.

creasing fairness in the 18th Century, the success of some reforms made existing inequities even more intolerable. And the government's refusal to reform the diocesan bureaux in general after having reformed the bureau of Troyes — what Préclin calls the "check" of the *curés'* success — compounded the frustrations of the *curés* and led to their open disobedience and revolt. Here as with other abuses of the Old Régime, it was less intolerable evil than the reasonable hope for reform and its partial victories which led to more violent dissatisfaction.

In seeking to determine what tax rate the bishops of the Gallican Church paid — that is, what proportion of their *real* revenue they were taxed — of invaluable assistance is a document in the Archives nationales first used by Chevaillier. The document entitled "Etat des revenus des bénéfices consistoriaux du royaume suivant les économats" lists the revenues and *décimes* of the large number of sees which fell under royal administration owing to the death of their bishops; they range from as early as 1721 until 1766. In managing vacant sees the government knew exactly the amount of income received by the bishops; the figures given by the *économat* were as free from error or fraud as possible.[84] Furthermore, so reliable were its figures that the Assemblies of the clergy, seeking a fiscal reorganization in the 1750's, informed itself about the true level of ecclesiastical revenue from this source. Of course, only bishoprics and other benefices in the royal gift were included. Thus, apart from whether the Assemblies utilized these figures honestly, their reliability was unquestionable.[85]

Comparing the revenue figures of the *économat* with those officially recognized by the Assemblies of the clergy in assessing taxes, Chevaillier found that the assessment was based on a fairly accurate statement of revenue. In the period 1750-60 for the vacated sees, the official assessment compared as follows with the real revenue listed by the *économat*:

[84]    R. Chevaillier, "Un Document sur la fortune du haut clergé au XVIIIᵉ siècle", *Bulletin de la Société d'histoire moderne*, April-May, 1921, pp. 65-66.
[85]    *Ibid.*, p. 75.

| See | Year | Official Assessment | Economat |
|---|---|---|---|
| Senlis | 1754 | 24,000 | 32,500 |
| Tours | 1750 | 35,000 | 54,000 |
| Blois | 1753 | 32,500 | 33,500 |
| Bayeux | 1753 | 70,000 | 65,000 |
| Castres | 1752 | 54,000 | 54,200 |
| Lombez | 1751 | 40,000 | 41,000 |
| Toulouse | 1752 | 90,000 | 107,318 |
| Angoulême | 1753 | 19,000 | 20,000 |
| Luçon | 1758 | 28,000 | 24,900 |
| Total | | 392,500 | 432,418 |

Thus the sees of Senlis, Tours, and Toulouse were under-evaluated fairly heavily, the Assembly having recognized only 76.88% of their real incomes. However, these nine sees as a unit were recognized as being worth 90.77% of their actual value.[86] Comparing the *décimes* paid by the bishops whose sees fell vacant in this period Chevaillier found that before 1755 the following was true:

| Tax Rate Paid | Number of Sees | Percentage of Total |
|---|---|---|
| | | % |
| More than 1/10 | 32 | 32.65 |
| 1/10 to 1/15 | 24 | 24.49 |
| 1/15 to 1/20 | 18 | 18.37 |
| 1/20 to 1/30 | 15 | 15.31 |
| 1/30 to 1/50 | 7 | 7.14 |
| Under 1/50 | 2 | 2.04 |
| | 98 | |

After the 1755 reforms the bishops whose sees fell vacant paid as follows:

| Tax Rate Paid | Number of Sees | Percentage of Total |
|---|---|---|
| | | % |
| More than 1/10 | 16 | 41.03 |
| 1/10 to 1/15 | 13 | 33.33 |
| 1/15 to 1/20 | 6 | 15.38 |
| Under 1/20 | 4 | 10.26 |
| | 39 | |

[86]   *Ibid.,* p. 76.

Using the same documents as Chevaillier.[87] I find that a more accurate comparison yields these results:

| Tax Rate Paid | Before 1755 | | 1755 and After | |
|---|---|---|---|---|
| | # | % | # | % |
| More than 1/10 (over 10%) | 17 | 17.35 | 18 | 34.62 |
| 1/10 to 1/15 (10% to 6.67%) | 28 | 28.57 | 12 | 23.08 |
| 1/15 to 1/20 (6.67% to 5%) | 21 | 21.43 | 14 | 26.92 |
| 1/20 to 1/30 (5% to 3.33%) | 18 | 18.37 | 6 | 11.54 |
| 1/30 to 1/50 (3.33% to 2%) | 11 | 11.22 | 2 | 3.85 |
| Under 1/50 (under 2%) | 3 | 3.06 | — | — |
| | 98 | | 52 | |

From the above it becomes clear that the bishops were taxed at a higher rate after the reforms of 1755-60 than before: the average tax before 1755 was 7.57% compared to 9.61% afterwards.[88]

It was unquestionably the reforms of 1755-60 which raised the bishops' share of the *décimes*. However, further study of the 29 sees which fell vacant in the period 1761-66 for which we have *économat* revenue figures, reveals that 28 of these 29 sees paid less than the rate indicated by the eight-class system — from as little as 1.20% less to a high of 11.33% less. The reduction by class was as follows:

| | | % |
|---|---|---|
| Class II: | 13 sees | —4.79 |
| Class III: | 2 sees | —5.25 |
| Class IV: | 6 sees | —5.59 |
| Class V: | 5 sees | —4.09 |
| Class VI: | 2 sees | —2.03 |
| Class VII: | 1 see | +4.82 |

The richest sees thus benefited most from the failure to apply the system vigorously: Coutances with an income of 40,114 livres paid 11.33% less; Auxerre with 49,028 livres 10.55% less; Noyon with 41,000 livres 7.98% less. The see of Vence with but 7,230 livres in revenue paid 4.82% above what its membership in Class VII indicated. If Chevaillier is correct in his contention that in the mid 18th Century the assessments of bishops' revenues were roughly equal to their real value as indicated by the *économat*, one can only conclude that there was no attempt really to apply the tax reform to the revenues of the bishops.

[87] AN, G8* 552, "Etat des revenus des bénéfices consistoriaux du royaume suivant les économats". *Ibid.*, V7 77-88, "Commissions extraordinaires du conseil: bureau des économats".
[88] See Appendix V for a list of the increases by bishopric.

Finally, if we compare the tax rate paid by the bishops listed in the *économat* with that paid by the *congruistes* of Lyon, we find that whereas before the reform the *congruistes* of Lyon paid *décimes* at the rate of 17%, the bishops paid only about 7.57%. After the reform, the Lyonnais *congruistes* paid much less, but not so much less than the bishops: 5%-6% compared with about 9.61% for the bishops. And the *curés à portion congrue* were receiving each less than 1% of the incomes of the bishops!

# VI

## ENGLAND: THE EPISCOPAL CORPORATION: CONVOCATION AND TAXATION

The Anglican equivalent of the General Assembly of the Gallican clergy was the Convocation of the Church of England. There were in England two Convocations: the Convocation of Canterbury under the presidency of the archbishop of Canterbury and including representatives from the twenty-two dioceses of the Southern Province; and the smaller Convocation of York under the presidency of the archbishop of York and including representatives from the four sees of the Northern Province.[1] The two assemblies, thus, were provincial assemblies, but the overweening importance of the Southern Province gave it the exclusive status of the national Convocation. The Convocation of Canterbury was a bicameral body: an upper house of twenty-two bishops and a lower house of 145 clergymen, among whom were two proctors representing the parochial clergy of each diocese, twenty-four capitular proctors, and seventy-seven minor dignitaries. The Convocation of York was unicameral and included the four bishops, thirty-one representatives of the parochial clergy, seven capitular proctors, and thirteen minor dignitaries — or fifty-five members in all. The proctors of the parochial and capitular clergy were elected by all the beneficed clergymen in the dioceses. To speak of Convocation in the period from the Restoration to the Age of Reform is to spreak only of the Canterbury Convocation, and of that only until 1717, the year of its suspension.

Because the business of Convocation was as much the fiscal support of the Crown as its own spiritual and temporal affairs, Convocation traditionally had met contemporaneously with every new Parliament. Before 1533 the archbishop of Canterbury had had the right to summon Convocation at his pleasure, but with the Reformation he lost all

---

[1] Although a part of the Province of York since the 16th Century, the see of Sodor and Man does not appear to have been represented in the Northern Convocation.

initiative in this area to the Crown. According to Sir Edward Coke's correct exposition of the limitations of Convocation, it could neither assemble, enact canons, nor execute them without royal assent; nor could it execute upon royal approval any canons which violated royal prerogatives, the common law, statutory law, or immemorial custom.[2] The archbishop did, nonetheless, retain the right to have his consent to the canons of Convocation made indispensable.[3] Like the Gallican General Assemblies the Anglican Convocation was assembled solely at the monarch's pleasure and proceeded to his business as directed.[4]

The representation of the clergy in Parliament — bishops and abbots in the House of Lords before the Reformation, and bishops alone afterwards — traditionally had not constituted a third estate of the realm alongside lords and commons. In medieval England the bishops sitting in the upper house of Parliament were regarded to be there by virtue of their baronial tenure. In 1295 Edward I had sought to create a Parliament of three estates by summoning higher and lower ecclesiastics alike to vote taxes in Parliament. The clergy, however, had preferred to tax itself separately in Convocation, and its wish had been honored. And while the clergy continued to be included in the traditional writs for the meeting of Parliament, except for slight lower clergy attendance in Parliament in the 14th Century, the clergy was not represented in Parliament.[5] Although in creating six new dioceses, with six additional episcopal seats in the House of Lords, Henry VIII had made no pretense that their non-existent baronial tenures were the cause of representation, still the bishops in Parliament did not represent the clergy, and Parliament as a whole did not represent it until after the Restoration. Only Convocation was the national assembly of the Anglican clergy.

Just as in France there developed controversy concerning the competence and authority of the General Assemblies of the clergy, so also in England was the Convocation a source of controversy. In France,

[2] Sir Robert Phillimore, *The Ecclesiastical Law of the Church of England* (London, Henry Sweet, 1873), Vol. II, p. 1929.
[3] Ollard and Crosse, *op. cit.*, p. 141.
[4] Charles II ordered the Northern Convocation to convene with an authorization "... to conferr, debate, treat, consider, consult, and agree of and upon such other points, matters, and things, as we from time to time should deliver ... unto you in writing under our signe Manuall or privy signett to be debated ... Wee do hereby authorize and require that you review ...", etc. Charles II to the archbishop of York, November 22, 1661. *The Records of the Northern Convocation* (= *The Publications of the Surtees Society, Durham*, CXIII) (1906), p. 315.
[5] Ollard and Crosse, *op. cit.*, p. 448.

with the purging of the Jansenists from the ecclesiastical hierarchy, the conflict over ecclesiastical independence became polarized into Parlements against bishops, with the royal government in the middle, trying to balance the one against the other. Because in England, however, the upper and lower clergy were deeply divided over low and high churchmanship and the Convocation was bicameral, the conflict over ecclesiastical independence took on the appearance of an intra-ecclesiastical feud – between the champions of ecclesiastical independence in the lower house of Convocation and the Whigs on the bench of bishops and in government and Parliament. During the Convocation controversy, roughly from 1689 until the end of Convocation in 1717, it was the lower clergy through its spokesmen in Convocation, and not the episcopate, which pressed for ecclesiastical independence. The result was different significantly from the French pattern of episcopate against magistracy.

Basically, the Convocation controversy in England was fought over the attempt of the Whig ministries and the bishops to lighten disabilities pressing down upon dissenters and sometimes to propagate latitudinarian views in theology and Church government. The battle developed at the beginning of King William's reign when the lower house of Convocation was able to obstruct the ministry's Parliamentary bill for the Comprehension of dissenters in the Church Establishment. The obstructionist tactics of the lower house of the clergy and its political partisanship on behalf of the Tories led King William to refuse to permit any new Convocation to assemble until 1701. This long delay sparked the pamphleteering of Francis Attersbury who became the champion of Tory clericalism. It was his propagandistic activity on behalf of the recalling of Convocation which made it politically inadvisable for the government to keep it in adjournment *sine die*.[6]

Atterbury shared fully the high Tory view that in the hands of Whig bishops and under a Whig ministry the Church of England was "in danger". He described the Church as besieged by its foes:

She has perhaps the least influence of any Church upon earth, by virtue of that discipline and authority which she is permitted to exercise; and no method hath been left unattempted to make her loose the hold she had in the affections and reverence of the people. That which supports her under these disadvantages is, the *incapacity* that lies on her enemies as to *places*

---

[6]   H. C. Beeching, *Francis Atterbury* (London, Pitman, 1909), pp. 123-124.

*and power* [that is, the Test Act]. Let this incapacity be ever removed, she is from that moment at mercy, and can subsist only . . . by miracle.[7]

Atterbury conceived of the Anglican clergy as a separate corporate order which expressed itself in Convocation. By deliberately confusing Edward I's summoning of clerics to Parliament with the prior institution of Convocation — a contention ably refuted by Edmund Gibson [8] — Atterbury sought to make Convocation an indispensable type of parliament for the ecclesiastical subjects of the Crown, a Church parliament whose two houses would parallel in mutual independence the two houses of Parliament. A preoccupation with the clerical *Order* characterized his activity on behalf of Convocation; he described himself as

. . . push'd on by an Hearty concern for the Interests of Religion, and of my Order (as far as the Latter of these is subservient to the Former), and by an Eager Desire of going somewhat towards supporting the Good Old Constitution I live under. . . .[9]

The opposition of the Whig bishops to his Tory sentiments led Atterbury to exalt the power of the lower clergy — a position in theory decidedly un-Tory but politically necessary. Having to admit that Henry VIII's ecclesiastical legislation indeed had curtailed ecclesiastical independence, Atterbury decided that such curtailment consisted solely in having deprived the archbishop of Canterbury of the right to summon Convocation at his pleasure. The archbishop, thereafter, required a royal writ. However, once licensed to convene, the clergy was free to discuss whatever it deemed necessary. Thus the Reformation had, in his view, only limited the powers of the archbishop — not those of the clergy.[10] He exalted an ecclesiastical independence which, given the Whiggery of the episcopate, meant nothing short of a presbyterian-like co-sovereignty of the lower clergy with the episcopate in the governance of the Church of England.

---

[7]  "Reflections on a late scandalous Report about the Repeal of the Test Act", *The Epistolary Corespondence, Visitation Charges, Speeches, and Miscellanies of the Right Reverend Francis Atterbury, D.D., Lord Bishop of Rochester* (London, J. Nichols, 1783-84), Vol. II, p. 94.

[8]  *Synodus Anglicana*, ed. by *Edward Cardwell* (Oxford, University Press, 1854); first published in 1702. It is Phillimore's view that Gibson's historical study of Convocation was the best ever made; Phillimore, *op. cit.*, Vol. II, p. 1926.

[9]  Francis Atterbury, *The Rights, Powers, and Privileges of an English Convocation* (London, Tho. Bennet, 2nd edition, 1701), p. iv.

[10]  *Ibid.*, pp. 130-131.

Above all, Atterbury emphasized that Convocation was a *parliamentary* Assembly. His endeavors were designed to demonstrate

... that the Inferior Clergy, tho' meeting and consulting apart from the Parliament, yet were still reckon'd to belong to it, and to be (in some sense; and to some Purposes) a Member of it; and together with the Prelates of the Upper House to compose (not indeed one of the Three Estates of Parliament, but however) an *Estate of the Realm*, assembling joyntly with the Parliament, and oblig'd by the Rules of our Constitution to attend always upon it.[11]

Characteristic of the 1788 position of the Gallican episcopate was Atterbury's protestation that his aim was not a revival of clerical privileges and preeminence but rather an attempt to insure the liberty of all. He warned the laity that an assault upon the traditional rights of Convocation concerned all Englishmen, for it could lead to an assault upon Parliament itself. Presupposing the existence, present or future, of a royal despotism which would seek to destroy the liberties of the different orders of the realm, he warned: "... If Slavery be once establisht in the Church, it will quickly spread it self into the State...."[12]

The failure of the English Convocation to survice under the 18th-Century Hanoverians meant, of course, that thereafter Parliament was to be the sole arena of ecclesiastical combat. This development may be seen as a small part of the gradual growth of parliamentary supremacy from 1688 until the reign of Victoria. It must be noted, however that as members of the House of Lords the archbishops and bishops of the Anglican Church were able to oversee their interests in Parliament when they could no longer do so in Convocation. The prelates comprised an important bloc in the Upper House, and as much as they were inclined to be slavishly subservient to their political patrons, where the welfare of the Church was involved they did dare to manifest a certain independence of the ministry.[13] As a united bloc in questions affecting the Church the spiritual lords, in union with like-minded temporal peers, could defeat many governmental bills. Whether the issue in question was the Quakers' Tithe Bill of 1736, the Mortmain Bill of the same year, the Dissenters' Relief Bill of 1772, or the measures of the Age of Reform for Catholic emancipation and the

[11]   *Ibid.*, p. 63.
[12]   *Ibid.*, pp. x; 63.
[13]   A. S. Turberville, *The House of Lords in the XVIIIth Century* (Oxford, Clarendon Press, 1927), p. 425.

reform of the Irish Church, the bishops did in Parliament what they would have done in Convocation: they defended their ecclesiastical interests. Indeed, Gibson's break with Walpole stemmed largely from the former's leadership of a national movement to defeat the Quakers' Tithe Bill. Lord Hervey regarded the activities of Gibson and his fellow bishops to defeat this measure as little short of seditious; [14] he, at least, didn't feel that the lack of Convocation was hindering ecclesiastical independence sufficiently.

If the bishops were to a certain extent able to compensate for the loss of Convocation by political participation in the House of Lords, many of them clearly saw this as insufficient. Gibson deplored the fact that there were certain advantages to Convocation which had been lost, in spite of its past record of indiscipline.[15] Typically, however, 18th-Century bishops were cautious about openly voicing their disapproval of the end of Convocation. Wake's position in 1697 was a model of smug satisfaction with the best of all possible Church establishments:

When a national church is once thoroughly established, and neither needs any further laws to be made for the enforcing of its discipline; or any new confessions to be framed for the security of its doctrine; when its liturgy and other offices are fixed and stated; and there is so far from being any need of altering or improving any of these, that it is thought a crime but even to suppose that it is possible to improve them, or to make any alterations in them but for the worse; then I cannot imagine, until something arises to unsettle such a constitution, what a convocation could have to meet about.[16]

The classic view of the advantages and disadvantages of Convocation, however, was stated by Richard Hurd later in the 18th Century. His observations on the Convocation controversy, before his elevation to the episcopate, revealed the conflict in the minds of good Hanoverian churchmen between their devotion to the State and their regard for the Church:

I could wish that Atterbury had considered the *expediency* of this practice [of Convocation], as well as the *right*. There is no doubt but the Church has lost very much of her dignity and authority, by this disuse of her Convocations; and, by this means, Religion itself may have been considerably disserved. But, in other respects, I have not light enough at present to determine for myself, whether these Church Synods would be of

14   Sykes, *Edmund Gibson* ..., pp. 168-173.
15   Sykes, *From Sheldon to Secker*, p. 56.
16   William Wake, *The Authority of Christian Princes*, pp. 277-278, cited in Sykes, *Church and State* ..., p. 312.

all the benefit to Religion, which Dr. Atterbury supposes. . . . It might be something difficult to say, whether the mischiefs or the advantages be greater. . . . I see there are some material benefits resulting from these Councils; the principal of which, as I imagine, is, that any *abuse* or *grievance*, which it concerned the Ecclesiastical State to take notice of, might be represented with more weight and effect to the Legislature. But then, on the other hand, have not the Bishops authority enough to regulate all material disorders within their Dioceses? Or, if they have not, does not their seat in Parliament and the easy opportunity they have of meeting and conferring together every year during the Session of Parliament, enable them to consult and provide for the rectifying of all disorders, either by procuring new laws, or more effectually enforcing old ones? [17]

Warburton agreed substantially with Hurd's position on Convocation, himself observing that indeed the right of Convocation was a matter quite separate from its expediency.[18] With such views, the 18th Century bishops had to make the most of their representation in the House of Lords. However, in overseeing the Church's welfare in the Parliament rather than in a Convocation, the bishops were integrated into the political life of the kingdom and lost their separate corporate identity. Herein lies the significance of the suspension of Convocation.

If the immediate causes of the almost permanent suspension of Convocation were the obstructionist tactics and political partisanship of its lower house — its attack on Comprehension, its support of Sacheverell, and its assault upon the theories of Hoadly, the royal favorite — the reason Convocation could be dispensed with was its abandonment in 1664 of separate ecclesiastical taxation. When the main reason for tolerating Convocation had been removed, its demise was only a matter of time and temperament. Atterbury had recognized this rather early, while Convocation yet drew breath. He noted that the clergy generally had coupled its granting of taxes with petitions for redress of its grievances.

Now they have left off to Tax themselves, they must no longer draw Occasions of Relief from the Wants of the Crown but from the Goodness and Justice of Him that wears it. It will be for the Honour of a Reign, founded in the Liberties of a People, and secur'd by maintaining 'em to suffer All Bodies of Men to enjoy their Rights, tho' they give nothing for it. . . .[19]

The irreversible limitation on the clergy's independence deriving from its loss of fiscal autonomy was for Atterbury unfortunate. But

[17]    Richard Hurd to William Warburton, no date, 1760, letter CXLIV, in Warburton, *op. cit.*, pp. 310-312.
[18]    Warburton to Hurd, October 14, 1760, letter CXLV, *ibid.*, p. 313.
[19]    Atterbury, *op. cit.*, p. 133.

he did not permit himself to believe it had sounded the necessary death knell of ecclesiastical assemblies. Accepting the fact that the fiscal autonomy and redressive petitioning of the clergy were forever lost, he nonetheless educed an added justification of Convocation:

But should the Clergy have no Representation, no Complaints to make to the King and Parliament, yet they themselves may be complain'd of to either; and it is fit they should be ready, to give answer to such Complaints. All other Bodies and Communities of Men, if any thing be mov'd in Parliament to their Prejudice, can immediately Assemble and Confer together, and lay before their Superiors the Consequences of it, as far as their Particular Interests are concern'd: The Clergy alone has no such Liberty or Opportunity, if their Parliamentary Assemblies [that is, Convocations] are not observed; and are, in this respect, therefore, in worse condition than the Pettiest Company, or Corporation in the Kingdom.[20]

Thus, the work of Atterbury on behalf of Convocation was the effort to establish the clergy as a separate corporate estate with its own rights and privileges — with the necessary restraint that much of previous ecclesiastical power in the face of public opinion, Whig intransigeance, and dynastic necessities, could never be regained. Atterbury would not have been too out of place in a General Assembly of the Gallican clergy. The significant difference between his predicament and that of the French episcopate, however, was, first, that with the demise of Convocation early in the 18th Century his hopes and those of his party were shattered, and, secondly, that Whig political control of the nomination of English bishops resulted in his movement's being one primarily of the lower clergy. The Anglican bishops, thus, did not strive for the corporate independence desired by Atterbury and the Tory clergy. The defeat of ecclesiastical independence in England and its non-episcopal leadership marked it off from the French clergy's success in holding on to a large measure of ecclesiastical independence. The ultimate cause of this divergence had undoubtedly been the Tudor Reformation; but the more immediate cause was the end of ecclesiastical taxation in 1664.

With the Restoration of the Anglican Church, also restored was its right to tax itself in supporting the Crown. Yet within but a few years the bishops agreed, without fanfare, to abandon this important privilege and submit the clergy to the taxes voted by Parliament. Very little direct evidence of the nature of this ecclesiastical concession exists, but this very fact is of greatest significance: a step which

[20]    *Ibid.*, pp. 134-135.

sounded the death knell of Convocation and integrated the clergy fully into the political life of the kingdom was taken with a perhaps characteristically English lack of excitement. The absence of contemporary comment on this essentially reformist measure and the informal and semi-private arrangements which produced it were indicative of English piece-meal reform. The lack of any opposition on the part of the bishops contrasted remarkably with the resolute position of French bishops, for whom the abolition of ecclesiastical fiscal autonomy seemed to mean the abolition of religion itself. The historian can almost applaud the lack of evidence concerning the *tax deal* of 1664; here, the void speaks more eloquently than a mass of documents.

Whatever contemporary comment on the clergy's abandonment of its fiscal autonomy existed generally held that the clergy had expected thereby to have its burden lightened; historians have followed suit. Gilbert Burnet wrote:

... The rule of subsidies being so high on the clergy, they had submitted to be taxed by the house of commons ever since the year 1665, though no memorials were left to inform us how that matter was consented to so generally, that no opposition of any sort was made to it. . . .

In a footnote to Burnet's account Speaker Onslow observed that the tax deal was arranged verbally between Archbishop Sheldon and Lord Chancellor Clarendon and tacitly accepted by the clergy in the hope of lightening its tax burden. As a result, all clerics who were neither bishops nor peers acquired the right to vote for Members of the House of Commons.[21]

An early 18th-Century historian of the Church, in discussing the Sheldon-Clarendon arrangements, recorded that the bishops and the rest of the clergy

... began to think this customary Method of taxing themselves, somewhat burthensome. They thought 'tis possible, the Expectations of the Court might be set too high upon them this way; and that the *Commons* were often discontented, unless they overcharg'd themselves and swell'd their Subsidies beyond a reasonable Proportion. How well these Jealousies were founded, I shall not examine. But 'tis supposed, the being apprehensive of such Inconveniences, brought Archbishop *Sheldon* and some other leading Prelates, into a Concert with the Lord Chancellor *Hide*, the Lord Treasurer,

[21] *Bishop Burnet's History of His Own Time*, Vol. IV, pp. 520-521. An act of 10 Anne, ch. 23, referred to ecclesiastical benefices as freeholds sufficient for conferring the franchise on their incumbents. *The Statutes at Large* (London, 1769), Vol. IV, p. 568.

and some others of the Ministry. . . . And to encourage their Assent to this Cession, two of their four *Subsidies* were to be remitted. . . .[22]

It is important to note that the clergy's apparent expectation that common taxation would weigh less heavily upon it than separate ecclesiastical taxation was not just a theoretical possibility. Under the system of taxation resorted to during the Interregnum the clergy had been taxed in common with the laity, and the former had indeed found its burden less onerous than under separate taxation.[23]

A letter to Archbishop Sheldon from John Hackett, bishop of Lichfield, at the time of the tax deal reveals that Sheldon had apparently invited his colleagues on the bench of bishops to offer their advice on the arrangements he was about to conclude with Clarendon. As evidence of what motivated the clergy in this silently executed reform the letter is invaluable and deserves quotation almost in full.

Your Grace is pleased to command my opinion how the clergie at the present should behave themselves if levyes of money should be raised upon us by others and not by ourselves in Convocation. I being ignorant in what manner the tax (which must be a great one) shall be raised, shall shoot in the dark, yet in obedience to your Grace I have presumed to deliver my conceptions. If the old way of subsidies be thought on by the house of Commons (for the supply of monies must be derived from them) the Exchequer Rolls do direct the imposing of the Clergy Subsidies: but that way will be frivolous at this Season. A subsidy was a sum of money 80 years since: now the prices of all things being so greatly enhanced subsidies are but small aids to the Kings treasure. The monthly tax upon land is farr the best way by experience and then our lands are subject to such proportions as Lay Commissioners think fitt, unless some restriction be inserted in the Act, and some of our Body be put in in all Counties for Assessors. This way I know is precondemn'd by an Act of Parliamt, but it is fit to be consider'd again. . . . If one large sum in the lump be exacted of the Clergy (as sometimes it hath been) I conceive better to be named by others than by ourselves for this reason. For let us name what we will, some ill willers will think it is not enough, but it we submit to that which is demanded, the mouth of detraction is stopt, since we do as much as is demanded. In all the Kings wants the Clergy should shew themselves freehearted and liberal because the Church is defended in the Kingdome, but in this [Dutch] warr wherein we of Staffordshire hear that the most illustrious Duke of York will adventure his person . . . his Grace . . . being so great and open a Patron to the Establisht Church of England, the Clergy must be very forward to

[22] Jeremy Collier, *An Ecclesiastical History of Great Britain* (London, Samuel Keble, 1708-14), Vol. II, p. 893.

[23] Stephen Dowell, *A History of Taxation and Taxes in England* (London, Longmans, Green, 2nd edition, 1888), Vol. II, p. 30.

advance his enterprises which will appear the more, when . . . we are willing to wave customs and privileges belonging to us.[24]

It is clear that at least for the bishop of Lichfield the expectation of a lower ecclesiastical tax burden through the inclusion of the clergy in common taxation was not the only motive for such willing acquiescence in the tax reform. He seems to have had a very healthy feeling that whether the clergy through its fiscal autonomy paid more or less than the laity, its separate status and privileges could only do it harm in the affections of the Parliament and the people. He also saw the need for a strong Church-State alliance. The Anglican bishops thus emerged as far less devoted — if at all — to the separate corporate identity of the clerical estate than the French prelates. The motive of the Parliament was not difficult to see. The clergy's surrender of its tax privileges correspondingly increased the position of Parliament which, in the reign of Charles II, was acquiring a monopoly in providing the king with revenue. No longer could the king, whether a despot or not, find an independent source of supply in the clergy's Convocation. The spectacle in Charles I's day of Convocation willingly granting the "tyrant" taxes while Parliament refused him any could never recur.[25] The contributions which the clergy made to Charles I in 1639 in the form of subsidies and benevolences were deemed violations of the Petition of Right by the Parliament.[26]

Before the Puritan Revolution the Anglican clergy had indeed borne a heavier tax burden than the laity. The clergy's direct taxes included first fruits, tenths, and subsidies. The first fruits and tenths had before the Reformation been internal ecclesiastical levies; with Henry VIII's break with Rome they had become regular contributions to the Crown. Since the Reformation, therefore, separate ecclesiastical taxation in England, unlike in France, had not constituted taxation for internal use.[27] The first fruits and tenths went directly and automatically to the king, where in France the former (annates) went to Rome and the tenths (décimes) for the internal use of the clergy. Since the ecclesiastical subsidy was paid at the rate of 4 s. on each pound of income remaining after the payment of tenths — totalling 5 s.

[24]   Bishop Hackett to Archbishop Sheldon, October 29, 1664; Bodleian Ms. Tanner 47, f. 201; reprinted in H. N. Mukerjee, "Parliamentary Taxation of the Clergy", Notes and Queries, Vol. CLXVI (January 20, 1934), p. 41.
[25]   William Henry Hutton, The English Church from the Accession of Charles I to the Death of Anne (London, Macmillan, 1903), p. 199.
[26]   Christopher Hill, Economic Problems of the Church . . ., pp. 195-196.
[27]   Ibid., p. 195.

7d. on each pound — there was nothing about it resembling a free gift. Thus the Anglican clergy did not enjoy immunity from taxes; rather, it paid tenths directly to the Crown and a subsidy which was levied at a fixed rate. All ecclesiastical taxation meant in England was the separate voting of taxes — a privilege far inferior to that of the French clergy.

The Anglican clergy paid first fruits and tenths on all vicarages worth £ 10 or more and on all rectories worth £ 6 13 s. 4d. or more, as valued in the Tudor *Valor Ecclesiasticus*. Thereby almost 3000 vicarages and rectories were exempt, in addition to university estates and the poor curates. The listings of the *Valor Ecclesiasticus* were not only obsolete because of the Price Revolution, but the provision that the value of vicarages (which, by definition, owned only a part of the tithes) be computed as if the great tithes appropriated by their rectors still belonged to them meant that vicarages over £ 10 paid as much as if they had been rectories. Thus, the middle clergy paid the stiffest taxes. In addition, benefices in corn-growing areas and those depending on income in kind were able to avoid taxation on the income added to their former revenues by economic growth, while those benefices dependent on money incomes were taxed more severely.[28]

The clergy were exempt from Parliamentary tenths and fifteenths, but their own tenths paid to the Crown offset this advantage. The clergy and laity paid their separate subsidies at the same rate. And clergy and laity alike paid other direct taxes such as shipmoney, forced loans, and benevolences, as they did also the indirect customs and excise taxes. Thus the clergy and laity paid virtually all taxes at the same rate. But the clergy, in fact, paid a higher percentage of their *real* income than the laity. In 1628 five lay subsidies voted by Parliament netted £ 275,000 while five clerical subsidies netted £ 94,000. Estimating the ecclesiastical population at .2% of the total, Hill finds that this .2% paid 25% of that year's principal direct tax — the subsidy.[29] If the clergy paid the subsidy at the same rate as the laity

---

[28]   *Ibid.*, pp. 188-190; 194.
[29]   *Ibid.*, p. 192. From 1610-1635 the sums raised by the ecclesiastical subsidies reached £ 290,448 or about £ 11,618 yearly; the laity's contribution through the subsidy in the period 1621-1628 was £ 750,104 or £ 93,763 yearly. Thus the clergy, but .2% of the population, paid about 11% of the subsidy spread out over several years in the early Stuart period. Frederick C. Dietz, *English Public Finance 1558-1641* (New York, Century, 1932), p. 396. In the period from the reign of Queen Elizabeth to the Long Parliament, the yield from lay subsidies

and at the same time paid a percentage of the total subsidy higher than its proportion of the population, one must conclude either that the clergy owned more property, per capita, than the laity or that the evaluation of lay wealth was lower than that of ecclesiastical wealth. As the first possibility, in the light of the dissolution of the monasteries, is clearly absurd, the only conclusion to be drawn is that the clergy's property, relative to the laity's property, was over-assessed. Actually, neither clergy nor laity was correctly assessed, but lay wealth was increasing more rapidly than ecclesiastical wealth and laymen escaped paying taxes on the increased revenue.[30] The clergy had reason to feel its separate taxation an inconvenience and a burden.

The financial needs of the Parliamentary and Cromwellian regimes necessitated a basic change in the pattern of direct taxation of the laity. The direct tax on income was the subsidy, and it was levied ordinarily at the rate of 4 s. per pound on the income of landowners and office-holders, and at the rate of 2 s. 8d. per pound on the net capital or movables of merchants, artisans, and tenant farmers.[31] The Puritan Revolution blurred the traditional distinction between taxes voted for the life of each monarch and those extraordinary grants voted as necessity demanded; during the Interregnum the direct taxes became regularly collected monthly assessments.[32] The Restoration period saw various taxing experiments employed, but the Act of 1693 established a land tax, the basic 18th-Century direct tax. Not only did the Restoration Parliaments maintain many of the fiscal expedients of the Rebellion, but the virtually last non-Parliamentary source of royal revenue was stopped up. In 1661 the Court of Wards was abolished, the king having to forego large fees from wardships, licenses on alienation of property, purveyance, respite of hommage, and other forms of dues from those who held land directly of the Crown. The abolition of this source of non-Parliamentary revenue not only constituted an augmentation of Parliamentary fiscal power; it must also be seen in the context of an increase in the power of the landed classes following the Restoration. The Court of Wards had not

---

declined steadily while ecclesiastical subsidies steadily yielded more. The gentry was better able to conceal its true revenues than was the clergy. *Ibid.*, p. 393.

[30] Hill, *op. cit.*, p. 193.

[31] William Kennedy, *English Taxation 1640-1799* (London, G. Bell, 1913), pp. 18-19.

[32] W. R. Ward, *The English Land Tax in the Eighteenth Century* (Oxford, University Press, 1953), pp. 1-2.

really been a *feudal* institution; it had, instead been a Tudor invention designed, not to enforce military service by the tenants-in-chief of the Crown, but rather to exact money in exchange for military service which the Crown did not desire. It had been a means of Tudor domination of the feudal aristocracy. In abolishing death and succession duties which had fallen upon a single class, the landed gentry, the Parliament succeeded in spreading this burden to all classes through an increase in taxes on beer, cider, and tea. The result was a lighter tax burden for the landed classes.[33] In this light, the clergy's tax agreement of 1664 was an additional triumph of Parliament's fiscal supremacy; while it is true that the clergy gained therefrom through lower tax rates, its common taxation with the gentry served to solidify further the Restoration alliance of clergy and gentry.

The 18th-Century land tax to which laity and clergy were both subject was ostensibly a tax of a shilling rate on each pound of income. Actually, in 1698 the government abandoned any further attempt to tax the increase in the national wealth through truly taxing a proportion of income. Instead, the 1693 assessments became fixed and a quota rather than a pound-rate became the method of assessment. Every shilling per pound granted amounted to a sum of £ 500,000 which was apportioned among the tax-payers. Even the rate of 4 s. per pound was not always applied: from 1698 to 1799 the average nominal rate of the land tax was 3.48 shillings per pound; that is, 17.4% of the income from land in 1693.[34] Even in 1693, however, the assessments had been incorrect: the areas around London and in the home counties probably were taxed at a 20% rate, but in the more distant counties of the West and the North the rate was more nearly 5%.[35] However, given the static assessment of 1693 — an assessment which meant that the land tax "had come to be a rent charge rather than a tax" [36] — the true rate collected was much less than either 20% around London or 5% in the West and the North. Contemporaries estimated that the land tax in the 18th Century yielded no more than one-half of what it nominally should have yielded — about one-tenth or one-twelfth.[37]

---

[33] David Ogg, *England in the Reign of Charles II* (Oxford, Clarendon Press, 1955), Vol. I, pp. 159-161.

[34] Dowell, *op. cit.*, Vol. II, pp. 85-88.

[35] Ward, *op. cit.*, p. 10.

[36] Kennedy, *op. cit.*, p. 128.

[37] *Ibid.*, p. 123.

## II

The above comparison of the deliberative and fiscal organization of the French and English episcopates further strengthens the argument that the French bishops significantly more than the English constituted a separate corporation or caste and were not integrated into the nation as a whole. The existence of national ecclesiastical assemblies or convocations competent to deliberate upon their own spiritual and temporal affairs was a unique expression of national corporate identity. Neither the French nobility, with its regional Parlements and several surviving provincial estates, nor the Third Estate during the two-century decline of the Estates-General had any comparable national organization. But though subject to the final authority of the Crown, the French clergy had retained a "liberty" lost by the other estates of the realm. In England, on the other hand, the nobility and higher ranks of the commonalty were nationally represented in a Parliament which in the 18th Century shared at least equal power with the Crown. The existence of Parliament in England and the absence of its equivalent in France had vital consequences for the relative power of the respective national ecclesiastical assemblies of the two nations. In any case, the French General Assemblies of the Clergy endured throughout the 18th Century: the clergy's retention of separate taxation had made the suspension or abolition of these assemblies unwise for the fiscal solvency of the State. In England, once the clergy had been subjected to national taxation, the demise of Convocation was foredoomed; until its suspension in 1717 it met only irregularly, and in the eyes of the government it repeatedly demonstrated the wisdom of abolishing it. Significant, then, were the survival of the French General Assemblies until the last days of the Old Régime and the corresponding failure of the English Convocation to have preserved enough importance to save itself from extinction.

In both countries the national Church assemblies and their exercise of power were challenged by the secularizers, by the Parlements and the Whig politicians, respectively. The Parlements wanted to limit the General Assemblies to the perfunctory voting of taxes in order to forestall their use in rekindling sectarian strife and propagating ecclesiastical independence. The Whigs feared the independence of the Church employed as a Tory political weapon, potentially capable of barring them from public office and even of toppling the new dynasty. Faced with opposition to the assemblies, the clergy of France and

England were both led to justify the activities of their assemblies and even to seek to win for them greater freedom and initiative. The significant difference between the French and English defense of ecclesiastical independence was simply that in France the bishops, who alone counted for something in the General Assemblies, led the defense of their deliberative body and, in the view of the magistrates, sounded the clarion of aggressive clericalism. But in England, owing to a bicameral Convocation which gave the non-episcopal clergy some deliberative identity and to the political control of the nomination of bishops, the defenders of ecclesiastical independence and Convocation included, not the majority of bishops, but the lower clergy; led by Francis Atterbury, later a bishop, the lower clergy pushed so far the pretended rights of Convocation as to threaten the episcopal order itself. The majority of bishops generally supported the position of the ministry and with great relief acquiesced in the final suspension of Convocation. The Anglican bishops, unlike the Gallican, were not the protagonists of the national ecclesiastical assemblies; nor did they come into conflict with the lay power over the activities of these assemblies. It was Atterbury who most resembled a French prelate, and he was a rare exception who had risen to prominence on the crest of a short-lived Toryism and Jacobitism under Queen Anne and had been made a bishop through the influence of the Tory extremists in spite of the apprehension of the Queen and some of her more moderate Tory ministers. As for Atterbury's episcopal foes — not only did they not constitute a closed caste; they did not even seek to constitute one.

The differing attitude of the French and English bishops towards the fiscal immunities of the clerical order alone would justify regarding the two groups as fundamentally unlike. It would not be an undue exaggeration to claim that no issue so aroused the concern of the French General Assemblies and the bishops who dominated them as the threat that their fiscal exemptions and autonomy might be modified or abolished. To them, the cause of fiscal independence — self-apportionment of internal taxes and free contributions to the royal treasury — was the cause of religion itself. In Lafont de Savine's defense of the Civil Constitution of the Clergy, quoted in a previous chapter, he took the position that the clergy's fiscal immunities were more imagined then real, but that its separateness in fiscal affairs from the rest of the nation caused its motives and its very patriotism to be called into question. While it has, I believe, been demonstrated above that the clergy enjoyed concrete fiscal advantages, still it remained true that the trappings of corporate privilege intensified popular hostility towards the clergy. Few in 18th-Century France knew how much the upper clergy really paid in taxes, but the mysterious workings of ecclesiastical privilege seemed to justify any suspicion. Lafont de Savine lamented that the episcopal leadership had so closely identified religion with fiscal independence that opposition to the one bred contempt for the other in an association of guilt. For, indeed, the bishops never so boldly opposed the government as when under Machault it systematically threatened their fiscal privilege and autonomy. It was not until 1789 when the government was hopelessly bankrupt, the nation demanding equality of taxation, and the *curés* in open revolt, that the bishops yielded their cherished rights.

We contrast this attitude of the French prelates to the English bishops' informal and unheralded relinquishment of clerical taxation and their willingness to be integrated into national and Parliamentary taxation. It is true that in 1664 the English bishops did not have left as much to yield to the secular authority as the French bishops were finally willing to yield in 1789; the Tudor Reformation had already transformed internal ecclesiastical taxation into a regular contribution at a fixed rate to the State. Also, the English clergy, in general, undoubtedly benefited from a lower tax rate after the tax agreement of 1664. Nevertheless, the views of Bishop Hackett do reveal that the desire to avoid lay jealousies and to support the public interest were also important determinants in the minds of the bishops. One has the impression that the French bishops would have opposed yielding their fiscal autonomy even if it had promised a lower tax burden; in any case, the French prelates did enjoy tax exemptions not enjoyed by their English counterparts even before 1664, and they had good reason for opposing reform. The 3%-5% of their annual income which the French clergy contributed to the royal treasury was significantly lighter a burden than the English land tax of 10%-12% to which the English clergy were subject. If the costs of the French clergy's fiscal autonomy made them pay *décimes* which were much higher than 3%-5%, such was the price of fiscal autonomy. Furthermore, the French clergy as a whole not only paid less in taxes than the English clergy; they also paid less than the Third Estate and less even than the French nobility. Contrast this with the fact that the English clergy paid roughly the same rate as the nobility and gentry, while the English bishops did not, like the French prelates, enjoy a self-apportionment which, at least for half of the 18th Century, shifted ecclesiastical taxation largely onto the shoulders of the lower clergy; and you again emerge with the picture of the French episcopate as a caste apart, separated in its tax privileges from the Third Estate, the nobility, and the lower clergy — a group whose inordinate privileges created an unbridgeable chasm between it and the rest of society. The English bishops in no such way were conspicuous; they paid their taxes like the other landed groups, taxes nationally voted and commonly assessed.

If the whole English clergy paid the same tax rate as the landed classes, it cannot be forgotten that the inequalities of income between the upper clergy and the lower clergy were as great in England as in France. In 1762 the average episcopal income was approximately £ 2180; while the average curate's income was somewhere between £ 40 and £ 70; thus, the average curate received about $2\frac{1}{2}$% of the bishops' incomes. In a later period the inequality of income appeared greater; according to the parliamentary report of 1835, the average episcopal income was £ 5937, compared to the curate average of £ 81 — or about 1.4%. Because the Land Tax was really collected at a fixed rate, fixed money incomes were increasingly at a disadvantage in the 18th Century as rising incomes were taxed according to the static assessment of 1693.

In all fairness, one must consider as an argument in favor of the Gallican clergy that if its actual contributions to the State, as *dons gratuits*, were small, it did pay the expenses of fiscal management in the form of interest and the salaries of tax collectors, which under a national system of taxation would have had to be borne by the State. In other words, had the government in taxing the clergy directly raised as much as the latter itself collected in *décimes*, a large proportion of this sum would have been consumed in the process of tax-farming — as was the case with the revenues already raised by the State, both in direct and indirect levies. For in spite of everything, the clergy was reputed to be expert in matters of finance. Still, the costs of a separate taxing system such as the clergy operated were probably greater than the costs of taxing the clergy within a national levy. Finally, when comparing the French and English episcopates, one still confronts in regard to the former a separate fiscal organization, stoutly defended, which even after the assessment reforms of 1755-60 allowed the prelates to pay a relatively low tax rate; the English bishops paid their taxes like the other landed classes. Both before and after the inauguration of the assessment reform in the collection of *décimes* the French prelates paid less than the English land tax. One is compelled to conclude that both subjectively and objectively, both in the popular consciousness and in concrete tax figures, the financial organization of the clergy gave to the Gallican episcopate a separate identity which divided it from the rest of the nation.

# CONCLUSION

Our statistical analysis of the social origins of the French and English-Irish episcopates in the pre-revolutionary, pre-reform era justifies the utilization of Tocqueville's aristocracy-caste distinction in describing respectively the English and French bishops. The Gallican episcopate emerges as a caste within the caste-like nobility, a group 87% of whose members in the period 1682-1790 were of noble birth. The admittance of a *roturier* into the ecclesiastical aristocracy became increasingly difficult as the 18th Century progressed; it must be noted, however, that even in the Golden Age of Louis XIV some 88% of the bishops were nobles as compared with 90% in the period 1774-1790 — not a great rise but one significant in that only two bishops in this later period were of *roturier* origin. There was, then, a century of overwhelming discrimination against the entry of plebeians into the Gallican episcopate; the episcopate was quite properly seen as a subdivision of the nobility, a "noblesse en camail".

Furthermore, the ministry's motives in preferring men to the episcopate were primarily dictated by the social prejudices of the king and his ministers. High Church benefices offered a means of supporting the nobility in its style of life. Where political factors were of great importance, they were still viewed in terms of social prejudice: the nobility was paid for its service to the state in the material and social advantages provided by the vacant bishoprics, but prejudice prevented the bourgeoisie from being rewarded in the same fashion. Also, the need to placate the provincial Estates saw the granting of Church benefices to families influential within the provincial Estates, but no appeasement of the aggressive Paris robe nobility was attempted through the same means of corruption. The end result of this policy was the exclusion of both the Third Estate and the robe nobility from the episcopate of the French Church. The episcopate became closed to all but a small group of the nobility; and it was estranged from the bourgeoisie by social prejudice and from the Parlements by its narrow recruitment and its theories of ecclesiastical independence and autonomous legal jurisdiction which clashed with aggressive magisterial nationalism. The episcopate was not merely unintegrated into the whole of society: it was shut off from the rest of society, and communication with it became a raging controversy over privileges and corporate independence, rarely a dialogue between citizens with any common interests to defend and extend.

The study of the English-Irish episcopate reveals on the other hand a body which though aristocratic in its function of leadership was recruited from a much wider section of the population and which had broader national roots. A trend towards the relative elimination of rank plebeians from the episcopate came only to any great degree in mid century and only became pronounced after the outbreak of the French Revolution when English society became more repressive. The motives for the preferment of men to the English and Irish episcopates were political: the need to have episcopal support for the governing ministry in the House of Lords and episcopal electioneering endeavors in the counties and boroughs. A very substantial number of bishops, 24% of the total number in the period 1660-1832 and 46% of our "uncertain" grouping, were the sons of clergymen below the rank of bishop. This clergy came from diverse social and economic backgrounds and had numerous blood, social, and occupational ties with a wide cross-section of the local population. The English episcopate (if not the Irish, by the very nature of the "colonial" problem in Ireland) was thus well integrated into society — estranged from neither the social or political life of the nation. England in the 18th Century was probably more aristocratic than France in that the English aristocracy ruled England while the French nobility was subject to the more or less despotic monarchy; but the English aristocracy did not monopolize the Church solely for its own offspring, admitting to its leadership men of diverse backgrounds whose political services were appreciated. The power of the English aristocracy being greater than that of the French nobles, the former less compellingly needed to take refuge in titles and privileges and to monopolize Church preferment. To be sure, under stress — when the danger of Jacobinism was felt — the English aristocracy showed an inclination for a more rigid system of episcopal preferment; but it was only an inclination. In short, then, both the Gallican and Anglican episcopates, in their degree of relative integration into and isolation from society as a whole, mirrored the two national aristocracies. We may with justice state that the Gallican episcopate was a caste while the Anglican episcopate was an aristocracy.

Finally, the Gallican episcopate's retention of ecclesiastical Assemblies for the purpose of self-taxation set it off from the other groups comprising French society. Until the Revolution of 1789 it remained true that "the clergy ... were ... the most independent body in the nation, the only one whose peculiar liberties were safe from assault" [1] For the French episcopate the retention of fiscal autonomy was the cause of heaven itself, and its tenacious will to avoid surrender caused it to demand increasingly greater independence for its Assemblies and brought it to repeated near-revolts against royal authority throughout the 18th Century, culminating finally in the open revolutionary defiance of 1788.

Of a different temperament entirely were the Anglican bishops who yielded up to Caesar their fiscal autonomy without a fuss and refused to follow the lead of Atterbury — perhaps the only genuine counterpart of a French prelate in England — in seeking to make Convocation an independent and indispensable institution. Finally, the French bishops not only were separately taxed but they also paid their taxes at a rate below that of both the privileged nobility and the unprivileged Third Estate. The bishops' fiscal independence before and after a long-procrastinated self-reformation enabled it also to shift much of the tax burden onto the lower clergy. In England, the land tax to which Parliament subjected ecclesiastics and laymen alike resulted in the bishops' paying in unison with the other propertied classes of society. Thus, the separate identity of the Gallican prelates, as opposed to their Anglican colleagues, manifested itself not only in social origins but also in fiscal institutions. Their birth and their privileges created that caste-consciousness which so pre-eminently characterized 18th-Century French prelates and which became the *bête-noire* of the democratic Revolution.

[1] Tocqueville, *op. cit.*, Vol. I, p. 170.

APPENDIX I

## THE FOUR ARTICLES OF 1682

From the French text given in Mention, *op. cit.*, I, pp. 27-31.

*Declaration of the Clergy of France Concerning the Ecclesiastical Power.*

Many strive to overthrow the decrees of the Gallican Church, the liberties which our ancestors have sustained with so much zeal, and their foundations resting on the holy Canons and the tradition of the Fathers. Also among these are they who, on the pretext of those liberties, do not fear to injure the primacy of St. Peter and the Roman Pontiffs, his successors instituted by Jesus Christ, the obedience which is due them by all Christians, and the majesty of the Apostolic See, so venerable in the eyes of all nations where the faith is taught and the unity of the Church conserved. On the other side, the heretics omit nothing in order to depict as insupportable to kings and peoples this power which embodies the peace of the Church, and by means of this cunning to separate simple souls from the communion of the Church and Jesus Christ.

It is with the intention of remedying these evils that we, archbishops and bishops assembled in Paris by the order of the king with the other deputies representing the Gallican Church, have deemed it proper, after due deliberation, to establish and declare:

I. That St. Peter and his successors, the vicars of Jesus Christ, and even the whole Church have received power from God only over spiritual things and those concerning salvation, and not over temporal and civil affairs; Jesus Christ teaching us Himself that *His kingdom is not of this world*, and in another place, that *one should render unto Caesar that which in Caesar's and unto God that which is God's*; and that this teaching of St. Paul the Apostle cannot be altered or overturned: *that everyone should be subject to the higher powers; for there is no power which does not come from God, and it is He who ordains those [powers] which are on the earth; those then who oppose these powers resist the order of God.* Consequently, we declare that kings and sovereigns are not subject to any ecclesiastical power in temporal matters by the order of God; that they can be deposed neither directly nor indirectly by the authority of the Keys of the Church; that their subjects cannot be dispensed from the submission and obedience which they owe them or absolved from their oath of loyalty, and that this doctrine, necessary for public tranquillity and no less advantageous for the Church than for the State, should be inviolably followed as conforming to the word of God, the tradition of the holy Fathers, and the examples of the Saints.

II. That the fullness of power which the Holy Apostolic See and the successors of St. Peter, the vicars of Jesus Christ, have over spiritual affairs is such that the decrees of the holy Ecumenical Council of Constance in its fourth and fifth sessions, approved by the Holy Apostolic See, confirmed by the practice of the whole Church and the Roman Pontiffs, and observed religiously at all times by the Gallican Church, remain in full force, and that the Church of France does not approve of the opinion of those who attack those decrees or who weaken them by claiming that their authority is not well established, that they are not approved, or that they apply only to times of schism.

III. That, thus, the exercise of apostolic power should be ruled by the Canons made by the Spirit of God and consecrated by general respect; that the rules, customs, and constitutions received into the kingdom should be maintained and the limits raised by our fathers kept firmly; that it is even [part] of the greatness of the Holy Apostolic See that the laws and customs established with the consent of this respectable See and the Churches continue without change.

IV. That, although the Pope has the principal part in questions of faith and his decrees apply to each and every Church, his judgment is, however, not irrevocable unless the [whole] Church consents.

We have had sent to all the Churches of France and to the bishops who preside over them by the authority of the Holy Spirit these maxims which we have received from our fathers in order that we may all proclaim the same thing, be all of the same mind, and follow all the same doctrine.

APPENDIX II

EPISCOPAL REVENUES IN FRANCE

The following table lists the annual revenues of the 130 sees of France according to the best available sources. The records of the *Économat*, the governmental administration of vacant benefices, provide information for most of the sees; according to a detailed study of these records, its information has been deemed exact and free of fraud.[1] The figures given by the *Almanach royal* have only been used where necessary; they are often erroneous, but in no consistent way — sometimes too high, sometimes too low.

| Bishopric | Year | Revenue (livres) | Best Source |
|---|---|---|---|
| Strasbourg | 1744 | 170,000 | Almanach royal |
| Strasbourg | 1789 | 400,000 | Almanach royal |
| Paris | 1746 | 162,000 | Economat (AN, G8* 552)[2] |
| Cambrai | 1744 | 100,000 | Almanach royal |
| Cambrai | 1789 | 200,000 | Almanach royal |
| Narbonne | 1719 | 85,800 | Economat (AN, V7 83)[3] |
| Narbonne | 1751 | 123,900 | Economat G8* 552 |
| Narbonne | 1762 | 119,000 | Economat G8* 552 |
| Metz | 1744, 1789 | 120,000 | Almanach royal |
| Albi | 1747 | 133,200 | Economat G8* 552 |
| Albi | 1764 | 130,900 | Economat G8* 552 |
| Auch | 1741 | 147,500 | Economat G8* 552 |
| Rouen | 1733 | 85,000 | Economat G8* 552 |
| Rouen | 1759 | 111,600 | Economat G8* 552 |
| Toulouse | 1720 | 92,300 | Economat V7 84 |
| Toulouse | 1732 | 113,900 | Economat G8* 552 |
| Toulouse | 1762 | 110,000 | Economat G8* 552 |
| Beauvais | 1728 | 53,200 | Economat G8* 552 |
| Bayeux | 1753 | 73,800 | Economat G8* 552 |
| Tours | 1750 | 58,300 | Economat G8* 552 |
| Arras | 1744 | 22,000 | Almanach royal |
| Arras | 1789 | 80,000 | Almanach royal |

[1]  R. Chevaillier, "Un Document sur la fortune du haut clergé au XVIIIe siècle", *Bulletin de la société d'histoire moderne*, April-May, 1921, pp. 60-80.
[2]  "État des revenus des bénéfices consistoriaux du royaume suivant les économats".
[3]  "Commissions extraordinaires du conseil: bureau des économats".

| Bishopric | Year | Revenue (livres) | Best Source |
|---|---|---|---|
| Verdun | 1744 | 50,000 | Almanach royal |
| Verdun | 1789 | 74,500 | Almanach royal |
| Condom | 1734 | 65,600 | Economat G8* 552 |
| Condom | 1763 | 87,500 | Economat G8* 552 |
| Lavaur | 1748 | 44,700 | Economat G8* 552 |
| Lavaur | 1764 | 53,700 | Economat G8* 552 |
| La Rochelle | 1729 | 56,600 | Economat G8* 552 |
| Comminges | 1739 | 51,800 | Economat G8* 552 |
| Comminges | 1763 | 62,100 | Economat G8* 552 |
| Cahors | 1741 | 50,300 | Economat G8* 552 |
| Castres | 1752 | 61,000 | Economat G8* 552 |
| Bordeaux | 1743 | 50,900 | Economat G8* 552 |
| Rodez | 1746 | 51,000 | Economat G8* 552 |
| Lisieux | 1744 | 40,000 | Almanach royal |
| Lisieux | 1789 | 50,000 | Almanach royal |
| Lyon | 1744 | 52,000 | Rhône 6G 65* |
| Lyon | 1769 | 60,000 | Rhône 6G 70* [4] |
| Orléans | 1753 | 33,500 | Economat G8* 552 |
| Orléans | 1757 | 54,000 | Economat G8* 552 |
| Nancy | 1744, 1789 | 50,000 | Almanach royal |
| Saint-Omer | 1744 | 40,000 | Almanach royal |
| Saint-Omer | 1789 | 50,000 | Almanach royal |
| Reims | 1721 | 46,100 | Economat G8* 552 |
| Reims | 1762 | 84,500 | Economat G8* 552 |
| Montpellier | 1748 | 54,100 | Economat G8* 552 |
| Montpellier | 1766 | 63,800 | Economat G8* 552 |
| Arles | 1746 | 62,900 | Economat G8* 552 |
| Sens | 1733 | 45,000 | Economat G8* 552 |
| Béziers | 1745 | 45,500 | Economat G8* 552 |
| Langres | 1735 | 39,200 | Economat G8* 552 |
| Agen | 1735 | 40,200 | Economat G8* 552 |
| Bourges | 1729 | 24,000 | Economat G8* 552 |
| Bourges | 1757 | 38,800 | Economat G8* 552 |
| Auxerre | 1754 | 40,600 | Economat G8* 552 |
| Auxerre | 1761 | 49,000 | Economat G8* 552 |
| Montauban | 1739 | 27,000 | Economat G8* 552 |
| Montauban | 1762 | 44,100 | Economat G8* 552 |
| Rieux | 1747 | 33,200 | Economat G8* 552 |
| Lambez | 1751 | 42,600 | Economat G8* 552 |
| Saint-Papoul | 1738 | 26,500 | Economat G8* 552 |
| Coutances | 1721 | 18,000 | Economat V7 82 |
| Coutances | 1757 | 28,400 | Economat G8* 552 |
| Coutances | 1764 | 40,100 | Economat G8* 552 |
| Nantes | 1746 | 28,000 | Economat G8* 552 |
| Mende | 1723 | 48,400 | Economat G8* 552 |
| Dijon | 1755 | 9,100 | Economat G8* 552 |
| Agde | 1740 | 44,800 | Economat G8* 552 |

[4]  *Archives du département du Rhône,* nouvelle côte 6G 65*, "Rôles des revenus et impositions des bénéfices, 1760"; nouvelle côte 6G 70*, "Extrait du rôle des décimes du clergé du diocèse 1744-69".

| Bishopric | Year | Revenue (livres) | Best Source |
|---|---|---|---|
| Agde | 1759 | 50,200 | Economat G8* 552 |
| Vannes | 1717 | 18,000 | Economat V7 82 |
| Vannes | 1742 | 16,700 | Economat G8* 552 |
| Grenoble | 1725 | 28,000 | Economat G8* 552 |
| Aix | 1744 | 32,000 | Almanach royal |
| Aix | 1789 | 37,400 | Almanach royal |
| Toul | 1744 | 17,000 | Almanach royal |
| Toul | 1789 | 37,000 | Almanach royal |
| Noyon | 1733 | 29,400 | Economat G8* 552 |
| Noyon | 1766 | 41,000 | Economat G8* 552 |
| Besançon | 1744, 1789 | 36,000 | Almanach royal |
| Carcassonne | 1729 | 52,200 | Economat G8* 552 |
| Saint-Pons de Tomières | 1729 | 31,300 | Economat G8* 552 |
| Vienne | 1751 | 36,400 | Economat G8* 552 |
| Saint-Malo | 1739 | 22,000 | Economat G8* 552 |
| Puy-en-Velay | 1742 | 21,600 | Economat G8* 552 |
| Luçon | 1736 | 23,200 | Economat G8* 552 |
| Luçon | 1758 | 25,500 | Economat G8* 552 |
| Rennes | 1732 | 12,000 | Economat G8* 552 |
| Rennes | 1761 | 19,200 | Economat G8* 552 |
| Laon | 1741 | 41,900 | Economat G8* 552 |
| Amiens | 1733 | 24,000 | Economat G8* 552 |
| Le Mans | 1723 | 27,100 | Economat G8* 552 |
| Saint-Dié | 1789 | 30,000 | Almanach royal |
| Bayonne | 1745 | 28,300 | Economat G8* 552 |
| Mirepoix | 1720 | 20,000 | Economat V7 84 |
| Mirepoix | 1737 | 31,200 | Economat G8* 552 |
| Marseille | 1744, 1789 | 30,000 | Almanach royal |
| Viviers | 1748 | 39,100 | Economat G8* 552 |
| Évreux | 1753 | 32,900 | Economat G8* 552 |
| Évreux | 1759 | 33,100 | Economat G8* 552 |
| Poitiers | 1748 | 35,500 | Economat G8* 552 |
| Poitiers | 1759 | 35,200 | Economat G8* 552 |
| Sarlat | 1747 | 22,700 | Economat G8* 552 |
| Aire | 1734 | 26,700 | Economat G8* 552 |
| Aire | 1757 | 30,700 | Economat G8* 552 |
| Tarbes | 1717 | 22,400 | Economat V7 81 |
| Tarbes | 1751 | 34,300 | Economat G8* 552 |
| Lodève | 1750 | 31,100 | Economat G8* 552 |
| Fréjus | 1739 | 28,300 | Economat G8* 552 |
| Châlons-sur-Marne | 1733 | 20,000 | Economat G8* 552 |
| Châlons-sur-Marne | 1763 | 32,400 | Economat G8* 552 |
| Saint-Claude | 1744, 1789 | 27,000 | Almanach royal |
| Lescar | 1729 | 23,100 | Economat G8* 552 |
| Lescar | 1762 | 28,600 | Economat G8* 552 |
| Nîmes | 1736 | 38,300 | Economat G8* 552 |
| Angers | 1731 | 24,200 | Economat G8* 552 |
| Uzès | 1736 | 26,100 | Economat G8* 552 |
| Alet | 1723 | 21,300 | Economat G8* 552 |
| Alet | 1762 | 26,100 | Economat G8* 552 |

| Bishopric | Year | Revenue (livres) | Best Source |
|---|---|---|---|
| Pamiers | 1741 | 29,700 | Economat G8* 552 |
| Chartres | 1746 | 44,500 | Economat G8* 552 |
| Blois | 1719 | 27,600 | Economat V7 84 |
| Blois | 1753 | 39,200 | Economat G8* 552 |
| Mâcon | 1731 | 17,100 | Economat G8* 552 |
| Mâcon | 1763 | 25,200 | Economat G8* 552 |
| Périgueux | 1719 | 20,800 | Economat V7 84 |
| Périgueux | 1731 | 24,300 | Economat G8* 552 |
| Acqs | 1736 | 18,700 | Economat G8* 552 |
| Couserans | 1732 | 29,900 | Economat G8* 552 |
| Soissons | 1738 | 22,000 | Economat G8* 552 |
| Soissons | 1764 | 26,600 | Economat G8* 552 |
| Meaux | 1737 | 23,300 | Economat G8* 552 |
| Meaux | 1759 | 33,200 | Economat G8* 552 |
| Autun | 1748 | 15,900 | Economat G8* 552 |
| Autun | 1758 | 41,400 | Economat G8* 552 |
| Embrun | 1740 | 33,700 | Economat G8* 552 |
| Vabres | 1764 | 30,100 | Economat G8* 552 |
| Boulogne | 1742 | 15,600 | Economat G8* 552 |
| Avranches | 1746 | 18,700 | Economat G8* 552 |
| Avranches | 1764 | 24,800 | Economat G8* 552 |
| Nevers | 1751 | 30,900 | Economat G8* 552 |
| Tréguier | 1731 | 15,500 | Economat G8* 552 |
| Tréguier | 1761 | 18,400 | Economat G8* 552 |
| Dol | 1748 | 20,100 | Economat G8* 552 |
| Limoges | 1739 | 23,000 | Economat G8* 552 |
| Limoges | 1758 | 23,300 | Economat G8* 552 |
| Angoulême | 1753 | 23,900 | Economat G8* 552 |
| Saintes | 1744 | 25,200 | Economat G8* 552 |
| Saintes | 1763 | 26,000 | Economat G8* 552 |
| Riez | 1751 | 18,600 | Economat G8* 552 |
| Senlis | 1754 | 32,500 | Economat G8* 552 |
| Perpignan | 1744, 1789 | 18,000 | Almanach royal |
| Lectoure | 1717 | 8,000 | Economat V7 81 |
| Lectoure | 1745, 1760 | 38,100 | Economat G8* 552 |
| Bazas | 1746 | 20,000 | Economat G8* 552 |
| Séez | 1740 | 17,500 | Economat G8* 552 |
| Alais | 1744 | 25,000 | Economat G8* 552 |
| Alais | 1755 | 25,100 | Economat G8* 552 |
| Quimper | 1739 | 11,000 | Economat G8* 552 |
| Toulon | 1737 | 10,700 | Economat G8* 552 |
| Toulon | 1759 | 13,600 | Economat G8* 552 |
| Sisteron | 1764 | 17,600 | Economat G8* 552 |
| Die | 1741 | 18,800 | Economat G8* 552 |
| St.-Paul-de-Léon | 1745 | 9,000 | Economat G8* 552 |
| St.-Paul-de-Léon | 1763 | 12,700 | Economat G8* 552 |
| Clermont | 1742 | 18,900 | Economat G8* 552 |
| Tulle | 1740 | 11,500 | Economat G8* 552 |
| Tulle | 1764 | 11,800 | Economat G8* 552 |
| Troyes | 1742 | 39,700 | Economat G8* 552 |
| Troyes | 1761 | 21,300 | Economat G8* 552 |

| Bishopric | Year | Revenue (livres) | Best Source |
|---|---|---|---|
| Châlon-sur-Saône | 1753 | 15,600 | Economat G8* 552 |
| Valence | 1725 | 15,600 | Economat G8* 552 |
| Oloron | 1742 | 16,000 | Economat G8* 552 |
| Saint-Flour | 1742 | 16,800 | Economat G8* 552 |
| Saint-Brieuc | 1744 | 16,300 | Economat G8* 552 |
| Saint-Brieuc | 1766 | 20,500 | Economat G8* 552 |
| Gap | 1754 | 24,800 | Economat G8* 552 |
| Gap | 1763 | 22,700 | Economat G8* 552 |
| Senez | 1740 | 11,600 | Economat G8* 552 |
| Senez | 1756 | 14,100 | Economat G8* 552 |
| Grasse | 1752 | 12,000 | Economat G8* 552 |
| Glandève | 1755 | 22,200 | Economat G8* 552 |
| Belley | 1751 | 7,300 | Economat G8* 552 |
| St.-Paul-Trois-Châteaux | 1743 | 8,700 | Economat G8* 552 |
| Apt | 1751 | 13,600 | Economat G8* 552 |
| Digne | 1746 | 11,500 | Economat G8* 552 |
| Digne | 1758 | 11,700 | Economat G8* 552 |
| Vence | 1754 | 6,600 | Economat G8* 552 |
| Vence | 1763 | 7,200 | Economat G8* 552 |
| Bethléem | 1744, 1789 | 1,000 | Almanach royal |

APPENDIX III

## LEDRAN'S MÉMOIRE

Nicolas-Louis Ledran (1687-1774), for a long period the archivist of the Ministry of Foreign Affairs and a man well worthy of belief, drew up a "Mémoire sur la grande affaire de la constitution *Unigenitus Dei Filius,* 1730-1769"[1] in which he described at length Fleury's attitude toward the Jansenists, the Parlements, and the filling of vacant bishoprics. The Cardinal was depicted by Ledran as continually under papal pressure to destroy the Jansenists with immediate rather than long-term measures. Ledran cites at great length one of Fleury's explanatory letters to Rome, this one to Clement XII, and it is well worth the reading:

"I dare to inform Your Holiness that he does not yet know the full extent of the sickness with which the kingdom and principally the capital city are afflicted. As one examines it thoroughly one discovers its excess and one is astonished by the number of rebels as much among churchmen as among laymen, and especially among the women and the religious.

If one wished to punish them all at once and to use extreme measures, one would aggravate and increase the malady rather than cure it. They would not fail to reunite themselves by new bonds. They would unite with the Calvinists from whom they hardly differ and who are still unfortunately only too numerous in France. It is certain that one would then see reborn the fatal troubles which have agitated France for more than a century; and one cannnot doubt their intentions.

One has but to read the history books to be convinced that violent remedies always have had fatal results and have never succeeded. It is necessary to add to these reflections that we still are unsure of the turn which the affairs of Europe will take, and that if we are forced to make war, there would be danger or at least great folly to attack without consideration of a sect which is so spread out and which wants no dependence or any kind at all.

I can assure Your Holiness with certitude that the zeal of the king for the faith is just what he could wish for, and that he [the king] will not lose sight of the plan to reestablish it to its former glory. But after having maturely weighed all the means which one is to use in achieving that, his Majesty

---

[1]  *AAE,* Mémoires et Documents, Fonds Divers, Rome, Vol. 92, folios 202-307.

has decided on the following four as the principal and most proper ones for the realization of the goal he proposes.

1. To destroy little by little all the schools where error is taught and thereby to arrest the progress of the malady if one does not cure it immediately. . . .

2. To name to the bishoprics, abbeys, canonries, and even to the sinecures persons who have declared in favor of the good doctrine. The king has in this matter the most exact attention, and thank God there has not been a single one in five years for which his Masjesty has had occasion to repent. The good seminaries are full and the bad ones are deserted, because it is known that those in the latter ones can hope for no favor. . . .

3. It is to change, to weaken, and to diminish as much as possible the religious congregations which are corrupted. . . .

4. It is to allow M. the archbishop of Narbonne to assemble the council of his province to try M. the bishop of Montpellier [Colbert de Croissy, a Jansenist] in the same way that the metropolitan see of Embrun dealt with M. the bishop of Senez [Soanen]. . . .

There remains a very essential matter which is that of the Parlements. It is with good reason that Your Holiness has taken it so much to heart, since they have become the chief support of the Jansenists. However, Very Holy Father, at the same time that we feel how important it would be to curb their audacity, nothing is more difficult than to find the means of doing it . . .

The Parlement of Paris has for two centuries sought only to have itself regarded as the tutor of the kings, the defender of the peoples, and as a sovereign tribunal which is to check the excessive power of the sovereign. It is in this light that it first favored Richerism whose principles reduced the power of the popes to the sole title of ministerial head of the Church and submitted that of the kings to the dominion of the community, that is to say, of the assembled people, in whom authority radically resided.

This detestable opinion was adopted after the death of Dr. Richer by the abbé de Saint-Cyran and afterward by the Jansenists; and one need not be astonished that the Parlement favors them, as it does so even openly. One need not conclude that this body is generally tainted, and in it there remain certainly men who think correctly; but the great number of ill-disposed persons prevails by far, and the well-disposed would not dare to speak with a certain force because they would end by discrediting themselves. . . ." [2]

Ledran also quotes a *mémoire* prepared by Fleury for the eyes of Delci, the papal nuncio, in which the Cardinal's general ideas on filling vacant bishoprics are mirrored:

"One should thus not believe that one can fill the vacant sees with perfect men, and one must be content to choose those who are the least undesirable — provided that they have the most essential qualities, which are morals and opinions; birth may not be neglected, and when of equal merit or even inferior, it is useful to prefer men of birth because the peoples have more

[2] Fleury to Clement XII, October 23, 1730, *ibid,* folios 216-223.

respect for them and religion needs to be supported by an imposing exterior." [3]

Fleury, himself, took an active interest in the genealogies of prospective nominees, civil and ecclesiastical. Replying to a request from the archbishop of Narbonne for a benefice for his nephew, the Cardinal replied much as Boyer would later: "You need not doubt, Monsieur, that I am very sincerely disposed to do what you desire for M. your nephew. He bears a name which is too great a consideration for him not to be eligible. . . .[4]

[3] Mémoire of August 5, 1737, *ibid.*, folios 245-246.
[4] Fleury to the archbishop of Narbonne, March 12, 1732, *AAE*, Mémoires et Documents, Fonds France, Vol. 1644, folio 199. For the Cardinal's interest in genealogies see: Bibliothèque nationale, nouvelles acquisitions françaises, MSS. 31, letters of April 24, 1727, and May 2, 1727.

APPENDIX IV

# NOTE ON BISHOP GIBSON

Gibson was a true reformer. He did not hesitate to attack the vexing problems of patronage, translations, and inequalities in episcopal revenues. His view of translation was that given the inequalities between bishoprics, the practice of translating bishops was desirable since it offered deserving prelates promotion and encouragement. Recognizing its abuses, however, abuses which permitted Benjamin Hoadly to obtain three translations within eighteen years, Gibson proposed that a limit of one translation be imposed — and that only after service of seven years in the previous diocese. Facing the problem of Church livings which bishops held *in commendam,* Gibson justified them with the fact of glaring inequalities in income: however, he wanted to regularize this system of supplementary income by distinguishing between bishoprics needing permanent supplementary sources of revenue, bishoprics needing such help temporarily until the expenses of translation or elevation were met, and those wealthy sees which required no livings *in commendam.* Gibson personally followed such a program, retaining several sinecures when elevated to Lincoln until he had liquidated the debts incurred in his preferment: first fruits, ceremonial fees, and so on.[1]

Gibson was acutely conscious that the unequal size and incomes of diocese were the root of the trouble with the government of the Anglican Church. He saw the need for altering the size of diocees, but he was realistic enough to perceive that any increase in the total number of sees would meet vigorous lay opposition, since an increase of spiritual lords in the upper house of Parliament would have been unwelcome in government quarters and among most politicians; the source of endowments for new sees also was an almost insurmountable barrier. Gibson seriously contemplated the resurrection of the suffragan bishops whose office had died out in the 16th Century, but again the factor of revenue intruded itself. Furthermore, he perceived that a revival of suffragan bishops would complicate the operation of royal patronage because suffragan bishops would expect to succeed to the bishoprics to which they had been assigned as auxiliaries: if the bishops themselves named their suffragans, the king's patronage over all episcopal appointments would soon be destroyed; if, on the other hand, the king named the suffragans, the bishops would be saddled with perhaps unwanted assistants. Viewing contemporary social trends, Gibson keenly saw

[1]  Sykes, *Edmund Gibson* . . ., p. 217.

the danger: " 'By degrees, episcopal care will all devolve on suffragans; and younger sons of nobility will be all the bishops and only attend parliament' ".[2] In view of these many obstacles, he was compelled to shun an increase in the total number of bishops; he did, nonetheless, seek a redistribution of existing episcopal boundaries — going so far as to advise the suppression of three bishoprics, Rochester, Bristol, and Gloucester, the first of which dated from the 7th Century, and the creation of three substitutes, Brecknock, Eton, and Southwell, whose formation would somewhat equalize the existing territorial boundaries and revenues of the twenty-seven sees. Such a reorganization can only be considered highly reformist in character — a portend of reforms to come. That Gibson failed to win approval for his proposals — as moderate and well-reasoned as they were — and only succeeded in transferring two deaneries from rich to poor bishoprics, was owing to the Whig oligarchy's extremely conservative policy. The ruling group desired to petrify the 18th-Century tension between conformity and dissent: abolition of Occasional Conformity and Schism Acts but retention of Test and Corporation Acts. Still suspicious of the high churchmen, the Whigs opposed any further power for the Church.[3] The reformation of ecclesiastical life which might have resulted from some of Gibson's ideas was not to their liking; the Church served their political and social purposes as it was.

[2]   Sykes, *From Sheldon to Secker* . . ., p. 194.
[3]   *Ibid.*, p. 216.

APPENDIX V

EPISCOPAL TAX RATES IN FRANCE:
CHANGES AFTER REFORMS OF 1755-60

|  |  | % |
|---|---|---|
| Meaux | 1737-59 | —2.66 |
| Orléans | 1753-57 | —1.20 |
| Autun | 1748-58 | —6.45 |
| Mâcon | 1731-63 | +1.25 |
| Rouen | 1733-59 | +3.61 |
| Rennes | 1751-61 | —1.57 |
| St.-Paul-de-Léon | 1745-63 | +3.45 |
| Tréguier | 1731-61 | —3.12 |
| Limoges | 1739-58 | +4.04 |
| Albi | 1747-59 | —1.57 |
| Albi | 1759-64 | +1.59 |
| Saintes | 1744-63 | +0.63 |
| Poitiers | 1748-59 | +1.61 |
| Condom | 1734-57 | +0.90 |
| Condom | 1757-63 | +4.04 |
| Luçon | 1736-58 | +2.10 |
| Lectoure | 1745-60 | +3.11 |
| Comminges | 1739-63 | +2.29 |
| Aire | 1734-57 | +7.31 |
| Lescar | 1729-62 | —0.09 |
| Narbonne | 1751-62 | +6.18 |
| Agde | 1745-59 | +2.37 |
| Montpellier | 1748-66 | +4.49 |
| Alet | 1723-62 | +3.11 |
| Alais | 1744-55 | —0.01 |
| Toulouse | 1732-58 | +3.89 |
| Toulouse | 1758-62 | +3.81 |
| Lavaur | 1748-64 | +2.02 |
| Toulon | 1737-59 | +5.97 |
| Gap | 1754-63 | +0.10 |
| Vence | 1754-58 | +0.37 |
| Vence | 1758-63 | —1.80 |

| Digne | 1746-58 | —0.32 |
| Senez | 1740-56 | —6.17 |
| Avranches | 1746-64 | —2.38 |
| Évreux | 1753-59 | +0.89 |
| Coutances | 1720-57 | +1.13 |
| Coutances | 1757-64 | —1.35 |
| Troyes | 1742-58 | —2.29 |
| Auxerre | 1754-61 | +1.74 |
| Reims | 1721-62 | +4.59 |
| Soissons | 1738-64 | +1.93 |

# BIBLIOGRAPHY

## A. THE GALLICAN EPISCOPATE

### 1. Archival and Manuscript Sources

I. *Archives nationales*:

AD XVII "Rondonneau Collection": cultes.

Ba 1, folio 7, no. 2: "Mémoire présenté au ministre et secrétaire d'état ayant le département du clergé, par les curés à portion congrues, 1788".

D XIX 23-26; 27; 44; 45; 46-98; 99-103: Comité ecclésiastique.

E 2125; 2134; 2141; 2149; 2157; 2163; 2175; 2182; 2192; 2203; 2212; 2222; 2233; 2244; 2253; 2264; 2276; 2287; 2293; 2306; 2313; 2322; 2330; 2344; 2353; 2362; 2373; 2381; 2386; 2396; 2404: "Minutes d'arrêts se rapportant au même département [conseil du roi] et relatifs principalement aux affaires ecclésiastiques, 1732-1763".

G8  43 Taxes of benefice-holders in Clermontois (Reims).

G8  68-80 "Augmentation des portions congrues, 1768".

G8* 339 "Département de 1726".

G8* 552 "État des revenus des bénéfices consistoriaux du royaume suivant les économats".

G8* 553 "Département de 1755".

G8* 706 "Procès-verbal de l'Assemblée générale extraordinaire du clergé de France, 1788".

G8* 2451-2467 "Recueil des conférences du 'conseil du clergé' 1766-88".

G8* 2468-2556 "Mémoires et requêtes du clergé 1727-1780".

G8* 2557-2626 "Lettres d'Agence 1721-1787".

G8* 2781-2834 "Consultations. Délibérations du conseil du clergé 1727-1788".

L 727-746: Évêchés.

O1* 276 Ecclesiastical Affairs 1703-1763. Maison du roi.

O1  362-436 Correspondence 1701-1791. Maison du roi.

O1  437-486 Ministerial Dispatches 1741-1789. Maison du roi.

O1  592-596 Letters to the Maison du roi.

O1  604 Episcopal Correspondence. Maison du roi.

U 877 Letter of Cardinal Fleury.

V7 77-88 "Commissions extraordinaires du conseil: bureau des économats".

## II. *Bibliothèque nationale*:

Fonds Français MSS.
6457-6458 "Recueils de droit ecclésiastique".
20969 "Feuilles des bénéfices 1672-1702".
6950; 12767; 17708; 19667; 19669; 20948; 23216; 23217; 23218; 23224; Correspondence of Cardinal Fleury.
Nouvelles Acquisitions Françaises MSS.
31 Correspondence of Cardinal Fleury.
2076-2077 Abbé Jean-Bruno de Ranchon, *Histoire de André Hercule Cardinal de Fleury, Principal Ministre*, 2 volumes, 1758.
22152, folios 170-171 "Discours de M. de Dillon, archevêque de Narbonne", September 7, 1785.


## III. *Archives du ministère des affaires étrangères*:

*Mémoires et Documents; Fonds France:*
  745-1415  "Affaires intérieures".
  1465-1474 "Petits Fonds" — Alsace.
  1477-1780 Angoumois.
  1484      Anjou.
  1487      Auvergne.
  1493-1499 Bourgogne.
  1520-1529 Bretagne.
  1556-1563 Dauphiné.
  1568-1577 Flandre.
  1581-1586 Franche-Comté.
  1596-1607 Ile-de-France.
  1640-1651 Languedoc.
  1652      Limousin.
  1661      Maine.
  1670-1674 Orléanais.
  1687-1695 Picardie.
  1698      Poitou.
  1730-1742 Provence.
  1743      Rouergue.
  1751      Touraine.

*Mémoires et Documents, Fonds Divers, Rome:*
  37; 41-66; 91; 92; 93; 94; 98 Concerning *Unigenitus*.

*Correspondance Politique, Rome:*
  849-860; 862-914 Corespondence of Cardinal de Bernis.


## IV. *Archives départementales du Rhône (nouvelles côtes)*:

6G 34  "Déclarations faites suivant la délibération du bureau diocésain du 11 novembre 1785".
6G 64* "Rôle de tous les bénéficiers qui payent les décimes dans le diocèse de Lyon, 1756-1759".
6G 65* "Rôles des revenus et impositions des bénéfices, 1760".
6G 70* "Extrait du rolle des décimes du clergé du diocèse 1744-69".

7G 10   "Lettres des agents généraux du clergé de France à l'archevêque et au syndic du clergé du diocèse de Lyon 1727-1788".

7G 38*  "Etat des impositions des bénéfices du diocèse dressé par les commissaires nommés par l'Assemblée du clergé du diocèse pour 1720".

7G 40   "Etat de répartition par classes des impositions du diocèse 1760-1771".

7G 42*  "Rôle du don gratuit dressé et arrêté par les commissionaires députés par l'Assemblée générale, 1690".

7G 45*  "Rôle du dixième dressé et arrêté par les commissaires députés par l'Assemblée générale, 1711".

7G 46*  *Ibid.*, 1718.

7G 47*  *Ibid.*, 1726.

7G 48*  "Rôle des décimes dressé et arrêté par les commissaires députés par l'Assemblée générale, 1760".

7G 49*  *Ibid.*, 1770.

7G 50*  *Ibid.*, 1781.

7G 56   "Pièces générales".

7G 57*-63*"Comptes rendus aux députés du clergé de Lyon par le receveur particulier alternatif des décimes du diocèse, 1692-1780".

## 2. *Printed Sources*

*Almanach royal* (Paris), 1715, 1755, 1789.

*Archives parlementaires de 1787 à 1860* (Paris, Librairie Administrative de Paul Dupont [1st series, 1787-99], 1904-1908).

*Arrest de la cour de parlement* (July 8, 1766, Paris, G. Simon, 1766); in the collection "Jansénisme: pamphlets", Vol. XXI, no. 31, in the Speer Library, Princeton Theological Seminary.

Bachaumont, *Mémoires secrets pour servir à l'histoire de la république des lettres en France depuis 1762 jusqu'à nos jours* (London, John Adamson, 1777-89), 36 volumes in 31.

Barbier, *Chronique de la régence et du règne de Louis XV (1718-1763), ou Journal de Barbier* (Paris, Charpentier, 1858), 8 volumes.

Ber[anger], Thomas-Guillaume, *Haro sur la f[euille] des b[énéfices]* (Grenoble, 1789).

Boisrouvray, Jacquelot de, *Journal inédit d'un député de l'ordre de la noblesse aux États de Bretagne pendant la régence (1717-1724),* edited by G. de Closmadeuc (= *Archives de Bretagne*, Vol. XIII (1905).

Calonne, "Mémoire sur le remboursement des dettes du clergé", (*Assemblée de Notables*, 1787), Bibliothèque nationale, Le21.7, Box I.

Campan, Mme., *Mémoires sur la vie privée de Marie-Antoinette, Reine de France et de Navarre,* ed. by Barrière (Paris, Baudouin Frères, 4th edition, 1823), 3 volumes.

*Collection des procès-verbaux des assemblées générales du clergé de France depuis l'année 1560* (Paris, Imprimerie de Guillaume Desprez, 1767-80), 8 volumes.

Correspondance administrative sous le règne de Louis XIV, ed. by G. B. Depping (Paris, Imprimerie Nationale, 1850-55), 4 volumes.

*Correspondance des contrôleurs-généraux des finances avec les intendants des provinces,* ed. by A. M. de Boislisle (Paris, Imprimerie Nationale, 1874-97), 3 volumes.

d'Hozier, Louis-Pierre, *Armorial général de la France* (Paris, 1738-1872), 7 vols.

Dulaure, Jacques-Antoine, *Vie privée des ecclésiatiques, prélats, et autres fonc-tionnaires publics, qui n'ont point prêté leur serment sur la Constitution civile du clergé* (Paris, Chez Garnéry, 1791-92).

Du Tems, Abbé Hugues, *Le Clergé de France* (Paris, Chez Delalain et Brunet, 1774-75), 4 volumes.

Du Tillet, G. L., évêque d'Orange, *Sentiment d'un évêque sur la réforme à intro-duire dans le temporel et la discipline du clergé* (Paris, Le Clere, 1790).

Expilly, Abbé Jean-Joseph, *Dictionnaire géographique, historique et politique des Gaules et de la France* (Paris, Desaint et Saillant, 1762-1770), 6 volumes.

Fauchet, Abbé, *De la Religion nationale* (Paris, Chez Bailly, 1789).

Fleury, Abbé Claude, *Institution au droit ecclésiastique* (Paris, Herissant Fils, 2 volumes.

Francheville, *Lettre à M. le curé de ... député aux États Généraux, sur les prin-cipaux abus qu'il faut réformer dans la cour de Rome, et dans le clergé de France* (Cosmopolis, 1789), Bibliothèque nationale, Lb39.7131.

*Gallia christiana in provincias ecclesiasticas distributa qua series et historia archiepiscoporum, episcoporum et abbatum* (Paris, V. Palme, 1856-99), 16 volumes.

Hébert, François, *Mémoires du curé de Versailles (1686-1704)* (Paris, Les Editions de France, 1927).

Héricourt du Vatier, Louis de, *Les Loix ecclésiastiques de France dans leur ordre naturel, et une analyse des livres du droit canonique conférés avec les usages de l'église gallicane*, New Edition (Neufchâtel, La Société Typographique, 1774; originally published c. 1735), 2 volumes in one.

*Les Idées gallicanes et royalistes du haut clergé à la fin de l'ancien régime, d'après la correspondance et les papiers inédits de Pierre-Augustin Godart de Belbeuf, évêque d'Avranches (1762-1803)*, ed. by Em. Sévestre (Paris, Alphonse Picard, 1917).

Isambert, François-André, *et al.*, eds., *Recueil général des anciennes lois fran-çaises depuis l'an 420 jusqu'à la Révolution de 1789* (Paris, Belin-Leprieur, 1821-33), 18th-Century and 17th-Century Volumes.

*Journal de l'abbé de Véri*, ed. by baron Jehan de Witte (Paris, Librairie Plon, 1933), 2 volumes.

*Journal et mémoires de Mathieu Marais, avocat au parlement de Paris, sur la régence et le règne de Louis XV (1715-1737)* (Paris, Firmin Didot Frères, 1863-68), 4 volumes.

*Journal et mémoires du marquis d'Argenson*, ed. by E. J. B. Rathery (Paris, Mme Ve. Jules Renouard, 1859-67), 9 volumes.

La Chesnaye-Desbois, François Alexandre Aubert de, *Dictionnaire de la noblesse* (Paris, Schlesinger, 3rd edition, 1863-76), 19 volumes.

Lafont de Savine, Charles, évêque de Viviers, *Examen des principes de la Con-stitution civile du clergé* (Lyon, J. B. Delamolliere, 1792).

Lainé, P.-Louis, *Archives généalogiques et historiques de la noblesse de France* (Paris, Lainé, 1828-50), 11 volumes.

Laurent, Abbé, *Essai sur la réforme de clergé, par un vicaire de campagne doc-teur de Sorbonne* (Paris, Durand, 1789), Bibliothèque nationale, Ld4.5982.

*Lettre du curé de M ... diocèse de T ... à un de ses amis à Paris, à l'occasion de l'Assemblée du clergé* (May 23, 1755), S. 1., Bibliothèque nationale, Ld4.2695.

*Lettres secrètes sur l'état du clergé de France* (attributed to the abbé J.-S. Maury or the abbé Thyrel de Boismont) (S.l., 1781).

*Mémoire du clergé citoyen en réponse aux attaques de la noblesse* (S.l., 1788), Bibliothèque nationale), Lb39.882.

"Mémoire inédit de Fénelon sur la cour de Rome", *La Revue politique et littéraire*, 2nd series, 4th year (January 23, 1875), pp. 695-702.

*Mémoires de l'abbé Baston*, ed. by abbé Julien Loth and Ch. Verger (Paris, Alphonse Picard, 1897-99), 3 volumes.

*Mémoires de l'abbé Morellet* (Paris, Baudouin Frères, 1823), 2 volumes.

*Mémoires de Saint-Simon*, ed. by A. de Boislisle (Paris, Librairie Hachette, 1879-1928), 40 volumes.

*Mémoires du duc des Cars* (Paris, Librairie Plon, 1890), 2 volumes.

*Mémoires du prince de Talleyrand* (Paris, Les Éditions Henri Javal, 1953), Vol. I.

*Mémoires et lettres de François-Joachim de Pierre Cardinal de Bernis (1715-1758)*, ed. by Frédéric Masson (Paris, E. Plon, 1878), 2 volumes.

*Mémoires secrets de J. M. Augeard, secrétaire des commandements de la Reine Marie Antoinette* (Paris, Henri Plon, 1866).

Mention, Leon, ed., *Documents relatifs aux rapports du clergé avec la royauté de 1682 à 1789* (Paris, Alphonse Picard, 1893-1903), 2 vols.

Mercier, L. S., *Tableau de Paris* (Amsterdam, 1783-89), 12 volumes.

Moréri, Louis, *Le Grand Dictionnaire historique* (Basle, Jean Louis Brandmuller, new edition, 1760), 6 volumes. *Supplement* (Basle, Jean Christ, 1743-45), 3 volumes.

Necker, Jacques, *De l'Administration des finances de la France* (Paris, 1784), 3 volumes.

Neuville, R. P. de, *Oraison funèbre de S.E. Monseigneur le Cardinal de Fleury, ministre d'état, &c., prononcée au service fait par ordre du roi, dans l'église de Paris, le 25 mai, 1743* (Paris, Chez Coignard et Guerin, 1743).

Nivelle, G. N., *La Constitution Unigenitus déférée à l'église universelle ou recueil général des actes d'appel interjettés au future concile général de cette constitution et des lettres pastoralis officii ... avec les arrests et autres actes des parlemens du royaume qui ont rapport à ces objets* (Cologne, 1757), 3 volumes.

*Nouvelles ecclésiastiques, ou mémoires pour servir à l'histoire ecclésiastique*.

*Oeuvres complètes de Jean-Georges Le Franc de Pompignan, archevêque de Vienne*, ed. by abbé Migne (Paris, Chez J.-P. Migne, 1855), 2 vols.

*Oeuvres complètes de Voltaire* (Paris, Garnier Frères, 1877-85), 52 vols.

*Oeuvres de d'Aguesseau* (Paris, Chez Napoléon Chaix, 1865), 2 volumes.

*Oeuvres de Fénelon, archevêque de Cambrai* (Paris, J.-A. Lebel, 1820-30), 35 volumes.

*Oeuvres de l'abbé Fleury* (Paris, Librairie Ch. Delagrave, 1884).

Picot, M., *Mémoires pour servir à l'histoire ecclésiastique pendant le dix-huitième siècle* (Paris, Librairie Adrien Le Clere, 3rd edition, 1853-57), 7 volumes.

*Procès-verbal de l'Assemblée générale du clergé de France, 1780* (Paris, Chez Guillaume Desprez, 1782), Bibliothèque nationale, Ld5.582.

*Procès-verbal de l'Assemblée extraordinaire du clergé de France, 1782* (Paris, Chez Guillaume Desprez, 1783), Bibliothèque nationale, Ld5.584.

*Procès-verbal de l'Assemblée générale du clergé de France, 1785-86* (Paris, Chez Guillaume Desprez, 1789), Bibliothèque nationale, Ld5.598.

Puisaye, Comte Joseph de, *Mémoires, qui pourront servir à l'histoire du parti royaliste françois durant la dernière révolution* (London, E. Harding, 1803-1806), 6 volumes.

*Rapport de l'Agence, 1720-1785* (Paris, Chez Pierre Simon et al., 1726-88), 13 volumes.

*Rapport de Messieurs les anciens agens, contenant les principales affaires du clergé qui se sont passées depuis l'assemblée de 1710 jusqu'à celle de 1715* (Paris, Chez Pierre Simon, 1725).

*Recueil des actes, titres et mémoires concernant les affaires du clergé de France* (Paris, 1768-1780), 14 volumes.

*Réimpression de l'ancien Moniteur* (Paris, Plon Frères, 1863-70), 32 vols.

*Remontrances du clergé, présentées au roi le dimanche 15 juin 1788, sur ses droits, franchises et immunités*, Archives nationales, AD XVII, 10A.

*Remontrances du clergé présentées au roi le 15 juin 1788*, Bibliothèque nationale, Ld5-6.599.

*Remontrances du parlement de Bretagne au XVIIIe siècle* (Textes inédits précédes d'une introduction), ed. by A. Le Moy (Angers, Imprimerie Burdin, 1909).

*Remontrances du parlement de Paris au XVIIIe siècle*, ed. by Jules Flammermont (Paris, Imprimerie Nationale, 1888-1898), 3 volumes.

Reymond, Abbé Henri, *Droits des curés et des paroisses, considérés sous leur double rapport, spirituel et temporel* (Paris, 1776).

Sandret, L., *L'Ancienne Église de France, ou état des archevêchés et évêchés de France avant la Constitution civile du clergé province ecclésiastique de Rouen* (Paris, J.-B. Dumoulin, 1866).

Soulavie, Jean-Louis, *Mémoires historiques et politiques du règne de Louis XVI* (Paris, Treuttel et Würtz, 1801), 6 volumes.

*Sur l'Ascendant aristocratique de la noblesse dans le clergé* (S.l., 178-), Bibliothèque nationale, Lb39.1213.

*Tableau moral du clergé de France, sur la fin du dix-huitième siècle, ou le clergé françois, avant les États-Généraux, et ce qu'il doit devenir après* (S.l., April 1789).

## 3. Secondary Works

Allain, Abbé, *L'Instruction primaire en France avant la Révolution* (Paris, Librairie de la Société Bibliographique, 1881).

Allain, Ernest, "Un grand diocèse d'autrefois. Organisation administrative et financière", *Revue des questions historiques*, Vol. LVI (October, 1894), pp. 493-534.

Amann, E., "Autour de l'histoire du gallicanisme", *Revue des sciences religieuses*, Vol. XXI (1947), pp. 17-52.

Appolis, Emile, "A Travers le XVIIIe siècle catholique. Entre jansénistes et constitutionnaires: un tiers parti", *Annales: Économies, Sociétés, Civilisations*, Vol. VI (April-June, 1951), pp. 154-171.

Bassieux, F., "Théorie des libertés gallicanes du parlement de Paris au XVIIIe siècle", *Nouvelle Revue historique de droit français et étranger*, Vol. XXX (1906), pp. 330-350.

Besnier, Elisabeth, *Les Agents généraux du clergé de France, spécialement de 1780 à 1785* (Paris, Bernard Frères, 1939).

Bickart, Roger, *Les Parlements et la notion de souveraineté nationale au XVIIIe siècle* (Paris, Félix Alcan, 1932).

Bien, David D., *The Calas Affair. Persecution, Toleration, and Heresy in Eighteenth-Century Toulouse* (Princeton, University Press, 1960).

Blet, Pierre, S.J., *Le Clergé de France et la monarchie. Étude sur les assemblées générales du clergé de 1615 à 1666* (Rome, Librairie Editrice de l'Université Grégorienne, 1959), 2 volumes.

Bloch, Camille, *L'Assistance et l'état en France à la veille de la Révolution* (Paris, Librairie Alphonse Picard, 1908).

Bluche, J., *L'Origine des magistrats du parlement de Paris au XVIIIe siècle* (Paris, Au Siège de la Fédération, 1956).

Boiteau, Paul, *État de la France en 1789* (Paris, Librairie Guillaumin, 2nd edition, 1889).

Bonnel, Abbé S., *Notice biographique sur Guillaume-Louis du Tillet, dernier évêque d'Orange* (Meaux, Librairie Ch. Cochet, 1880).

Bourgain, L., "Contribution de clergé à l'impôt sous la monarchie française", *Revue des questions historiques*, Vol. XLVIII (July, 1890), pp. 63-132.

Bourlon, J., *Les Assemblées du clergé et le jansénisme* (Paris, Bloud, 1909).

Brette, Armand, "La Dette du clergé en 1789", *La Révolution française*, Vol. XLVI (Janurary-June, 1904), pp. 412-423.

Cagnac, Moïse, *De l'Appel comme d'abus dans l'ancien droit français* (Paris, Librairie Ve. Ch. Poussielgue, 1906).

Cans, Albert, *La Contribution du clergé de France à l'impôt pendant la seconde moitié du règne de Louis XIV (1689-1715)* (Paris, Librairie A. Picard, 1910).

——, *L'Organisation financière du clergé de France à l'époch de Louis XIV* (Paris, Librairie A. Picard, 1909).

Carré, Henri, *La Noblesse de France et l'opinion publique au XVIIIe siècle* (Paris, E. Champion, 1920).

Carrière, Victor, *Introduction aux études d'histoire ecclésiastique locale* (Paris, Letouzey, 1934-40), 3 volumes.

Chassin, C. L., *Les Cahiers des curés* (Paris, Charavay Frères, 1882).

Chevallier, Pierre, "Une Affaire maçonnique sous Louis XVI", *Revue d'histoire moderne et contemporaine*, Vol. II (July-September, 1955), pp. 212-218.

Chevaillier, R., "Les Revenus des bénéfices ecclésiastiques au XVIIIe siècle d'après les comptes de la régale et de la garde", *La Révolution française*, Vol. LXXIV (April-June 1921), pp. 113-149.

——, "Un Document sur la fortune du haut clergé au XVIIIe siècle", *Bulletin de la société d'histoire moderne*, April-May, 1921, pp. 60-80.

Coudy, Julien, *Les Moyens d'action de l'ordre du clergé au conseil du roi (1561-1715)* (Paris, Sirey, 1954).

Crousaz-Crétat, P. de, *L'Église et l'état ou les deux puissances au XVIIIe siècle* (Paris, Victor Retaux et Fils, 1893).

Denys-Buirette, A., *Les Questions religieuses dans les cahiers de 1789* (Paris, E. de Boccard, 1919).

D'Illiers, Louis, *Deux Prélats d'ancien régime, les Jarente* (Monaco, Editions du Rocher, 1948).

Durand, Abbé Valentin, *Les Évêques au XVIIIe siècle en Languedoc* (Montpellier, Imprimerie de la Manufacture de la Charité, 1907).

Duranlot, Ernest, "La Situation temporelle et le rôle social de l'épiscopat français avant la Révolution", *La Réforme sociale*, 3rd series, Vol. X (July-December, 1895), pp. 323-337.

Dutil, Léon, "Philosophie ou religion: Loménie de Brienne, archevêque de Toulouse", *Annales du Midi*, Vol. LXI (1948), pp. 33-70.

Esmein, A., *Cour élémentaire d'histoire du droit français* (Paris, Librairie du Recueil Sirey, 15th edition, 1925).

Fisquet, Honoré, *La France pontificale* (Paris, E. Repos, 1864-73), 21 vols.

Floquet, A., *Histoire du parlement de Normandie* (Rouen, Édouard Frère, 1840-42), 7 volumes.

Ford, Franklin, L., *Robe and Sword: The Regrouping of the French Aristocracy After Louis XIV* (Cambridge, Harvard University Press, 1953).

Gagnol, P., "Les Décimes et les Dons gratuits", *Revue d'histoire de l'église de France*, Vol. I (1910), pp. 167-173; Vol. II (1911), pp. 465-481.

Gay, Peter, *Voltaire's Politics: the Poet as Realist* (Princeton, University Press, 1959).

Gazier, Augustin, *Histoire générale du mouvement janséniste, depuis ses origines jusqu'à nos jours* (Paris, Librairie Ancienne Honoré Champion, 1922), 2 volumes.

Gérin, Charles, *Recherches historiques sur l'assemblée du clergé de France de 1682* (Paris, Librairie Jacques Lecoffre, 2nd edition, 1870).

Ghestin, Jacques, "L'Action des parlements contre les 'mésalliances' aux XVIIe et XVIIIe siècles", *Revue historique de droit français et étranger*, Vol. XXXIV (January-March, 1956), pp. 74-110; *Ibid.* (April-June, 1956), pp. 196-224.

Giraud, *Histoire de l'esprit révolutionnaire des nobles en France, sous les soixante-huit rois de la monarchie* (Paris, Baudouin Frères 1818), 2 volumes in one.

Glasson, E., *Le Parlement de Paris. Son rôle politique depuis le règne de Charles VII jusqu'à la Révolution* (Paris, Librairie Hachette, 1910), 2 volumes.

Greenbaum, Louis S., "Talleyrand and His Uncle: the Genesis of a Clerical Career", *The Journal of Modern History*, Vol. XXIX (September, 1957), pp. 226-236.

——, "Talleyrand and the Temporal Problems of the French Church from 1780 to 1785", *French Historical Studies*, Vol. III (Spring, 1963), pp. 41-71.

——, "Talleyrand as Agent-General of the Clergy of France: A study in Comparative Influence", *The Catholic Historical Review*, Vol. XLVIII (January, 1963), pp. 473-486.

——, "Ten Priests in Search of a Miter: How Talleyrand Became a Bishop", *The Catholic Historical Review*, Vol. L (October, 1964), pp. 307-331.

Guettée, René F. W., *Histoire de l'église de France, composée sur les documents originaux et authentiques* (Paris, V. Masson, 1847-56), Volumes XI and XII.

Guitton, Georges, S.J., *Le Père de la Chaize, confesseur de Louis XIV* (Paris, Beauchesne, 1959), 2 volumes.

Hardy, Georges, *Le Cardinal de Fleury et le mouvement janséniste* (Paris, Librairie Ancienne Honoré Champion, 1925).

Hoefer, Jean-Chrétien Ferdinand, *Nouvelle Biographie générale depuis les temps les plus reculés jusqu'à nos jours* (Paris, Firmin Didot Frères, 1855-66), 46 volumes.

Hutt, M. G., "The Curés and the Third Estate: the Ideas of Reform in the Pamphlets of the French Lower Clergy in the Period 1787-1789", *The Journal of Ecclesiastical History*, Vol. VIII (1957), pp. 74-92.

Jager, Abbé Jean N., *Histoire de l'église catholique en France d'après les documents les plus authentiques, depuis son origine jusqu'au concordat de Pie VII* (Paris, A. Le Clere, 1862-75), Volumes XVIII, XIX, and XX.

Jean, Armand, *Les Évêques et les archevêques de France depuis 1682 jusqu'à 1801* (Paris, Alphonse Picard, 1891).

Kerbiriou, Louis, *Jean-François de la Marche, évêque-comte de Léon. Etude sur un diocèse breton et sur l'émigration* (Quimper, Le Goaziou, 1924).

La Gorce, Pierre de, *Histoire religieuse de la Révolution française* (Paris, Librairie Plon, 1912-24), 5 volumes.

Laplatte, C., "L'Administration des évêchés vacants et la régie des économats", *Revue d'histoire de l'église de France*, Vol. XXIII (1933), pp. 161-225.

Lavaquery, Abbé E., *Le Cardinal de Boisgelin 1732-1804*. Vol. I: *Un Prélat d'ancien régime* (Paris, Librairie Plon, 1921).

Laveille, Abbé A., "Les Revenus du clergé breton avant la Révolution", *Revue des questions historiques, New series*, Vol. XLVIII (October, 1912), pp. 461-471.

Lepointe, Gabriel, *L'Organisation et la politique financières du clergé de France sous le règne de Louis XV* (Paris, Receuil Sirey, 1923).

Levasseur, E., *La Population française* (Paris, Arthur Rousseau, 1889), Vol. I.

Levesque, E., "Fénelon et les candidats à l'épiscopat", *Bulletin de littérature ecclésiastique*, Vol. XXIII (1922), pp. 182-186.

Lévy Schneider, L., *L'Application du concordat par un prélat d'ancien régime, Mgr Champion de Cicé, archevêque d'Aix et d'Arles* (Paris, F. Rieder et Cie., 1921).

——, "L'Autonomie administrative de l'épiscopat français à la fin de l'ancien régime", *Revue historique*, Vol. CLI (January-February, 1926), pp. 1-33.

Maistre, Joseph de, *De l'Église gallicane dans son rapport avec le souverain pontife* (Lyon-Paris, J. B. Pélagaud, 1863).

Marion, Marcel, *Dictionnaire des institutions de la France aux XVIIe et XVIIIe siècles* (Paris, Auguste Picard, 1923).

——, *Histoire financière de la France depuis 1715* (Paris, Arthur Rousseau, 1914-31), Vol. I.

——, *Machault d'Arnouville* (Paris, Librairie Hachette, 1891).

Martin, Victor, *Le Gallicanisme politique et le clergé de France* (Paris, Auguste Picard, 1929).

Maury, Alfred, "Les Assemblées du clergé en France sous l'ancienne monarchie; Part IV: Les Assemblées du clergé à la fin du XVIIe et au XVIIIe siècle", *Revue des deux mondes*, Vol. XL (July-August, 1880), pp. 621-667.

Mautouchet, Paul, "Les Questions politiques à l'Assemblée du clergé de 1788", *La Revolution française*, Vol. XLII (January, 1902), pp. 5-44.

McCloy, Shelby T., *Government Assistance in Eighteenth-Century France* (Durham, Duke University Press, 1946).

McManners, John, *French Ecclesiastical Society Under the Ancien Regime. Angers in the Eighteenth Century* (Manchester, University Press, 1960).

Metz, René, *La Monarchie française et la provision des bénéfices ecclésiastiques en Alsace, de la paix de Westphalie à la fin de l'ancien régime (1648-1789)* (Strasbourg-Paris, F.-X. Le Roux, 1947).

Michaud, J. F. and L. G., *Biographie universelle ancienne et moderne* (Paris, A. Thoisnier Desplaces, 2nd edition, 1843-65), 45 volumes.

Monternat, Abbé Charles, *Yves Alexandre de Marbeuf, ministre de la feuille des bénéfices, archevêque de Lyon (1734-1799)*, (Lyon, H. Lardanchet, 1911).

Nau, Paul, "A l'Origine des encycliques modernes: un épisode de la lutte des évêques et des parlements, 1755-56", *Revue historique de droit français et étranger*, 4th series, Vol. XXXIV (April-June, 1956), pp. 225-267.

Orcibal, Jean, *Louis XIV contre Innocent XI. Les Appels au future concile de 1688 et l'opinion française* (Paris, Librairie Philosophique J. Vrin, 1949).

Palmer, Robert R., *The Age of the Democratic Revolution* (Princeton, University Press 1959-64), 2 volumes.

——, "The National Idea in France Before the Revolution", *Journal of the History of Ideas*, Vol. I (January, 1940), pp. 95-111.

Pastor, Ludwig, Freiherr von, *The History of the Popes*, English translation (London, Kegan Paul, Trench, Trubner & Co., 1940-41), volumes 32 ff.

Perrin, Joseph, *Le Cardinal de Loménie de Brienne, archevêque de Sens* (Sens, Imprimerie de Paul Duchemin, 1896).

Pradt, Dominique G. F. de, *Les Quatre Concordats* (Paris, F. Béchet, 1818), 3 volumes.

Préclin, E., *Les Jansénistes du XVIIIe siècle et la Constitution civile du clergé. Le développement du richerisme, sa propagation dans le bas clergé* (Paris, Librairie Universitaire J. Gamber, 1928).

Proyart, Abbé Liévain Bonaventure, *Louis XVI détroné avant d'être roi* (Liége-Brussels, new edition, 1814; original edition, London-Hamburg, 1800).

Raduget, Xavier, "La Carrière politique de l'abbé Maury de 1786 à 1791", *Revue d'histoire de l'église de France*, Vol. III (1912), pp. 505-515; 613-643.

Rebillon, Armand, ed., *Département d'Ille-et-Vilaine, La Situation économique du clergé à la veille de la Révolution* (Rennes, Imprimerie Oberthur, 1913).

Rebillon, Armand, *Les États de Bretagne de 1661 à 1789* (Rennes, Imprimeries Réunies, 1932).

Regnault, Émile, *Christophe de Beaumont, archevêque de Paris (1703-1781)* (Paris, Librairie Victor Lecoffre, 1882), 2 volumes.

Remacle, L., *Ultramontains et gallicans au XVIIIe siècle. Honoré de Quinqueran de Beaujeu, évêque de Castres, et Jacques de Forbin-Janson, archevêque d'Arles* (Marseille, Cayer, 1872).

Robert, P.-Albert, *Les Remontrances et arrêtés du parlement de Provence au XVIIIe siècle* (Paris, Arthur Rousseau, 1912).

Sabine, George H., *A History of Political Theory* (New York, Henry Holt, revised edition, 1955).

Sambucy, Abbé de, *Vie de Mgr de Beauvais, ancien évêque de Senez* (Paris, Chez Dufour, 1842).

Schmitt, Thérèse-Jean, *L'Organisation ecclésiastique et la pratique religieuse dans l'archidiaconé d'Autun de 1650 à 1750* and *l'Assistance dans l'archidiaconé d'Autun aux XVIIe et XVIIIe siècles* (Autun, Société d'Imprimerie L. Marcelin, 1957).

Sicard, Abbé Augustin, *L'Ancien Clergé de France: les évêques avant la Révolution* (Paris, Librairie Victor Lecoffre, 5th edition, 1912).

——, "Un Monde disparu. Les dispensateurs des bénéfices ecclésiastiques avant 1789", *Le Correspondant*, New series, Vol. CXX (1889), pp. 856-894.

Tans, J. A. G., "Les Idées politiques des jansénistes", *Neophilologus*, Vol. XL (January, 1956), pp. 1-18.

Vaissière, Pierre de, *Curés de campagne de l'ancienne France* (Paris, Éditions Spes, 1932).

Verlaque, Abbé V., *Histoire du cardinal de Fleury* (Paris, Victor Palmé, 1878).

## B. THE ANGLICAN AND IRISH EPISCOPATES

### 1. *Printed Sources*

*Anecdotes of the Life of Richard Watson, Bishop of Llandaff* (written by himself) (Philadelphia, Abraham Small, 1818).

Atterbury, Francis, *The Rights, Powers, and Privileges of an English Convocation* (London, Tho. Bennet, 2nd edition, 1791).

*Bishop Burnet's History of His Own Time* (Oxford, University Press, 2nd edition, 1833), 6 volumes.

Blackstone, Sir William, *Commentaries on the Laws of England* (Philadelphia, George W. Childs, 1868), 2 volumes.

Burke, Edmund, *Reflections on the Revolution in France* (London, Everyman's Library, 1910).

Burn, Richard, *Ecclesiastical Law* (London, T. Cadell, 3rd edition, 1775), 4 volumes.

Burtchaell, George Dames, and Sadleir, Thomas Ulick, eds., *Alumni Dublinenses* (London, Williams and Norgate, 1924).

Cardwell, Edward, ed., *Documentary Annals of the Reformed Church of England* (Oxford, University Press, 1844), Vol. II.

*The Clerical Guide and Ecclesiastical Directory.* . . . compiled from the report of the commissioners appointed "to inquire into the Established Church in England and Wales" and presented to both houses of Parliament in June 1835 . . . (London, J. G. and F. Rivington, new edition, 1836).

C[okayne], G. E., *The Complete Peerage* (London, The St. Catherine Press, revised edition, 1910-53), 12 volumes.

Collier, Jeremy, *An Ecclesiastical History of Great Britain* (London, Samuel Keble, 1708-14), 2 volumes.

*Comparative Account of the Population of Great Britain in the Years 1801, 1811, 1821, 1831* (By Order of the House of Commons, Oct. 19, 1831).

*A Complete Collection of the Protests of the Lords,* ed. by J. E. T. Rogers (Oxford, Clarendon Press, 1875), 3 volumes.

"Correspondence of Archbishop Stone and the Duke of Newcastle", *English Historical Review,* Vol. XX (1905), pp. 508-542; 735-763.

*The Correspondence of Jonathan Swift, D.D.,* ed. by F. Elrington Ball (London, G. Bell, 1910-14), 6 volumes.

*The Correspondence of King George the Third,* ed. by John Fortescue (London, Macmillan, 1927-28), 6 volumes.

Coxe, William, *Memoirs of the Duke of Marlborough, With His Original Correspondence* (London, George Bell, new edition, 1876-85), 3 volumes.

*Diary of the First Earl of Egmont, Viscount Percival* (London, Historical Manuscripts Commission, 1920-23), 3 volumes.

*Dictionary of National Biography.*

*English Historical Documents 1660-1714,* ed. by Andrew Browning (New York, Oxford University Press, 1953).

*English Historical Documents 1714-1783,* ed. by D. B. Horn and Mary Ransome (New York, Oxford University Press, 1959).

*English Historical Documents 1783-1832,* ed. by A. Aspinall and E. Anthony Smith (New York, Oxford University Press, 1959).

*The Epistolary Correspondence, Visitation Charges, Speeches, and Miscellanies of the Right Reverend Francis Atterbury, D.D., Lord Bishop of Rochester* (London, J. Nichols, 1783-84), 3 volumes.

"First Report From His Majesty's Commission Appointed to Consider the State of the Established Church with Reference to Ecclesiastical Duties and Revenues", *Sessional Papers, House of Commons,* 1835, Vol. XXII, pp. 1 ff., microprint.

"First Report of His Majesty's Commissioners on Ecclesiastical Revenue and Patronage in Ireland, March, 1833", *Sessional Papers, House of Commons,* 1833, Vol. XXI, pp. 242 ff., microprint.

Foster, Joseph, ed., *Alumni Oxonienses (1500-1714)* (Oxford, James Parker, 1891), 4 volumes.

——, *Alumni Oxonienses (1715-1886)* (London and Oxford, Joseph Foster and Parker & Co., 1888), 4 volumes.

Gibson, Edmond, *Synodus Anglicana,* ed. by Edward Cardwell (Oxford, University Press, 1854); first published in 1702.

*Handbook of British Chronology,* ed. by F. M. Powicke (London, Royal Historical Society, 1939).

Hervey, John, Lord, *Some Materials Towards Memoirs of the Reign of King George II,* ed. by Romney Sedgwick (London, KEP, 1931), 3 volumes.

Holland, Henry Richard Vassall Fox, Third Lord, *Further Memoirs of the Whig Party 1807-1821* (New York, E. P. Dutton, 1905).

King, William, *Correspondence,* National Library of Ireland, microfilm.

*Letters of Spencer Cowper, Dean of Durham 1746-74,* ed. by Edward Hughes

(= *The Publications of the Surtees Society*, Vol. CLXV) (1950), published in 1956.

*Letters Written by His Excellency Hugh Boulter, D.D., Lord Primate of All Ireland to Several Ministers of State in England* (Dublin, George Faulkner, 1770), 2 volumes in one.

*The Lives of Dr. Edward Pocock, the Celebrated Orientalist, by Dr. Twells; of Dr. Zachary Pearce, Bishop of Rochester, and of Dr. Thomas Newton, Bishop of Bristol, by Themselves; and of the Rev. Philip Skelton, by Mr. Burdy* (London, Rivington, 1816), 2 volumes.

*Memoirs and Correspondence of Viscount Castlereagh*, ed. by Charles Vane, Marquess of Londonderry (London, Henry Colburn, 1848-51), 8 volumes.

*Memoirs of Viscountess Sundon*, ed. by Mrs. Thompson (London, Henry Colburn, 1847), 2 volumes.

*Private Correspondence of Chesterfield and Newcastle, 1744-46*, ed. by Richard Lodge (= *Camden Society Publications*, series 3, Vol. XLIV) (1930).

Pyle, Edmund, *Memoirs of a Royal Chaplain, 1729-1763* (London, John Lane, 1905).

*The Records of the Northern Convocation* (= *The Publications of the Surtees Society, Durham*, Vol. CXIII) (1906).

*Reports on the Manuscripts of J. B. Fortescue, Esq., Preserved at Dropmore. The Papers of William Wyndham, Lord Grenville* (London, Historical Manuscripts Commission, 1892-1927), 10 volumes.

"Summary of Digest of Inquiry into Revenues and Patronage in Ireland", *Sessional Papers, House of Commons*, 1833, Vol. XXVII, pp. 449 ff., microprint.

Swift, Jonathan, *The Prose Works of Jonathan Swift*; Vol. XII: *Irish Tracts, 1728-1733* (Oxford, Shakespeare Head Press, 1955).

*Synodalia. A Collection of Articles of Religion, Canons, and Proceedings of Convocations in the Province of Canterbury*, ed. by Edward Cardwell (Oxford, University Press, 1842), 2 volumes.

"Third and Fourth Report of Commissioners of Ecclesiastical Inquiry, Ireland", *Sessional Papers, House of Commons*, 1837, Vol. XXI; 1836, Vol. XXV.

Tone, Theobald Wolfe, *Autobiography of Theobald Wolfe Tone* (London, Unwin, 1893), 2 volumes.

Venn, J. A., ed., *Alumni Cantabrigienses, Part II, 1752-1900* (Cambridge, University Press, 1940-51), 4 volumes.

Venn, John and Venn, J. A., eds., *Alumni Cantabrigienses, Part I, From Earliest Times to 1751* (Cambridge, University Press, 1922-27), 4 volumes.

Wade, John. ed., *The Extraordinary Black Book: An Exposition of Abuses in Church and State . . .* (London, Effingham Wilson, new edition, 1832).

Walpole, Robert, *Four Letters to a Friend in North Britain, Upon the Publishing the Tryal of Dr. Sacheverell* (London, 1710).

Warburton, William, *Letters From a Late Eminent Prelate to One of His Friends* (London, T. Cadell, 2nd edition, 1809).

## 2. Secondary Works

Abbey, Charles J. and Overton, John H., *The English Church in the Eighteenth Century* (London, Longmans, Green, 1878), 2 volumes.

Ball, J. T., *The Reformed Church of Ireland (1537-1886)* (London, Longmans, Green, 1886).

Barnes, Donald G., "The Duke of Newcastle, Ecclesiastical Minister, 1724-54", *The Pacific Historical Review*, Vol. III (June, 1934), pp. 164-191.

Beckett, J. C., "The Government and the Church of Ireland under William III and Anne", *Irish Historical Studies,* Vol. II (March, 1941), pp. 280-302.

Beeching, H. C., *Francis Atterbury* (London, Pitman, 1909).

Bosher, Robert S., *The Making of the Restoration Settlement, The Influence of the Laudians 1649-1662* (Westminster, Dacre Press, 1951).

Carpenter, Edward, *Thomas Tenison, Archbishop of Canterbury, His Life and Times* (London, S.P.C.K., 1948).

Chase, Eugene Parker, "The Struggle for the Autonomy of the Church of England", *Essays in History and Political Theory in Honor of Charles Howard McIlwain* (Cambridge, Harvard University Press, 1936), pp. 109-137.

Cornell, K. H. *The Population of Ireland 1750-1845* (Oxford, Clarendon Press, 1950).

Dietz, Frederick C., *English Public Finance 1558-1641* (New York, Century, 1932).

Dowell, Stephen, *A History of Taxation and Taxes in England* (London, Longmans, Green, 2nd edition, 1888), 4 volumes.

Every, George, *The High Church Party 1688-1718* (London, S.P.C.K., 1956).

Gwatkin, H. M., *Church and State in England to the Death of Queen Anne* (London, Longmans, Green, 1917).

Hill, Christopher, *Economic Problems of the Church, From Archbishop Whitgift to the Long Parliament* (Oxford, Clarendon Press, 1956).

——, *Puritanism and Revolution, Studies in Interpretation of the English Revolution of the 17th Century* (London, Secker & Warburg, 1958).

Holdsworth, Sir Williams S., "The Conventions of the Eighteenth Century Constitution", *Iowa Law Review,* Vol. XVII (January, 1932), pp. 161-180.

Hutton, William Henry, *The English Church from the Accession of Charles I to the Death of Anne* (London, Macmillan, 1903).

Kennedy, William, *English Taxation 1640-1799* (London, G. Bell, 1913).

Landa, Louis A., *Swift and the Church of Ireland* (Oxford, Clarendon Press, 1954).

Lathbury, Thomas, *A History of the Convocation of the Church of England* (London, John W. Parker, 1842).

Makower, Felix, *The Constitutional History and Constitution of the Church of England* (London, Swan Sonnenschein, 1895).

Mant, Richard, Bishop of Down, *History of the Church of Ireland from the Reformation to the Revolution* (London, John W. Parker, 1841).

——, *History of the Church of Ireland from the Revolution to the Union of the Churches of England and Ireland* (London, John W. Parker, 1840).

Mayo, C. H. "The Social Status of the Clergy in the Seventeenth and Eighteenth Centuries", *English Historical Review,* Vol. XXXVII (1922), pp. 258-266.

McCracken, J. L., "Irish Parliamentary Elections 1727-68", *Irish Historical Studies,* Vol. V (March, 1947), pp. 209-230.

Morgan, William Thomas, *English Political Parties and Leaders in the Reign of Queen Anne 1702-1710* (New Haven, Yale University Press, 1920).

Mukerjee, H. N., "Parliamentary Taxation of the Clergy", *Notes and Queries. Vol. CLXVI* (January 20, 1934), p. 41.

Namier, Sir Lewis B., *Monarchy and the Party System* (Oxford, Clarendon Press, 1952).

——, *The Structure of Politics at the Accession of George III* (New York, St. Martin's Press, 2nd edition, 1957).

O'Brien, George, *The Economic History of Ireland in the Eighteenth Century* (Dublin-London, Maunsel, 1918).

Ogg, David, *England in the Reign of Charles II* (Oxford, Clarendon Press, 1955), 2 volumes.

Ollard, S. L. and Crosse, Gordon, eds., *A Dictionary of English Church History* (London, A. R. Mowbray, 2nd edition, 1919).

Overton, John H. and Relton, Frederick, *The English Church from the Accession of George I to the End of the Eighteenth Century* (London, Macmillan, 1906).

Phillimore, Sir Robert, *The Ecclesiastical Law of the Church of England* (London, Henry Sweet, 1873), 2 volumes.

Phillips, C. S., "L'Église de France et l'église anglicane au XVIIIe siècle", *Oecumenica*, Vol. IV (April, 1937), pp. 415-421.

Phillips, Walter Alison, ed., *History of the Church of Ireland*, Vol. III: *The Modern Church* (Oxford, University Press, 1933).

Plumb, J. H., *Sir Robert Walpole* (London, The Cresset Press, 1956-60), 2 volumes.

Sharp, Thomas, *The Life of John Sharp, D.D., Lord Archbishop of York* (London, Rivington, 1825), 2 volumes.

Switzer, Gerald B., "The Suppression of Convocation in the Church of England", *Church History*, Vol. I (September, 1932), pp. 150-162.

Sykes, Norman, "Archbishop Wake and the Whig Party, 1716-23", *The Cambridge Historical Journal*, Vol. VIII (1945), pp. 93-112.

——, *Church and State in England in the XVIIIth Century* (Cambridge, University Press, 1934).

——, "The Duke of Newcastle as Ecclesiastical Minister", *English Historical Review*, Vol. LVII (January, 1942), pp. 59-84.

——, *Edmund Gibson, Bishop of London, 1669-1748* (Oxford, University Press, 1926).

——, *From Sheldon to Secker, Aspects of English Church History 1660-1768* (Cambridge, University Press, 1959).

——, "Queen Caroline and the Church", *History*, Vol. XI (January, 1927), pp. 333-339.

——, "Queen Anne and the Episcopate", *English Historical Review*, Vol. L (July, 1935), pp. 433-464.

——, *William Wake, Archbishop of Canterbury 1657-1737* (Cambridge, University Press, 1957), 2 volumes.

Trevor-Roper, H. R., *Archbishop Laud 1573-1645* (London, Macmillan, 1940).

Turberville, A. S. *The House of Lords in the Age of Reform 1784-1837* (London, Faber and Faber, 1958).

——, *The House of Lords in the XVIIIth Century* (Oxford, Clarendon Press, 1927).

——, *The House of Lords in the Reign of William III* (= *Oxford Historical and Literary Studies, Vol. III*) (Oxford, Clarendon Press, 1913).

Walcott, Robert, *English Politics in the Early Eighteenth Century* (Cambridge, Harvard University Press, 1956).

Ward, W. R., *The English Land Tax in the Eighteenth Century* (Oxford, University Press, 1953).

Watson, J. Steven, *The Reign of George III 1760-1815* (Oxford, Clarendon Press, 1960).

Williams, Basil, *Carteret and Newcastle* (Cambridge, University Press, 1943).

——, "The Duke of Newcastle and the Election of 1734", *English Historical Review*, Vol. XII (July, 1897), pp. 448-488.

——, *The Whig Supremacy 1714-1760* (Oxford, Clarendon Press, 1939).

# INDEX

# STUDIES IN EUROPEAN HISTORY

1. S. GULDESCU: *History of Medieval Croatia.* 1964. 351 pp., 15 maps. Cloth.                                        Glds. 45.–

2. E. D. TAPPE: *Documents concerning Rumanian History (1427-1601), collected from British Archives.* With an Introduction by C. Marinesco. 1964. 164 pp. Cloth.                  Glds. 22.–

3. PETER JAMES KLASSEN: *The Economics of Anabaptism (1525-1560).* 1964. 149 pp. Cloth.                                        Glds. 22.–

4. MELVIN J. TUCKER: *The Life of Thomas Howard, Earl of Surrey and Second Duke of Norfolk (1443-1524).* 1964. 170 pp., map, 3 plates, 3 tables. Cloth.                  Glds. 24.–

# STUDIES IN AMERICAN HISTORY

1. HEINZ K. MEIER: *The United States and Switzerland in the Nineteenth Century.* 1963. 208 pp. Cloth.                  Glds. 18.

2. JACK AUTREY DABBS: *The French Army in Mexico, 1861-1867.* A Study in Military Government. 1963. 340 pp., 10 plates, map. Cloth.                                        Glds. 30.–

3. DAVID H. MAKINSON: *Barbados. A Study of North-American–West Indian Relations, 1739-1789.* 1964. 142 pp., 6 plates. Cloth.                                        Glds. 22.–

4. ODIE B. FAULK: *The Last Years of Spanish Texas, 1778-1821.* 1964. 156 pp. Cloth.                                        Glds. 20.–

MOUTON & CO. · PUBLISHERS · THE HAGUE